SMUT

SMUT

Erotic Reality/Obscene Ideology

Murray S. Davis

The University of Chicago Press
Chicago and London

✳ MURRAY S. DAVIS is the author of *Intimate Relations*.

The University of Chicago Press, Chicago 60637
The University of Chicago Press, Ltd., London

© 1983 by The University of Chicago
All rights reserved. Published 1983
Printed in the United States of America
90 89 88 87 86 85 84 83   5 4 3 2 1

Library of Congress Cataloging in Publication Data

Davis, Murray S., 1940–
  Smut : erotic reality/obscene ideology.

  Bibliography: p.
  Includes index.
    1. Sex.   2. Sexual deviation   3. Pornography.
  I. Title.
  HQ21.D32   1983   306.7   82–16061
  ISBN 0–226–13791–0

* For C. S.,
  my tenth Muse

Gloucester. The trick of that voice I do
    well remember.
Is't not the King?
Lear. Ay, every inch a king!
When I do stare, see how the subject
    quakes.
I pardon that man's life. What was thy
    cause?
Adultery?
Thou shalt not die. Die for adultery! No:
The wren goes to't, and the small gilded
    fly
Does lecher in my sight.
Let copulation thrive; for Gloucester's
    bastard son
Was kinder to his father than my
    daughters
Got 'tween the lawful sheets.
To't, luxury, pell-mell! for I lack soldiers.
Behold yon simp'ring dame,
Whose face between her forks presages
    snow,
That minces virtue, and does shake the
    head
To hear of pleasure's name,—
The fitchew nor the soiled horse goes to't
With a more riotous appetite.
Down from the waist they are Centaurs,
Though women all above;
But to the girdle do the gods inherit,
Beneath is all the fiends';
There's hell, there's darkness, there's the
    sulphurous pit,
Burning, scalding, stench, consumption;
    fie, fie, fie!

King Lear, 4.6.108–31

Contents

Approaches and Acknowledgments

I have tried to lay out in this book everything modern science does *not* know about sex. That is, I have tried to display here all the aspects of sex ignored by positivist science in the narrow sense. My goal is to present the nonscientific—though not *un*scientific—tradition of sexual knowledge in coherent form by synthesizing the personal, literary, philosophical, and theological perceptions that constitute this antipositivist position. I am not saying the scientific approach to sex should be rejected; I am saying it should be broadened. For I believe sex can be studied thoroughly and meaningfully only by including components that have been neglected in what passes today for a "science" of sex.

As I organized the materials that helped me reconceptualize sex in this way, it occurred to me that I was unintentionally following the phenomenological "reduction"—the method of intentionally doubting the received wisdom about a topic on deeper and deeper levels. In retrospect, I came to see that the earliest materials I could make sense of concerned not sex itself but its interpretation. These I brought together in what is now part two. Other materials indicated that sex was capable of more than one interpretation. These other interpretations of sex and their interplay comprise what is now part three. Only after I had cleared away these interpretations of sex could I see that my remaining materials concerned the pure experience of sex. These I organized in what is now part one. Finally, I arranged the parts into their present sequence because I felt the reader would find it clearer to transverse my reconceptualization of sex in the logical order of its development rather than in the phenomenological order of its discovery.

The complexity of my topic, my resources, and my approach obliged me to go through many drafts to produce this book. Several readers of these earlier versions helped to lead me out of the conceptual mazes in which I often got lost when my arguments had reached what seemed dead ends. In particular, I wish to thank Bennett Berger and Aaron Cicourel, of the University of California, San Diego, and Gary Marx, of MIT, for their detailed comments. Elizabeth Vodola, of the University of California, Berkeley, has my appreciation for editing my sometimes circumlocutory prose in these early drafts. Once again I am indebted to Donald Levine, of the University of Chicago, for bringing my manuscript to publishers' attention. I am also grateful to the entire sociology department of the University of California, San Diego, for its sustained support during the many years it took me to bring my project to fruition.

Finally, I would like to thank my wife, Catherine Schmidt, for sharing her numerous insights into my topic, and especially for her amused forbearance whenever I made notes on unseemly matters at untimely times.

Introduction

*F*or many years I have been puzzled by two questions: Why does a person want to have sex with others? And why do other people attempt to stop him or her from doing so? I first tried to find answers for these questions in the enormous literature on these topics already available.

One large group of books revealed the way we *should* have sex, either morally ("spontaneously," "lovingly," etc.) or technically ("rhythmically," "imaginatively," etc.). But their cognitive value seemed to me to lie less in what they claimed to demonstrate about sex than in what they inadvertently disclosed about a society that reduces every problematic activity to a homily or a diagram.

A second large group of books revealed the way we *do* have sex, describing the wide variations in sexual behaviors in different societies and subgroups of our society as well as in different stages of social history and individual development. But many of these books were merely anecdotal, displaying the diversity of sexual activities in the same way some early naturalists displayed butterflies and other species: merely as a haphazard collection with little attempt to integrate them into a more general system. Too often the surface variety of sexual relations has discouraged any attempt to search for their underlying unity.

The relatively few books that did postulate a principle for sex usually fell back on the "instinct theory." They treated sex as a "natural instinct" in the organism which manifests itself in various ways under various conditions. Sigmund Freud, the main proponent of this doctrine, believed the sexual instinct to be an irrational force, which periodically manifests itself to consciousness in the form of a swelling tension which strives for its own negation (see especially Freud 1961). He ingeniously describes what occurs when the sexual instinct, madly and blindly seeking the satisfaction of extinction, smashes into the obstacles society places in its path; for only after colliding with social restrictions do its trajectories become apparent in dreams, neuroses, slips of tongue, jokes, and so on, just as the tracks of certain subatomic particles become visible only after colliding with the water droplets of a cloud chamber.[1] But on the precollision nature of sex Freud had much less to say.

There are several problems in conceiving of sex as a natural instinct. First, whoever refers to something as "natural" or "instinctual" implies he has explained it fully and need say no more. But these rhetorical terms of conceptual closure inhibit further exploration of often the most crucial topics. Although powerful theories (like Newton's and Darwin's) have been spun around a key element called "natural" (e.g., gravity) or "instinctual" (e.g., self-preservation), they all contain this conceptual weakness at their core.

Second, by focusing on the taboos that restrain sexual expression, Freud's work has deflected attention from sex itself. Our current age of "liberation" has undermined these taboos, however, reducing the relevance of Freud's expression-repression model while increasing interest in sex's original, pre-impeded state.

Finally, the general acceptance of the instinct theory today itself has rendered this theory less provocative than it once was, has reduced its potential to generate the intellectual excitement necessary to stimulate further explorations of the unknown. (On the characteristics of "interesting" theories, see Davis 1971.)

For all these reasons, I decided to abandon the instinct theory and to try to develop new answers to the questions that motivated my search, starting from scratch. In this book, therefore, I will take the ball away from Freud's psychoanalytic disciples and pass it on to some more recent schools of thought. I hope that reconceptualizing sex in terms of these new paradigms will make it a more attractive and available topic for researchers who are not psychoanalytically oriented[2]—"turning out"[3] sex, as it were, from the exclusive possession of one kind of social scientist to the more comprehensive pleasure of others.

Let me stress, however, that I do not wish to disparage Freud's achievement, for his elaboration of his theory of sex is, without question, brilliant, even if the assumption on which it is based remains questionable. I merely wish to begin from a different starting point to see if another perspective can illuminate many of the aspects of sex that Freud's point of view has obscured.

To consider the first question concerning the appeal of sex I will analyze the erotic *phenomenologically* in part one. By synthesizing the phenomenology of Alfred Schutz and the existentialism of Jean-Paul Sartre, I will develop a perspective on sexual experience very different from the Freudian one. Whereas the Freudians see sex as basically biological (with some experiential consequences), I will conceive of it as essentially experiential (with some biological consequences). The Freudians regard human experience mainly as epiphenomena derived from more fundamental sexual desires.[4] In contrast, I will argue that sexual desires are also derived from human experience, being dependent as well as independent variables. In short, in part one I will treat sex as an *experience* that the individual wants to undergo and that society may encourage, rather than as an *instinct* that the individual wants to express and that society may repress.

To consider the second question concerning the persecution of sex I will shift from the level of individual experience to the level of its social interpretation. In part two I will analyze the obscene *ideologically*, synthesizing Mary Douglas's structuralism and George Herbert Mead's symbolic interactionism to create a perspective on sexual restrictions that again differs from the psychoanalytic one. The Freudians ask why the individual who wants to engage in forbidden sex acts deviates from the norms of our society, examining his or her personal history to explain sexual deviations in terms of earlier family relations. I will ask why our society traditionally has had norms that prohibit certain sex acts, examining their interrelation to explain these sexual prohibitions in terms of their logical structure. The Freudians, who assume that sexual desires will be "normal" unless something obstructs the usual course of their development, seek the cause of deviance. I, who assume that sexual desires will be diverse unless something channels them, seek the cause of normality.

Of course, to interpret sexual experience as obscene is only one way to look at it. In part three, therefore, I will contrast this conservative interpretation (disseminated mostly by theologians) that *fears* sex will disrupt society with the radical interpretation (disseminated mostly by literati) that *hopes* sex will disrupt society as well as with the liberal interpretation (disseminated mostly by social scientists) that minimizes the effect of sex on society.

Today many people in our society, caught between these world views, find our ambiguous age painfully confusing. But the theorist should find exhilarating the potential for clarification it offers, for only during the relatively brief transition periods between dominant world views can we come to understand their nature, their differences, and the process of their acceptance or rejection. If the world view currently in ascendance ever becomes taken for granted, the new clichés about sex will seem as obvious and unquestionable as did the old ones.

My nonstandard approach to sex calls for some remarks. First, although I am trying to describe the ways people experience and interpret sex, the only "evidence" I will offer for the validity of my descriptions are individual examples. Those who object to nonquantitative research argue, correctly, that "for example" is not proof. But if the same sexual experience or interpretation has been observed or commented on from three diverse viewpoints—my own, the example's author, and the reader's—its validity becomes at least plausible, if not yet fully proved. (When I could find no published example to confirm my own observation, I had to settle for the lesser degree of certainty supported by two viewpoints out of three; I hope the reader feels there were no instances where my viewpoint score was only one out of three.) Furthermore, I would rather present a small amount of support for a series of interesting assertions than a large amount of evidence for a few trivial ones. Researchers who devote most of their time and energy to documenting their assertions often end up with ones not worth documenting.

Second, although I am trying to develop a description of sex that is comprehensive, the resources from which I infer this description have been neither collected nor examined systematically. At the early stage of investigation, systematic method produces deceptive results. "Rigorous" researchers tend to focus only on dimensions of a topic for which data are easy to gather or analyze systematically, rather than on dimensions that are important for theory development or for the research subjects themselves. Thus rigorous researchers often feel they have exhausted a topic when others feel they have barely begun. For this reason, I chose to gather and analyze materials in ways that best manifested aspects of sex that are important in both senses mentioned above, even if I had to rely on some serendipity to do so.[5]

Third, although I am trying to concentrate on sex in this book, I cannot avoid some discussion of the interpersonal context in which it takes place, a topic I have treated more extensively elsewhere (see Davis 1973). Intimate relations and sexual relations are so closely connected that it is impossible to peel them apart without some particles of the one coming off on the analysis of the other.

Fourth, although I am trying to construct a universal model of sex, it will soon become obvious that this book was written from the male and heterosexual point of view. I do not believe this limitation is serious because I hope to show that sex—the topic of this book—is related to gender and orientation only incidentally. Consequently, I have emphasized the major aspects of sexual experience about which men and women, heterosexuals and homosexuals, share the same perspective while merely noting the minor ones about which their perspectives differ. Nevertheless, I hope this book will motivate other researchers to analyze sexual experience from the female or homosexual points of view to determine whether the gender and orientation differences I consider insignificant are actually significant. It would also be especially worthwhile for them to examine what might be called "romantic reality" and its relation to the sexual experience.

Fifth, a related issue concerns the "correct" use of pronoun gender, which is a touchy subject today for some people, especially in a book on sex. Although in general I have tried to match these pronouns to their appropriate reference, the desire to avoid awkward or incomprehensible sentences has sometimes forced me to use the masculine (and occasionally the feminine) pronoun alone when I mean to refer to both genders.

Finally, I am *not* trying to convince the reader that there is only one correct way to look at sex and that all the other ways people have conceived of it previously are worthless. I have no ax to grind, although on occasion I do sharpen a few knives.

Ever since the Cynic philosopher Diogenes was criticized for publically fornicating in the forum of Athens in the fourth century B.C., it has been the norm in Western society—as in most others—that sex should occur only in private.[6] Behavior in private places is, by definition, difficult to study. But none of the alternatives to observing sex in its natural settings is fully satisfactory. Observing sex in laboratory settings can change it in unknown ways (see Leslie Farber's critique [1978, pp. 123–145] of Masters and Johnson's research [1966]). And interviewing people about the sex they have in natural settings can motivate them to report only what they believe is acceptable to the interviewer or to society (see Paul Robinson's critique [1977, pp. 45–47] of Kinsey's method [1948, 1953]).[7] Since these distortions defeat the attempt to investigate sex both objectively and directly, I have fallen back on other means that are either objective or direct.

The main objective resource I will use to study sex is pornography.[8] Pornographers must achieve some verisimilitude in their work or they would lose their audiences. Occasionally, of course, they use fictive genre conventions for display purposes. For example, the "external ejaculation," in which the male comes outside—and usually on—the female, is as common in pornographic movies as it is rare in real life. But on the whole pornographers portray sex in a way that their readers find at least conceivable, if not common.

The pornography I will examine is more "soft core" than "hard core." When I began this project, I was surprised to discover that hard-core pornography is usually more abstract and less explicit than soft-core pornography. With the major exceptions of Pauline Réage's and Marco Vassi's writings, most hard-core pornographic books simply describe sexual *behavior*. (More precisely, they use four-letter words to induce the reader to imagine the corresponding behaviors: "First we sucked, then we fucked," etc.) Most hard-core pornographic movies are also abstract and behavioristic, for they seldom inform their audience about their characters' personality types and social categories. Soft-core pornography usually describes sexual *experience* in more detail, often depicting the subtle phenomenological effects that result when a character's sexual behavior clashes with his or her personal and social characteristics. Luis Buñuel's film *Belle de Jour*, for instance, captured the experiential distortions that occur when the prudish wife of a bourgeois spends her afternoons in a brothel. By analyzing these pornographic works I hope to combine the artist's perceptive descriptions of particular sexual episodes with the scientist's precise generalizing concepts.

Moreover, social scientists should find examining the lowest-status literary genres, like pornography, as fruitful as investigating the lowest-status human groups (bums, criminals, freaks, etc.). The most proscribed literary forms—like the most persecuted social deviants—must reveal unsettling truths about society that it does not want to hear.

A second objective resource I will draw on are classical theologians and philosophers—Augustine, Kant, and others. Although it may seem strange to juxtapose literary traditions as far apart as are theology and philosophy from pornography, their portrayals of sex are actually complementary; for these classical theologians and philosophers have directed attention to its harmful features whereas pornographers have pointed out its beneficial characteristics. In the last several centuries—until respectable authors and scientists could tolerate the topic again—theologians, philosophers, and pornographers were almost the only writers to deal with the sex act itself.

Sex must have at least the potential of being one of life's boundary experiences if it could be treated by only the highest and the lowest literary genres. (Freud himself observed, "The highest and the lowest are always closest to each other in the sphere of sexuality" [1972, p. 52].) As such, it should be studied in the social science traditions that attempt to connect the extremes of human existence rather than in those that confine their concerns to mankind's middle range.[9]

The most direct resource available to the sex researcher is his own sexual experience. But a participant-observation study of sex entails several risks. For one thing, the investigator may mistake his personal peculiarities for universal features of social life, painting a portrait of intercourse that his readers will find unrecognizable. For another, he may inadvertently reveal his own sexual preferences and discover, to his embarrassment, that he has exposed himself in public as completely as any confessional writer (for the way a person wants to copulate is thought to manifest his true nature). Finally, he may feel obliged to neutralize sex's sinister properties by using various appurtenances of "scholarly detachment" such as statistics, jargon, abstractness, and blandness. Otherwise some of his colleagues may feel that his topic has contaminated him personally by seeping across the boundary between research and researcher, just as sexual contamination sometimes crosses the boundary between character and actor (Goffman 1974, pp. 227–28) or between story and author (Roth 1977, p. 51).

All this may disgust some of his readers (for reasons discussed in part two), causing them to slam his book, snub his person, and try to deprive him of his job. Nevertheless, the intellectual benefits derived from drawing on direct subjective resources in the study of sex far outweigh the personal risk involved. The maxim, "nothing ventured, nothing gained," is nowhere more aptly applied than to sex research.

Some words on words. There are no neutral English terms for sexual organs and activities. Instead there are:

1. Usages implying that acceptable words for sex do not exist, such as asterisks (replacing an entire word or running through its middle like a lexical chastity belt), meaningless or onomatopoeic words ("oomph"), and adjectives describing sex as "unspeakable" or "unmentionable." Until recently most dictionaries omitted virtually all words referring to sex.

2. Allusions to sexual matters through the most abstract concepts possible, such as "it" or "thing":

> She that's a maid now and laughs at my departure
> shall not be maid long, unless things be cut shorter.
> Shakespeare, King Lear 1.5.55–56

3. Metaphors. The lexicographer Eric Partridge (1969, pp. 22–28, 35–36) found that Shakespeare analogized sexual parts and performances to geography and topology; agriculture and horticulture; war, archery, and jousting; sports, games, and athletics; business, trading and commerce; shapes and music; and religion and domesticity. Sexual metaphors drawn from nature vary with the society, as the literary critic John Atkins tell us:

> Just as the Arabs tended to see a desired body as a fruit and the Chinese as a tree, so the Western Europeans turned, characteristically, to landscape, and often landscape on such a scale that it resembled more a map. [1972, p. 184]

John Donne provides an example of the Western tendency to cartographize the sexual aspects of the human body:

> Licence my roaving hands, and let them go
> Before, behind, between, above, below.
> O my America! my new-found-land,
> My Kingdome, safeliest when with one man man'd,
> My myne of precious stones, My Emperie,
> How blest am I in thus discovering thee!
> Elegie xix, "Going to Bed"

Sexual metaphors used to be organic: "Thy two breasts are like two young roes that are twins, which feed among the lilies," sings the biblical Song of Solomon (4:5). Today they are mechanical: "The thought of screwing her turns me on."

4. Euphemisms, especially those that substitute a general area for the genitals (like lap) or a peripheral activity for sex

("sleep with"). The Victorians even euphemized matters only remotely connected with sex, as the popular historian and science writer G. Rattay Taylor reports:

> In the Middle Ages, the Church had preached the strongest condemnation of sex, but it had never hesitated to call a spade a spade. Neither had it objected to representations in art of the sex organs and even of the sexual act, in both normal and perverted forms. . . . It is, of course, quite inconceivable that the Victorians could have placed any such representations in their churches. . . . Thus not only standard nouns, used repeatedly by the Bible, such as "whore" and "fornication" became taboo, but references to childbirth became indelicate: the word "accouchement" began to replace "delivery" and "pregnant" the more native "with child." But in time even "pregnant" . . . became objectionable and led to the more ambiguous "in an interesting condition." [1973, pp. 212–13]

Even the term "sex" itself is a euphemism for sex, since it originally meant "gender" (from the Latin *'secare'*: to cut, divide).

5. Vulgar terms implying that sex is a lower-class activity (prick, fuck, suck) and Latin terms implying that sexual activity is confined to the educated upper class (penis, intercourse, fellatio). The lack of middle-class nomenclature for sexual organs and behaviors suggest a middle-class belief that they do not exist in the respectable world. Yet it is interesting that only the lower-class words have been censored as obscene:

> One of the strangest manifestations of the obscenity delusion is the idea that words in themselves have magical power and that two words, each describing the same thing, may be of quite different orders of "dirtiness." Thus "to fuck" is dirtier than "to copulate," "prick" is dirtier than "penis," "cunt" is dirtier than "vagina," and so on. Even the Kronhausens, whom one would hardly suspect of squeamishness, found it necessary to use circumlocutions like "vernacular for the

female sex organ" when quoting excerpts from pornographic
books. Yet these very authors point out the absurdity of
regarding as obscene an Anglo-Saxon monosyllable while
accepting a Latin polysyllable having the same meaning. [de
Ropp 1969, pp. 207–8]

Sexual censorship seems designed to suppress lower-class
mores whenever they intrude on middle-class morals (see
Bullough and Bullough 1977, pp. 166ff).

The sexual terminology of one class becomes comical
when used by another class. During a performance I
attended of the pornographic movie *The Story of Joanna*, the
audience convulsed with laughter whenever a supposedly
aristocratic character talked about sex in lower-class terms by
saying: "I want you to lick my pussy." The converse is
equally comical: "Please perform cunnilingus on my vagina," I overheard a truckstop waitress say to a trucker,
cracking up the other customers.

6. Overlapping the educated upper-class terms for sex are
scientific terms like "coition" and "genitalia." They make
sex seem like an engineering problem rather than a human
experience, accounting for their use in sex manuals: "Posi-
tioning his genitalia for coition, the male. . . ."

7. Ordinary words that have acquired sexual connotations. Unable to speak adequately in its own tongue, sex has
broken out of its linguistic quarantine and insinuated itself
into the rest of language. Chevy Chase, the mock newscaster
on NBC TV's *Saturday Night Live*, got a knowing laugh from
his audience by whispering into a telephone to his offstage
girlfriend, "No. *First* you fill your mouth with hot water, *then*
put in the ice cubes. . . ." Similarly the *New York Times* once
innocently carried an advertisement describing a pornographic movie as "Showering the Golden Screen with Love"
("golden showers" being the connoisseur's code words for
"urolagnia," which in turn is the psychologist's code word
for "liking to be pissed on"). The increasing prevalence of
these double entendres recalls Shakespeare's time.

The vocabulary for sex is changing. Lower-class terms like "prick" are gradually creeping upward while upper-class terms like "penis" are gradually creeping downward. Scientific terms like "coition" are gradually creeping into popular use while popular terms like "screwing" are gradually creeping into scientific use. Nevertheless a wide gap remains at the center: there are still no neutral terms—especially verbs—to use for discussing sex. Consequently, I have felt free to choose terms from all the above categories, as the context requires. This procedure has the advantage of dissociating me from social groups whose perspective on sex is restricted by their limited terminology. But since the entire sexual vocabulary currently available contains only high notes and low notes, this book might sometimes sound as though it were written by an adolescent whose voice is changing with puberty—alternately too crude with its "fucks" and too formal with its "fornicates."

Literary illustrations and interpretations of sex are not easy to produce. From about 1800 until very recently the sex act was the most conspicuous lacuna in literature: it occurred literally between the lines. Authors wrote around this subject, focusing only on the intimate relations in which intercourse was embedded. Even as sophisticated a writer as Stendhal used the technique of compressing time to get through a sexual episode:

> On seeing [Julian] enter, Mme. de Renal jumped out of bed. "Wretch!" she cried. . . . His only answer to her reproaches was to throw himself at her feet and clasp her knees. Since she said some very harsh things to him, he burst into tears.
> When Julian left Mme. de Renal's bedroom some hours later, it might be said, in the style of the novel, that he had nothing more left to desire. [1970, p. 95]

Film directors also advanced the art of sexual evasion. Like novelists, they compressed time, quickly cutting or slowly

dissolving to the next scene; but their main technical contribution was expanding space: panning the camera away
from the copulators and into their surroundings in order to
examine some natural process that symbolically paralleled
the sexual activities going on off camera. Pornographic
filmmaker Gerard Damiano disparages this technique:

> For some reason it's acceptable to *imply* that two people are
> fucking. Hollywood has been doing that for years. There's an
> embrace, and then you pan away to the fireplace, or the
> raging sea. But that's inadequate. That's bullshit. I do think
> that the amount of time you see actual penetration should be
> cut down to a bare minimum, but I do not want to go back to
> panning to that blazing fireplace. [*Village Voice*, 2 February
> 1976, p. 119]

If novelists and filmmakers have looked away from sex,
social scientists have looked at it from the wrong distance—
either presbyopically or myopically. Sociologists like Kinsey
looked at sex from so far away (as though with the wrong
end of a telescope) that they observed only an exterior behavior without human meaning (Trilling 1953, pp. 223–25,
229; Robinson 1977, pp. 56–57). Psychologists like Freud
looked at sex so closely (as though with X-ray eyes) that they
saw through it to observe only an inhuman and meaningless
interior instinct. In this book I will try to find the distance
that brings human experiences and interpretations of sex
into sharpest focus, even if it blurs sexual behaviors in the
foreground and sexual instincts in the background.

Clearly, this view of sex is one that inspires great fear. All
these artists and scientists have averted their eyes in one
way or another during the "sex scenes" in art and life, as if
they dreaded that their glance would disclose some terrifying crack in their cosmos. But those who do not fear that sex
will fragment their firmament believe the time has come to
look.

Part One
Sexual Experience

Erotic Reality and Everyday Reality

Writing in the 1920s, the Austrian novelist Robert Musil observed that sex was one of those activities that pull consciousness away from the ordinary concerns of everyday life:

> The sight of her had stirred him and moved him to caresses. Now, when it was all over, he felt again how little it concerned him. The incredible swiftness of such transformations, which turn a sane man into a frothing lunatic, now became all too strikingly clear. But it seemed to him that this erotic metamorphosis of consciousness was only a special case of something far more general; for nowadays all manifestations of our inner life, such as for instance an evening at the theatre, a concert, or a church service, are such swift appearing and disappearing islands of a second state of consciousness temporarily interpolated into the ordinary one.
>
> 'And yet a short time ago I was still at work,' he thought, 'and before that I was walking down the

street to buy a paper. . . . Yet in the mean time we have been
flying through a cloud of madness, and it is no less uncanny
how the solid experiences close up again over that vanishing
gap and re-assert themselves in all their tenacity.' [1965, p.
132]

The perspective from which we shall study these interpola-
tions of specialized experience within the broader experience of everyday life is the *phenomenological*.

Phenomenology was first defined in its modern form by
the German philosopher Edmund Husserl, who conceived
of it as a method to discover the foundations of the physical
world in human experience rather than in matter, where the
natural sciences sought them. His student, the Austrian
philosopher-sociologist Alfred Schutz, reoriented phenomenological research from the physical to the social
world. Schutz undertook a series of investigations into the
human experience of various temporary social roles, asking
how it felt to be a stranger, a homecomer, a scientist, a
musician, a fantasizer, a dreamer. But he did not investigate
the experience of what his contemporary Robert Musil considered the paradigm of all temporary social roles: the copulator. This topic was left for the French Existentialist Jean-
Paul Sartre to explore in his major work *Being and Nothingness*
(1956). But even Sartre was less interested in describing
sexual experience than in using it to prove the durability of
the individual in contrast to the ephemerality of all relations
between individuals, of which sex is the prototype. Recently, in *Frame Analysis* (1974), the Canadian-American
sociologist Erving Goffman greatly increased the power of
the phenomenological perspective by examining the borders
that distinguish experience inside a situation from experience outside the situation, as a "frame" differentiates what
is experienced as "picture" from what is experienced as
"wall." He extended phenomenology's concerns, applying
it particularly to "an evening at the theater" (as suggested by
Musil); and he refined its concepts, above all in his distinction between an individual's sense of "what is real" and

"what it is he can get caught up in, engrossed in, carried away by" (p. 6). But apart from some brief peeks at pornography (pp. 54–56, 70–71, 277–78), Goffman—uncharacteristically reticent—refrains from framing sex, the most obvious application of frame analysis.

In sum, these theorists have chiseled many facets into the phenomenological prism; but to my knowledge neither they nor anyone else have used it to scrutinize sex as comprehensively, systematically, and concretely as I believe this topic requires.

The sexual phenomenology I will develop here is based on the following observation: Those who copulate—and those who merely want to—experience the world in a manner strikingly different from those who go about their ordinary activities in everyday life. Like certain psychedelic drugs, sexual arousal alters people's consciousness, changing their perception of the world. Sex, in short, is a *reality-generating activity*.

My investigation of this topic will be an exercise in applied, rather than theoretical, phenomenology. I will attempt to articulate a specific experience rather than to discover the foundations of all experience, the task that has preoccupied phenomenology proper. Since I am more concerned with characterizing erotic experience than with searching for its pure "essence," I can drop much of the conceptual apparatus and bizzare jargon elaborated by the phenomenological tradition for the further stages of this inquiry, retaining only the simple descriptive concepts with which it begins this quest. A brief explication of these aspects of phenomenology will be useful for understanding the difference between the realities generated by sexual arousal and by everyday life. They are presented most clearly in the works of Alfred Schutz.

Schutz held that we experience our life as a primary everyday life-world that contains such secondary "other-worldly" enclaves as dreams, fantasies, and science (1973, p. 21). He calls our everyday life-world and its several secondary subworlds "finite provinces of meaning" (p. 23). As long as they do not contradict one another, we will regard as "real" whichever one we happen to be in at the moment (p. 22). All experiences are harmonious and compatible within a single finite province of meaning but inharmonious and incompatible between different ones (pp. 23–24). Therefore, we will experience all transitions between finite provinces of meaning as a "shock." Schutz cites as examples:

> going to sleep as a leap into a dream, awaking, the theater curtain rising, "being absorbed" in a painting . . . the shifting of consciousness when one begins to play, the lived experience of the "numinous," the jolt by which . . . the scientist shifts after dinner to the theoretical attitude, and also laughter as a reaction to the displacement of reality which is the basis of a joke. [1973, p. 24]

Schutz distinguishes the everyday life-world from others on the attentive dimension or what he calls the "tension of consciousness." Our everyday life-world requires our consciousness to be at its highest tension level, requires us to be "wide-awake." In contrast, our fantasy- or dream-world allows our consciousness to operate on lower tension levels, allows us to be less concerned with encountering actual everyday life (pp. 25, 35–36).

The pragmatic dimension or what Schutz calls the "form of spontaneity" also distinguishes these finite provinces of meaning. In daily life, "we act and operate not only within the life-world but also upon it" (p. 6). Through our bodily movements we actively "gear into" the outer world in order to transform its objects through "work." In contrast, scientific theorizing requires only "acts of thought" and dreaming is mostly passive (1973, pp. 26–27; 1962, pp. 212, 240–42).

These worlds differ as well along the communicative dimension or the "form of sociality." True communication is unique to everyday life because it is inherently intersubjective whereas dreaming is inherently solitary. Since scientific theorizing is also a solitary activity, the scientist must "drop the pure theoretical attitude . . . [and] return to the world of daily life . . . in order to communicate [his] theoretical thought to [his] fellow-men" (1973, pp. 27, 34; 1962, pp. 218, 244, 256). (We will examine other dimensions that, Schutz claims, distinguish the everyday life-world in chapter 1.)

The everyday life-world, then, differs from all other finite provinces of meaning because it is the wide-awake world of work and talk. Since only in this world are we most conscious, most affecting and affected physically, and most able to communicate verbally with others, Schutz concludes that is must be the "paramount reality," although he concedes that it does not always look this way to those caught up on other worlds (1973, p. 25; 1962, pp. 341–42).

In adapting phenomenology to study sex I shall replace Schutz's cumbersome "finite province of meaning" with the simple term "reality."[1] Thus I will refer to the experience of the world generated by our ordinary round of life as "everyday reality" and to that generated by our actual or potential sexual activities as "erotic reality."

Furthermore, I will not assume with Schutz that everyday reality is the "paramount reality" that superordinates all others (presumably including erotic reality; see also Goffman's critique of this assumption, 1974, pp. 560–63.) Schutz, who earned his living as a lawyer, banker, and broker, reveals his bourgeois bias in believing everyday reality more basic than the others. There may be many lawyers, bankers, and brokers who experience erotic episodes as nothing more than insignificant interruptions contained within the larger organization of their everyday lives. But prowling the halls of office buildings there are also many lovers (incidentally employed as lawyers, bankers, and brokers) who experience their everyday existence in the workaday world as merely the unimportant and unpleasant interlude between their erotic activities. When undistracted by work, their consciousness continually returns to this most significant and satisfying segment of their lives. Whoever has experienced how boring jobs dull awareness and how sexual fantasies

(not to mention activities) sharpen it will be extremely skeptical of Schutz's assertion that the former require a "higher
tension of consciousness" than the latter.

Most sex theorists agree that people lead split-level lives,
experiencing everyday reality and erotic reality as two distinct realms.[2] Nevertheless, components of one realm sometimes appear in the other.

Erotic elements may migrate into everyday reality, sub-
jecting ordinary consciousness to painful strain. For example, words that conjure up erotic reality blurted out in an
everyday setting may be as shocking as "a pistol shot at a
concert" (to borrow Stendhal's famous image of a revolution). This was especially true in eras when sexual activities
were unmentionable, as the cartoonist Al Capp recalls in
speaking about his early sexual experiences in the 1920s:

> You never talked about sex. It simply wasn't mentioned. The
> whole point was to have sex but never to admit to the other
> one that you'd had it. Even while you were buttoning up your
> fly, you just didn't admit it. Nice people simply never talked
> about it at all. [Fleming and Fleming 1975, p. 39]

Psychoanalysis underscores the role of language in evoking
each reality by trying to teach people to use the vocabulary of
erotic reality without going into it.

> Much of the character of the early periods of psychoanalysis
> involves training the patient in how to talk without arousal
> about this [sexual] aspect of his life. Even when this process is
> successful it creates the capacity to talk only in the context of
> the specialized therapeutic relationship and often with a
> highly abstract vocabulary that protects both the therapist
> and the patient from directly confronting sexual content. This
> is learning a capacity to neutralize the topic of sexuality, not
> learning to talk about it without concomitant anxiety or
> arousal. [Gagnon and Simon 1973, p. 105]

Also, certain parts of the body are citizens of both erotic

and everyday realms, for we must suppress our awareness of their sexual allegiances to put them to ordinary uses.

> Most of the physical acts . . . in the . . . sexual sequence occur in many other situations—the palpation of the breast for cancer, the gynecological examination, the insertion of tampons, mouth-to-mouth resuscitation—all involve homologous physical events. But the social situation and the actors are not defined as sexual or potentially sexual, and the introduction of a sexual element is seen as a violation of the expected social arrangements. [Gagnon and Simon 1973, pp. 22–23]

Everyday objects too, like cigars and donuts, may act as "sex symbols"—carnal forms lurking behind casual contents. Sex symbols seduce their viewers' unsuspecting consciousness out of the everyday into the erotic, causing them to wonder why so much trivia should evoke so much anxiety.

If erotic elements do not succeed in transforming or shocking everyday consciousness, they may end up merely annoying or embarrassing it. Some people—often reviewers of ordinary films—find boring and pointless the pornographic films that enthrall the rest of their audience. Unable to "get off" into an erotic reality that would inject excitement and meaning into the sexual images on the screen, they must watch them in the bright light of everyday reality, which washes out much of the shade and color of their sense.

Although the consumption of pornography may inadvertently occur in everyday reality, many aspects of its production must occur there. An editorial apprentice in a pornographic book factory reports her first reaction to the irony of having to deal with erotic elements in a matter-of-fact everyday way:

> I would have to replace all the author's boring physiological terms and charming euphemisms with hardcore, right-to-the-point grabbers. . . . Here I was, fumbling and fidgeting

while my new boss recited terms for the male sex organ in the
same tone of voice he might use to discuss the weather.
  "It seems strange to be discussing these things, doesn't it?"
he asked, seeing my embarrassment.
  I barely giggled out my agreement. [Lane 1978, p. 14]

Finally, when those locked into everyday reality are forced
to copulate, they will find even the sex act itself absurd. An
excellent illustration of the difference between the everyday
and the erotic perceptions of the world can be found by
comparing two classic passages from D. H. Lawrence's *Lady
Chatterley's Lover*. In the first Connie Chatterley is engaging
in outer erotic behavior without inner erotic experience:

> And this time the sharp ecstasy of her own passion did not
> overcome her; she lay with her hands inert on his striving
> body, and do what she might, her spirit seemed to look on
> from the top of her head, and the butting of his haunches
> seemed ridiculous to her, and the sort of anxiety of his penis
> to come to its little evacuating crisis seemed farcical. [1968,
> p. 184]

In the second she is engaging in similar behavior, but this
time sees it through an entirely different lens:

> And now in her heart, the queer wonder of him was
> awakened. . . . And now she touched him, and it was the
> sons of god with the daughters of men. . . . Her hands came
> timorously down his back, to the soft, smallish globes of the
> buttocks. Beauty! What beauty! a sudden little flame of new
> awareness went through her. How was it possible, this
> beauty here, where she had previously only been repelled?
> [1968, pp. 187–88]

Conversely, elements of everyday reality sometimes trespass upon erotic reality. Copulators who import instrumental criteria of "performance" or "adequacy" from
the everyday world of work quickly dispel the magic of erotic

reality, as the French phenomenologist Paul Ricoeur observes:

> Eros . . . belongs to the pretechnical existence of man. . . . Sexuality remains basically foreign to the "intention-tool-thing" relationship. It is a surviving example of noninstrumental immediacy. The body to body relationship—or better, person to flesh to flesh to person—remains basically nontechnical. As soon as attention is drawn to and settles on the technique of adjustment or the technique of sterility, the charm is broken. [1964, p. 141]

He also notes that the erotic world is essentially silent:

> Sexuality . . . belongs to the prelinguistic existence of man. . . . It mobilizes language, true, but it crosses it, jostles it, sublimates it, stupefies it, pulverizes it into a murmur, an invocation. Sexuality demediatizes language; it is Eros and not Logos. [1964, p. 141]

Therefore, copulators who direct their sexual interaction verbally also threaten to shatter the fragile goblet of erotic reality ("Roll over and put your head down there.").

Manipulating their environment through work and talk, then, is part of the everyday world that lovers are trying to forget. Erotic reality is often too delicate to contain these alien processes without disintegrating.[3] Thus erotic reality and everyday reality must each be whole and self-contained. Those shifting from one gestalt to the other usually want to go all the way if they want to go at all.

Occasionally, however, someone may attempt to cling to everyday reality while being dragged into erotic reality, trying to retain his or her ordinary technical competence even while being seduced. In Phillip Roth's novel *Portnoy's Complaint*, Portnoy's girlfriend fantasizes herself testing the ability to maintain military composure under extreme duress:

Around a big conference table, at rigid attention, sit all the boys in West Virginia who are seeking admission to West Point. Underneath the table, crawling on her hands and knees, and nude, is our gawky teen-age illiterate, Mary Jane Reed. A West Point colonel with a swagger stick tap-tapping behind his back, circles and circles the perimeter of the table, scrutinizing the faces of the young men, as out of sight Mary Jane proceeds to undo their trousers and to blow each of the candidates in his turn. The boy selected for admission to the military academy will be he who is most able to maintain a stern and dignified soldierly bearing while shooting off into Mary Jane's savage and knowing little weapon of a mouth. [1969, pp. 213–14][4]

It is one of the most remarkable features of human existence that we live not in one reality but in two (at least) and that we continually alternate between them, often against our will. Sometimes we are pulled into erotic reality when we want to remain in everyday reality, like the professor who finds himself with an erection in the middle of a lecture; at other times we are forced to fall back into everyday reality when we want to enter erotic reality, like the lover who finds himself without an erection when he has finally bedded his beloved. The sixteenth-century French essayist Montaigne voices the male side of this classical complaint about the capriciousness of sexual desire:

We have reason to remark the untractable liberties taken by this member, which intrudes so tiresomely when we do not require it and fails so annoyingly when we need it most, imperiously pitting its authority against that of the will, and most proudly and obstinately refusing our solicitations both mental and manual. [1958a, p. 42]

An exaggerated but eloquent version of the female side appears in the French pornographic film *Pussy Talk* where a voluble vagina gains control over its possessor's consciousness and conduct, forcing her into erotic reality whenever she wants to enter it least.

Oscillating between these two realities, we continually encounter the difficulty of integrating these two separate aspects of our existence. How different human life would be if people remained constantly in only one realm! If asexual, they need live only in everyday reality as eunuchs do and as monks and nuns aspire. If hypersexual, they need live only in erotic reality like sexual psychopaths, satyrists, and nymphomaniacs or like some of the fictional characters of the Marquis de Sade, Jean Genet, and William Burroughs as well as (to a lesser extent) Vladimir Nabokov, Phillip Roth, and Erica Jong. We might sometimes envy those who live only in one world, experiencing no transitional shocks and problems. But we who live in both worlds usually find the diversity worth the difficulty, and feel as superior to those reclused in one reality as the tourist does to stay-at-home.

In chapter 1 I will contrast our experiences of everyday and erotic realities. In chapter 2 I will examine the movement of our minds between them.

1.
The Lascivious Shift out of Everyday Reality

Someone who is sexually aroused experiences the world much differently from someone who is not (and from his or her own world-experience before and afterward). Sexual arousal brings new phenomena to one's attention while old phenomena fade from it; previously minor aspects loom larger in importance while previously major aspects shrink in significance.

In Alfred Schutz's terms, a person's "system of relevances" changes as soon as he or she becomes sexually aroused. Schutz uses this concept to describe our experience of the everyday world in his essay "On Multiple Realities":

> But we are not *equally* interested in all the strata of the [everyday world]. The selective function of our interest organizes the world in both . . . space and time in strata of major and minor relevance. . . . Those objects are selected as primarily important which are . . . ends or means . . . or . . . dangerous or enjoyable or otherwise relevant to me. [1962, p. 227][1]

Schutz's concept of a "relevance system" can be used to compare our experiences of everyday and erotic realities, and to account for their disjuction. For instance, it explains why someone who discovers that a same-gendered friend is homosexual is often stunned by the news, for he suddenly realizes that his sexual aspects, whose irrelevancy to their relationship he had taken for granted, may actually have been relevant all along—and vice versa for his nonsexual aspects. (Of course, he could be wrong.)

Whoever moves from everyday to erotic reality, then, experiences a *lascivious shift* in relevances in the temporal, spatial, social, and physical dimensions along which he organizes his world—a sexual effect analogous to the Doppler effect in physics.[2] In this chapter I will describe this perceptual distortion in each of these dimensions and point out the factors that generate ("turn-ons") or negate ("turn-offs") it.

Time

As far as the experience of time is concerned, sex really is "fun and games."[3] Like a game, sex is an objectively contained interruption in the temporal flow of everyday life. Like fun in a game, subjective involvement is normally confined to the sex act itself. Those preoccupied with preceding or succeeding events are not fully caught up in erotic reality.

But unlike most games, it is often uncertain exactly when sex has started. Erotic reality begins less sharply than it ends, as we shall see in the next chapter. And unlike the closed temporal horizon of most games, whose endings are determined by objective constraints (time, score, course), the temporal horizon of sex is open because it usually ends only when both partners subjectively feel finished.

Men and women, however, often disagree about the precise point a sexual episode starts or concludes. If the term *erotic inertia* can be used without negative connotations, women seem to have more of it than men, taking longer to get into erotic reality but also longer to get out of it. The phenomenological psychiatrist Leslie Farber observes:

The act of sex, for the male, is a contained event. Its onset of desire, or need, or even compelling urgency, its crescendo of development and its final climax and rapid denouement, constitute a drama of rise and fall. . . . His disinclination to linger . . . , usually felt and expressed as an abrupt urge to turn his attention elsewhere, to rejoin the world, is not a failure of affection on his part or a wishful repudiation of his larger tie to his mate—although it is sometimes so interpreted by her. . . .

A woman's experience of the act of sex is different. For her the event may be entered into with, or arise out of, desire—though seldom the undistractable urgency men sometimes feel. . . . Her inclination, unlike his, is to prolong the denouement of passion in order specifically to mark the relation of sex to the larger affection they share. [1978, p. 184]

Objective temporal constraints are usually distant enough to be disregarded. But they may encroach upon the sex act enough to kill its subjective spontaneity, compressing it into a mechanical activity. The American pornographer Marco Vassi provides an extreme example in *The Saline Solution*:

"I'm at George's." [Beverly said on the phone.] "I'm coming over there." . . . I look at Alice's body and remembered where we had left off. Perhaps I could give it twenty minutes.

It was Swiss. I had to take the entire sexual act and miniaturize it, leaving nothing out, rushing nothing, making it perfect but reducing the scale. . . .

Seven minutes, first vaginal caresses; eight and a half minutes, lick clitoris with tongue; twelve minutes, penetration; fifteen minutes, accomplish six variations from behind; seventeen and a half minutes . . . , penetrate to deepest upper point; now, two and a half minutes to ride . . . , she responds, she moans, she cries out, the vegetative tremors begin in my spine; nineteen and a half minutes, and throw open all the switches, pump pump fuck fuck whee whistle bang bang whoosh, and come. Huff huff. [Vassi 1976a, pp. 93–94]

As in such games as boxing and baseball, the objective time within the boundaries of the sex act is divided into rounds or innings. The subjective experience of the duration within these temporal subunits differs from the experience of the duration between them. Within each round, the partners exhaust the possibilities of some preliminary sexual activity (like fellatio or breast play) before moving on to the next after a brief break.

Erotic time must be synchronized more closely than everyday time. Each participant must continually try to harmonize his or her personal sexual rhythm with the partner's, during both the active periods and their interludes. Making music together (Schutz 1964, pp. 159–78) and sustaining good conversations (Davis 1973, pp. 180ff) are among the very few other activities that depend on time sharing so crucially. As soon as one partner's rhythm gets out of phase with the other's, they must readjust it immediately; otherwise accelerating disrhythmia will soon shatter the entire experience.

Certain periods of time are more likely than others to generate erotic reality. A person passes through intervals of these *eroticizing times* during the course of a day, a week, a year, even a lifetime. Although the hormonal cycles that help produce these periods may be regular, the interference between cycles of different lengths would make entrance into erotic reality an almost random disruption of everyday life if its generation were left solely to biology.

For this reason all societies smooth out the temporal flow of everyday life by regulating the occurrence of the erotic episodes that interrupt it. Some societies prescribe the times for intercourse in great detail:

> According to Eliezer the Great [in the ancient Jewish Mishnah] "the duty of marriage enjoined in the Law is: every day for them that are unoccupied; twice a week for labourers; once a week for ass-drivers; once every thirty days for camel drivers; and once every six months for sailors." [Quoted in Cameron 1976, p. 22]

Our society merely attempts to restrict sexual arousal to the vague temporal ghetto we call "bedtime."

One of the first to comment on the prevalence of this

custom, the seventeenth-century English satirical poet Samuel Butler, speculated in his *Notebooks* that it was responsible for the most serious social problem of his age (and perhaps of ours):

> These children that are begotten in the day, are commonly born in the day, and those in the Night by night: for Nature for the most part keepe's a Punctuall account of time: and that is one reason, why more are born in the Night than by Day, when men are commonly diverted by many other occasions. And in great Cities men are often in Drink before they goe to Bed which Makes the Children they get prove soe foolish. . . . [Quoted in Atkins 1972, p. 349]

Bedtime can be an eroticizing time because it occupies the residual period that remains after the duties and diversions of everyday existence are over. Its time horizon is infinite enough to allow the copulators to couple at their own pace, unrushed by the external deadlines of daily life.

Bedtime usually occurs at night, when many of the rules required for more formal daily interaction are suspended. The darkness that envelopes bedtime obscures the visual distortions of the close clinch of intercourse, the behavior that is more embarrassing when seen than when felt, and the inappropriate involvement (or lack of involvement) with one's sex partner or his/her parts. Bedtime occurs during the change-over from one day to the next that temporarily liquifies the solidity of everyday reality, producing the same fearful freedom of all transitional periods. Finally, sex is related to the other activity associated with bedtime: sleep. Besides reducing consciousness of everyday life, going to sleep provides a convenient utilitarian pretext both to begin and to end the sex act. It is not by chance that one of the main euphemisms for fucking in our society is currently to "sleep with."

The period preceding bedtime, when most social institutions are shutting down for the night, is also an eroticizing time. In a popular song sung by country and western artist

Mickey Gilley, this time period itself is observed to amplify the erotic reality generated by otherwise low-power faces and physiques:

> Don't the Girls all get Prettier at closin' time.
> Don't they all begin to look like movie stars. . . .
>   When the change starts taking place
>   It puts a glow on every face
> Of the fallen angels of the back street bars. . . .
> [Knight 1976]

Other periods are supposed to hinder the formation of erotic reality. *Uneroticizing times* in our society include "daytime" ("At least pull down the shades!"), "worktime," ("Stop fooling around: we've got work to do!"), and "mealtime" ("Now? How nauseating! Besides everything'll get cold.").

These temporal prohibitions against sex, however, are so weak in our society today that they are more honored in the breach. In fact, some people prefer to intensify their experience of erotic reality by socially violating these obsolescent norms while sexually violating each other. In *The World of Sex*, Henry Miller describes his daytime sexual adventures:

> Occasionally I would pay her a call in the middle of the day. I always had to proffer the excuse that I came to hear her play. . . . If I took a seat in the corner and listened to her attentively she might stop half way through a sonata and come over to me of her own accord, let me run my hand up her leg, and finally straddle me. With the orgasm she would sometimes have a weeping fit. Doing it in broad daylight always awakened her sense of guilt. [1965, p. 57–58]

Gospel singer Lou Rawles describes a sexual encounter while working:

> It was exciting, first of all because it was wrong—in the back seat of a car during a thirty-minute intermission between

singing "Jesus Loves Me," which was like our opening theme
song, and "He'll Never Let Go Your Hand," which was our
closing song.

A few minutes later I'm standing up there singing in front
of five thousand people and I look down and there was white
all over the front of my blue serge pants. The dudes ribbed me
to death about that for a month. . . . [Fleming and Fleming
1976, pp. 193–94]

Since temporal prohibitions against sex were weaker before and after the nineteenth century, the eighteenth-
century novelist Henry Fielding could portray the attempted
seduction of Tom Jones during dinner in a scene that would
become the celebrated centerpiece of Tony Richardson's
twentieth-century film:

Now, Mrs. Waters and our hero had no sooner sat down
together than the former began to play this artillery upon the
latter. . . .

First, from two lovely blue eyes, whose bright orbs flashed
lightning at their discharge, flew forth two pointed ogles, but,
happily for our hero, hit only a vast piece of beef which he
was then conveying into his plate and harmless spent their
force. . . . Many other weapons did she assay; but the God of
Eating . . . preserved his votary; . . . for as Love frequently
preserves from attacks of hunger, so may hunger possibly in
some cases defend us against love. [1963, pp. 429–30]

Two variables complicate the transition from unerotic to
erotic time: desire and availability.

A person must harmonize the various biological, psychological, and social pressures that put him "in the mood" for
sex, not only with one another but also with those of his
potential partner. Adding to the difficulty are the different
biosexual rhythms of each gender, the different psychosexual rhythms of each person, and the indefinite sociosexual
rhythms of our society. Moreover, the sexual "expectation"
demanded by social rhythms often interferes with the
"spontaneity" demanded by biological and psychological
rhythms, for one partner or both.

Once a couple establish their own rhythm for having intercourse, it becomes normative for them. One partner may
interrupt it occasionally for physical problems. ("Not
tonight, dear—I have a headache"). But whoever interrupts
it too frequently is accused of having "psychological problems," which are much lower status. (Consequently, real
psychological problems are often disguised as physical ones,
especially those with no external symptoms. Despite growing suspicions, one sex partner can never prove the other
has no headache.) The mid-1970s TV soap opera spoof *Mary
Hartman! Mary Hartman!* began with a five-week hiatus in
Mary's conjugal sex life—much too long, she thought. Thus
this program unwittingly disseminated a social norm about
how long one partner may suspend intercourse before the
other begins to attribute this lapse to troubles with motivation or the relation.

Even if both partners are in the mood for sex, each may
find himself or the other unavailable for it. Consequently
each must harmonize his own availability with his partner's.
The possibility that each may not know his partner's availability when planning his own creates a fourfold scheduling
problem often extremely difficult to resolve. The French
author Pauline Réage describes how two lovers overcome
this obstacle to the temporal integration of their erotic and
everyday lives:

> They met two or three times a week, but never during
> vacations, and never on weekends. Each of them stole the
> time they spent together from their families or their work. . . .
> They did not have a full night together. All of a sudden, at
> such and such an hour agreed upon ahead of time—the watch
> always remained on the wrist—they had to leave. . . . It was
> already a stroke of luck that he had been able to get away at
> all. Otherwise she would have waited an hour and then come
> back the following day at the same time, the same place, in
> accordance with the classic rules of clandestine lovers. . . . The
> idea that they would have to return home gave a special
> meaning to that stolen time, which came to exist outside the
> pale of real time, in a sort of strange and eternal present.
> [1973, pp. 3, 5, 7, 8]

As connoisseurs of love, the French have even institutional-
ized a trysting time for adulterous lovers, setting aside the
period between the end of work and the beginning of dinner, which they call "de cinq en sept" (from five to seven).

Finally, the two partners must harmonize *both* desire and
availability. When desire for sex is mutual, neither may be
available; when availability for sex is mutual, neither may
desire it. (As more partners are added for various levels of
group sex, the difficulties of getting everyone together increase exponentially.)

Considering the obstacles, one wonders how two people
ever manage to copulate at all. The love affair maximizes
mutual desire but not availability; marriage maximizes
mutual availability but not desire. Prostitution has traditionally compensated for the scheduling deficiencies of both:

> The fact that the single man turns up [at a brothel] mostly
> after eleven P.M. is testimony in itself as to why he came.
> He has taken a girl on a date, wined and dined her, enjoyed
> her company, been turned on, made the eternal overture, and
> she has responded with some unflattering excuse such as: "I
> have to go home and wash my hair."
> His ardor for her dimmed, but his appetite not sated, he
> takes out his black book and calls his favorite madam, and for
> less money than the cost of his evening out in most cases, can
> discharge his desires without any hassle. [Hollander 1972,
> p. 176]

Space

During erotic time, one's experience of the spatial expanse
of the everyday world shrinks drastically. The boundaries of
consciousness contract to room, bed, and body; whatever
lies outside these concentric spatial zones of awareness—
Where is her husband now? Is the door locked?—cease to be
matters of concern. A character of Marco Vassi's *The Saline
Solution* describes this cosmic contraction during intercourse
thus: "I am being fucked. I am being fucked. There is nothing in the world but being fucked" (1976a, p. 21).

Those who leave everyday reality to enter erotic reality, in short, become less attentive to both spatial (distant) and temporal (past and future) extremities but more attentive to their centers (local and present). Since sexual arousal intensifies the here and the now while attenuating the there and the then, it can bleach pain and anxiety from the experience of adverse environments. Those in prison often attempt to remain in erotic reality because it is one of the few palliatives available there that are powerful enough to blot out the constraint of the bars and the length of the sentence. Many soldiers, detectives, fugitives, revolutionaries, and inmates of the urban jungle are obsessed with eroticism for a similar reason. (Conversely, we will see that this power of erotic reality to reduce awareness of customary social concerns is partly responsible for the social taboos against entering it.)

The spatial setting is not only affected by the transition from everyday to erotic reality, it may either facilitate or hinder this transition. Barbara Harton found women's sexual fantasies commonly stress the physical setting: "I dream I am in a different place like a car, motel, beach, woods, etc." (1973, p. 43). Some people feel their experience of erotic reality is enhanced by benign settings (e.g., those bathed in moonlight or candlelight); others feel theirs is enhanced by hostile settings (e.g., those immersed in darkness or danger; see Davis 1973, pp. 211–17).

In order to minimize contact between realities our society has restricted public *sexy settings* to clearly circumscribed spatial ghettos. Commercial locations that expedite their inhabitants' passage from everyday to erotic reality include pornographic bookstores and movies, topless bars and burlesque houses, and high-class bordellos and massage parlors:

> Before and after your session, enjoy free drinks and *turn on* to wild and exotic topless dancers just "inches away" in our intimate, circular, bamboo lounge. [Ad for Tahitia Massage Parlor, *Screw* #371, 12 April 1976, p. 14]

Despite their boundaries, however, these ghettos of sexuality leak eroticism in space and time.

Spatially, they project an amorous overhang, a field of erotic reality that envelopes the sidewalks they front like fog. Their signs and pictures spray a mist of temptation over passersby, who can also catch glimpses of activities inside. In America detailed regulations control the extent and intensity of their erotic field by limiting the explicitness of the terms permitted in their signs (in Europe they are frankly called "sex houses"), the portrayal of erogenous zones permitted in their pictures, and the visibility of their interior permitted through windows and doors.

Temporally, they prolong an amorous hangover, a predisposition toward eroticism felt by their clientele for hours after its original impetus was removed. Robert Evens points out that his movie *Love Story*, although not pornographic, produced this hysteresis of desire:

> The movie became a great aphrodisiac. Guys went back to see the picture seven or eight times and brought a different girl every time, because when the girl walked out of that picture, for the next few hours she was in love. I think there was more sex that came from *Love Story* than from any porno film. . . . They went home and made love after seeing that picture. What a great thing to make a turn-on like that. . . . [*The New York Times* 15 August 1976, p. D 13]

The private arena where erotic reality is most often generated is the "bedroom." "To go to bed with" is another of the most frequently used euphemisms for sexual intercourse.

Those who go to bed together for sex shift from vertical to horizontal interaction, a form of interaction that occurs in very few other activities (sunbathing being perhaps the most common). Many rules governing the behavior of the "upright" are suspended for the prostrate, whether they be relaxing, fucking, giving birth, drunk, sleeping, sick, dying, or in the grave.[4] The horizontal position itself implies sexual activity. The terms "lie with," "lay," "tumble," "upend," and "go down" all have sexual connotations. In Shakespeare's *Henry IV* (part I, 3.1.229) Hotspur describes Kate as "perfect at lying down."

Those wishing to copulate usually move away from the furniture that anchors their everyday reality to the bedroom. The bedroom is the only major room in the house named after a piece of furniture instead of its central activity, probably because what takes place there (beside sleeping) has been unmentionable. Motel and hotel rooms have an erotic aura because they impose no spatial barrier between living room and bedroom, between everyday reality and erotic reality—the bed being their largest and most commanding piece of furniture. Gustave Flaubert filled with sexual imagery his description of the hotel room where Emma Bovary is carrying on one of her extramarital affairs:

> The bed was a large mahogany one, shaped like a boat. Red silk curtains, curved at the bottom, hung down very low from the ceiling beside the flaring headboard: and there was nothing in the world so lovely as her dark hair and white skin against that crimson background when, in a gesture of modesty, she brought her bare arms together and hid her face in her hands.
>
> The warm room, with its discreet carpet, its whimsical ornaments and its tranquil light, seemed expressly designed for the intimacies of passion. The arrow-tipped curtain rods, the brass curtain hooks, and the big knobs on the andirons would all begin to gleam when the sun shone in. On the mantel piece, between the candlesticks, were two of those large pink shells in which you can hear the ocean when you hold them to your ear.[1959, p. 228]

Unsexy settings hinder the formation of erotic reality in different degrees. Ordinary settings designed for utilitarian activities—work places, mass transportation, etc.—discourage their users from actually going into erotic reality but permit them to fantasize going there. Sacred settings like churches and cemeteries take precautions to prevent even reveries of erotic reality (which imply that the officially sanctioned sacred world may be intrinsically less enthralling than its officials care to admit). Traditionally, they have required full attire[5] and have sometimes even segregated the sexes:

It seems bizarre that as late as 1948 the eminent Professor of English constitutional history [at Radcliffe] was instructed to sit behind a screen at morning chapel services. All other women in the Harvard community had apparently accepted this restriction as a small price to pay for being there. Dr. Cam, however, astonished the college community by refusing to be kept in purdah and succeeded in having the screen removed. [Kendall 1976, p. 156]

Medical and scientific settings are unsuited to the formation of erotic reality, even in fantasy, because they have been sterilized of precisely the human symbols that make settings sexy, and thereby potentially dirty. Leslie Farber criticized Masters and Johnson's research on precisely these grounds, pointing out that only a supersexual "Our Lady of the Laboratory" could sustain "sexual excitement in the setting of the laboratory, the paraphernalia, the cameras, the technicians, the bright lights . . . while being measured and photographed" (1978, pp. 133–34).

Perhaps the least erotic of all settings are crises—settings in which everyday definitions have been suddenly ripped away and have not yet returned. Safeguards against sexual fantasy, let alone activity, in these limbos are superfluous. (Common, of course, are erotic fantasies *of* crises in which the fantasizer rescues, or is rescued by, an attractive social type. Rare, however, are erotic fantasies *during* crises.) The comedian Lenny Bruce once presented a sketch about going into erotic reality during a disaster:

You can *idolize* your wife, just be so crazy about her, be on the way home from work, have a head-on collision with a Greyhound bus, in a *disaster* area. Forty people laying dead on the highway—not even in the hospital, in the *ambulance*—the guy makes a play for the nurse:
OUTRAGED FEMALE VOICE: How could you *do* that thing at a time like that?
ASHAMED MALE: I got horney.
"*What?*"
"I got hot."
"How could you be hot when your *foot* was cut off?

People were *dead* and *bleeding* to death!"
(Apologetic): "I dunno." . . .
"He's a *moron*, that's all, he's just an *animal*! I don't know
how you could *think* of it. Your foot was cut off and you
could—*ugh, disgusting!*" [Cohen, 1967, p. 194]

There are two techniques to facilitate the transition from
unsexy to sexy settings. First, one can transform the setting
itself. Magazines like *Playboy* and *Cosmopolitan* inform the
unsophisticated how to transform a house or apartment
from an ordinary living place into a swinging single's pad.
Second, one can transport potential sex partners from
one kind of setting to another, perhaps by providing a minor
pretext—"Would you like to come up and see my
etchings?"—to disguise a move that may have metaphysical
ramifications (as we will see). The nineteenth-century
French novelist Joris Karl Huysmans describes both techniques as his hero, an inept and self-conscious seducer,
ponders how to transport his potential sex partner from his
living room to his bedroom or, failing that, how to transform his living room into a bedroom:

> I can't bear to think of getting her into the bedroom. Un-
> dressing and going to bed! That part is appalling unless you
> know each other very well. . . . The nice way is to have a cosy
> little supper for two. The wine has an ungodly kick to it. She
> immediately passes out, and when she comes to she is lying
> in bed under a shower of kisses. As we can't do it that way . . .
> I must possess her here, in this very spot. . . . It's hard to
> arrange in this room, because there isn't any divan. The best
> way would be to throw her down on the carpet. She can put
> her hands over her eyes as they always do. I shall take good
> care to turn down the lamp before she rises. Well, I had better
> prepare a cushion for her head. . . . [1972, p. 146]

Although the thought that unsexy settings could ever
become lascivious locales appalls many people, it arouses
others. Those who prefer to intensify their sexual excitement
by violating obsolescent social norms may copulate in unusual places—the bathroom instead of the bedroom, the

floor instead of the bed, or a work place like an office in the evening. The boiler room of a rooming house became the setting for unanticipated intercourse in Lawrence Durrell's novel *The Black Book*:

> 'She came down 'arf an hour ago. 'Ere. By the boiler.'. . . 'She come to me with nothing under her dress. She said: "Do you want it, Mister Morgan?" Gor but it was surprising like. [1962, p. 39]

A contributor to the pornographic newspaper *Screw* described intercourse in the john of a Trailways bus and bragged: "I've fucked and sucked in a church, in a school, in a hangar at Floyd Bennett Field, and in a lifeguard's chair . . ." [Greer 1976]. Mass transportation can become a sexy setting that is especially tempting for the adventurous because it often induces erotic fantasies but is a risky place to be actually risqué. The pornographic film *The Opening of Misty Beethoven*, however, imagines air transportation offically transformed from an unsexy to a sexy setting, with the ticket seller asking, "First class or tourist? Smoking or nonsmoking? Sex or nonsex?" Thus sex in unusual places (or times)—unusual because ordinary activities usually occur there (or then)—can intensify experiences of erotic reality by exaggerating its break with the surrounding everyday world.

In sum, the all-seeing eye, which can sense human experience as well as material substance, will perceive the great city as though it were a colossal carbonated beverage spilled upon a map, effervescing with little bubbles of erotic reality: individually appearing and disappearing; collectively clustering and dispersing over space, proliferating and subsiding over time.

Social

During the shift from everyday reality to erotic reality, one's experience of social space—where one plots people on social coordinates—changes even more noticeably than one's experience of physical space. Ordinary perception of social space is transformed in two ways.

First, people who were important in everyday reality now recede from attention. For the heterosexual with standard sexual tastes, persons of the same gender, members of one's immediate family, and merely utilitarian role partners like colleagues and service personnel fade from consciousness. Sex with any of them is inconceivable. Those with less conventional sexual inclinations, of course, experience a different form of fade-out: the opposite gender disappears for homosexuals, everyone but those in his immediate family disappears for the incestuous, and so on. Erotic reality erases fewer associates for those whose sexual preferences are less exclusive. "The nice thing about being bisexual," the comedian Woody Allen somewhere remarked, "is that it doubles your chance of getting a date on saturday night."

Second, people who were unimportant in everyday reality now advance to the forefront. The *lovable* are those to whom the aroused individual now wants to make love. Although in everyday reality he may have already noted certain individuals as potential lovables (because presumably he knows his own erotic tastes), in erotic reality they come to crowd everyone else out of his consciousness. Lovables are drawn from two populations. A person selects cosmopolitan lovables from everyone he has ever seen in person or in picture, especially models and movie stars. He selects local lovables from everyone currently in his immediate vicinity, such as his shipmates on the singles' cruise.

The *attainable* are those who will want to make love to the aroused. Type 1, "those who do" are not only sharply distinguished from type 2, "those who don't," but are also internally differentiated into 1a, "those who do easily," and 1b, "those who do but with difficulty." One of the first things an adolescent learns about sex is to distinguish all these categories accurately, according to Bob Guccione, editor of *Penthouse*:

When I was a kid, finding a girl who screwed was like
finding gold. It was a great piece of news if you heard about a
girl who screwed, because it was extraordinarily unusual for a
girl to screw without a lot of problems—having to take her
out, court her, spend money on her. When you did hear
about one, she was inevitably the object of many a gang bang.
[Fleming and Fleming 1976, pp. 77–78]

Since 1a and 1b come with different sets of operational procedures to actualize their potential attainability, it is extremely important for someone to recognize the category
with which he is dealing. A male who proceeds on the
assumption that the girl he would like to seduce is a 1a girl
may find that in fact she is a 1b girl. After making him aware
of his categorical mistake ("What kind of girl do you think I
am?") she may no longer be potentially attainable by him,
having become a type 2 girl.

One of the melancholy aspects of human existence is that
there are not enough lovables to go around. Since lovers far
outnumber lovables (especially for erotic eccentrics with deviant desires; see Ullerstam 1966, p. 149), competition for the
relatively few lovables available is fierce. Consequently, the
many lovers who find their lovables unattainable are forced
to settle for those attainable but not lovable, if they are
actually to make love at all.

Another way to conceptualize this problem is to see that
the populations of the lovable and of the attainable overlap
only slightly. Only a few of the lovable are attainable (as
Goethe's Werther discovered to his sorrow during his hope-
less one-sided affair with Lotte, who married someone else)
and only a few of the attainable are lovable (as Judith Ross-
ner's Theresa Dunn discovered to her mortification after
picking up Gary Cooper White at a singles spot called Mr.
Goodbar.) Even those of extremely high erotic status (like
rock music stars) or those in extremely unusual circumstances (like the few women at a mostly male army base)
who find almost everyone attainable are likely to find far
fewer of them lovable. Although our mass culture dissemi-

nates the illusion that worthiness and effort will always make lovables attainable and that increasing acquaintance will always make attainables lovable (that Mr. and Ms. Right will always meet and fall in love), such conjunctions actually occur only often enough to make everyone else believe it will someday happen to him or her.

Every society displays social types that should sexually arouse its citizens and social types that shouldn't. Unless specific ideals of sexual attractiveness have restricted the number of people generating erotic reality, everyone might find themselves sexually aroused by everyone else all the time. The sociologist Hans Zetterberg (1966, p. 134) refers to the system by which a society stratifies its members according to their ability to sexually arouse others as its "erotic ranking."[6]

Those with the highest erotic rank are the *sexy* or the *attractive*. This social type comprises those who are outstanding physically (the handsome and the beautiful), personally (the charming), or socially in regard to class (the wealthy), life style (the cultured, including the brilliant and the talented), or power (the influential). (Although the specific ranking within this top group is uncertain, Henry Kissinger—a member of the last category but not the first—once declared, "Power is the ultimate aphrodisiac.") If the sexy are those capable of turning on others to erotic reality and the *horny* are those capable of being turned on by others to erotic reality, the meeting between the sexy and the horny is one of the archetypal encounters of social life. Their confrontation produces far different experiential and interactional consequences than that between the sexy and the unarousable or between the horny and the unarousing. Of course, there is no reason why the horny cannot also be sexy, turning on to erotic reality whomever turned *them* on to it. But the horny often find to their dismay that, no matter how hard they try, they can induce the sexy neither to enter erotic reality themselves nor to shut off their maddening erotic field.

Midway down the scale are the *plain* or the *tolerable*. This social type neither generates erotic reality nor frustrates its formation if other factors favor it. They are by far the most numerous.

Those with the lowest erotic rank are the *repulsive*. The mere sight or thought of any member of this social type inhibits any sexual inclination. Someone may be repulsive physically (the ugly), personally (the "creep"), or socially (whoever is rated low in class, life style, or power). The repulsive are truly the "untouchables" of the erotic caste system. Unable to achieve mobility by their own efforts, they are given to Cinderella fantasy. Zetterberg (1966, p. 139) observes that they have never revolted against their erotic rank, though they have nothing to lose but their illusions.[7] Certain primitive tribes sacrificed their most sexually attractive members, ostensibly to honor their gods but (cynics believe) actually to equalize the erotic ranking of those remaining. We moderns are not so savage, but some have suggested taxing the attractive to compensate the repulsive for their sad lot in life, continually condemned as they are to collapsing the erotic reality of nearly everyone they encounter.[8]

Some individuals find their erotic ranking to be ambiguous, high on some dimensions but low on others. Woody Allen, who has become a spokesman for those whose physique and personality prevent others from entering erotic reality, was once asked if his newfound fame has helped his sexual success. He replied, "Yes. I now fail with a higher class of women," indicating that his physique and personality must be unappealing enough to counteract even so powerful an eroticizer as his high social status.

Some people prefer to copulate with social types the majority regards as unsexual or even antisexual. Al Capp, the cartoonist, described an encounter with a person who liked to go slumming in the lower erotic ranks:

> I got quite sick recently in London. I have a wooden leg and one that works, and the one that works wasn't working. So I

operated in a wheelchair. I was taken to a party, pushed in by an attendent, and as I came in there was this nine-foot-high girl, all navel, and she said to me, "I never fucked anybody in a wheelchair. Would you like to?" I disapprove of that kind of talk. I consider it distasteful and crawly. [Fleming and Fleming 1976, p. 41]

But even those who enjoy the intensification of erotic reality that results from breaking a weak social norm usually draw the line at unsexy personalities. It is one thing to want to copulate during times, in places, or even with anatomies others regard as unerotic; it is quite another to be sexually aroused by those others regard as "creeps."

Since sexual arousal increases a person's sensitivity to the erotic transmissions of others, it decreases his selectivity among those who turn him on. Thus someone already sexually aroused may promote the plain to the attractive, and sometimes even the repulsive to the tolerable[9]—though usually rescinding their new rank upon returning to everyday reality. The Mickey Gilley song quoted above, "Don't the Girls all get Prettier at Closin' Time," continues:

If I could rate 'em on a scale of one to ten,
I'm lookin' for a nine but eight would fit right in.
A few more drinks and I might slip to five or even four,
    But when tomorrow mornin' comes
    And I wake up with number one
I swear I'll never do it any more.

[Knight 1976][10]

The barriers of this erotic caste system, however, are not completely impermeable. A person can raise his local erotic score relatively by associating only with those whose score is lower than his own. The plain can hang out with the repulsive, making themselves seem the most attractive sex objects in the vicinity. And a person can raise his cosmopolitan erotic score absolutely by enhancing its physical, economic, cultural, or political components—one of the main motivations for upward mobility. Unhappily, this increase in erotic status often comes too late in life to be exploited fully, as Irving Wallace reports Art Buchwald once complained:

> Now, I'd been freelancing when Art Buchwald was a stringer in Paris for the *Herald Trib* . . . Art had just begun to make it when my first big best-seller came out, and here I was getting all this attention, and Art and I went out to breakfast one morning in Paris. We were alone, without our wives, and Art looked at me and said, "Jesus, you know, before, when we wanted all these broads, here we were, two unattractive guys and nobody gave a damn about us, and today—is it true with you?—you can have anybody, the whole Copacabana line. They're all name-fuckers, you know. . . . But we married and went public. Isn't life horrible? Before, you wanted it and couldn't get it. Now you can get it all, but you can't have it." He was moaning all morning about it. [Fleming and Fleming 1976, pp. 276–77]

The personality component of erotic status is perhaps the most difficult to improve. Having congealed in childhood, it may require years of psychoanalysis to alter in adulthood. Nevertheless there is a growing literature on the suavification techniques that can turn creeps into Casanovas almost instantly. The "How to Make Love to Men or Women Made Simple" series, which constitutes most of this literature, includes such titles as the following:

> *Picking up Girls Made Easy:*
> PICKING UP GIRLS CAN BE AS EASY AS OPENING A BEER! This amazing new pick up system is so easy to master, you can learn it without even trying. *Automatically* you will be transformed into an expert picker upper and seducer. . . . The day your album arrives will be a fantastic experience. Sit down, pour yourself a glass of wine, and put PICKING UP GIRLS MADE EASY on your record player. Your life won't be the same again! What you'll hear is so exciting and foolproof that the next time you spot a chick you'll pick her up without even thinking. After just one hearing you'll have

the style and confidence of a master. [in *Penthouse*, April
1976, p. 145]

Such books usually consist only of platitudes about changing "attitudes," but the "self-confidence" they recommend
acquiring is more the result of social success than its cause.
Those who do manage to eroticize their personality,
moreover, are not always pleased with the result, as in the
following letter to the editor of *The Village Voice*:

> I am by nature a gentle and nonaggressive 27-year old man
> who often finds women turned off sexually by my tenderness
> and non-macho view of the world. . . . After several fruitless
> years as a gentle poet-man, I now turn myself into heavy
> machismo when I go out with women. It works. *I* open the
> doors, *I* order the food and drinks, *I* decide which movie or
> play we will see, I keep my shirt unbuttoned down past my
> nipples and wear a gold chain around my neck with a carved
> elephant tusk medallion, and if the relationship is not work-
> ing out, *I* make the first move and tell my companion that I'm
> sorry but we're through.
> The sad thing about all this is that it *works*. After all those
> years of being naturally sensitive and gentle, and now I've got
> to turn myself inside-out just to appear sexy. It's fun, and it's
> nice, but I do wish I could just be myself again. [*Village Voice*,
> 12 May 1976, p. 3]

Physical

Moving from everyday into erotic reality changes the way
people perceive the body. First, it seems to intensify their
experience of physical characteristics relative to social and
psychological ones.[11] Goffman (1959, pp. 252–53) asserts that
the body is only a "peg" on which we hang a person's self.
But only in everyday reality is the body so inert. In erotic
reality the body becomes an "icon" that gives life to the self
as much as a "peg" that takes life from it. Second, the
sexually aroused experience the body as more sharply segregated from its circumstances than do the sexually
unaroused.[12] In short, the self, abstract and dispersed in

everyday reality, becomes embodied and localized in erotic reality.

Not only the body as a whole but also certain of its parts—especially its orifices—seem to stand out for the sexually aroused:[13]

> Lucinda came out of the bathroom. She was naked. For an instant her body seemed to glow and surge forward, her nipples radiating and cunt gaping like the mouth of a landed fish. [Vassi 1976a, p. 4]

These portions of the anatomy acquire a new meaning for those in erotic reality that is incomprehensible to those who remain in everyday reality.

> I looked at the tuft of hair between her legs. It seemed utterly trivial. Even in square or cubic inches, it assumed a tiny percentage of the body's total area or volume. It was, literally, a hole. That is to say, an emptiness. And was all this torment over a nothingness. [Vassi 1976a, p. 112]

It is not immediately apparent why the human body should be so sexy, especially since "all we ever see of each other—skin and hair—is dead." (The *National Geographic* television program on the human body from which this quotation comes was referring to the dead cells that constitute our topmost layer of skin and hair.) But it does not take much phenomenological reflection to articulate the arousing features of the body. I will briefly describe these physical "erons" that shift into erotic reality whomever receives their radiations.

Bodily *curves* stimulate sexual arousal at visual distance. Three different wavelengths of erotic radiation are generated by the macrocurves of the body as a whole, the middling curves of bodily sections (breast, buttocks), and the microcurves of the face (eyes, nose, lips). These physical forms can be sexually arousing in themselves: independent of their own substance (some Victorians found piano legs embarrassingly erotic enough to cover them with crinolines), independent of any substance (some find photos or portraits sexually stimulating), independent of the illusion of substance (some find mere cartoons of people sexy), and even independent of the visual representation of the curves (some men are sexually aroused merely by hearing the numbers that measure a woman's proportions, like 37-23-35).

Bodily *kinesics*—the anatomy in motion—intensifies the erotic radiation of its static forms. The "wiggle" of women and the "strut" of men exaggerate each gender's respective curves, kinetic movements in time that amplify their erotic power in space. Like curves, these dynamic forms can be sexually arousing even apart from their content, as in the "bump and grind" of burlesque, belly, or go-go dancing. The postures and gestures that distinguish each gender also seem to sexually arouse the other: the angle at which the legs are crossed, the distance upper arms are held from the trunk, the tilt of the pelvis, and the way eyelids are closed or opened (see Birdwhistell 1972, pp. 54–55).

Bodily curves and kinesics are the far-distance artillery of sexual attraction, catching the individual's attention and enticing him closer until the medium-distance sexual stimulators of *complexion, voice,* and *smell*[14] can open fire. Still more closely, the *texture* (smooth or rough) of hair and skin as well as the *density* (firm or flabby) of muscle/fat ratio are sexual arousers at touch distance. Finally, the *genitals* themselves generate eroticism by combining in their own way curves, kinesics, complexion, smell, texture, and density. (All that seems to keep them from becoming miniature human beings as far as sexual arousal is concerned is voice.)

In order to generate erotic reality, these physical features must affect the mind. Since one dimension common to both body and mind is time, it is in this dimension that the body/mind dualism can be overcome. The point of contact is rhythm, the cyclical change in tension over time. Each of the body's erotic generators establishes a specific tension/release cycle, which the mind experiences as an *erotic rhythm*. Ultimately, mind and body come to "vibrate" on the same frequency.

But the body does not always generate erotic reality. It can be not only unarousing but even antiarousing, undoing the erotic effects produced by personality and social type. The too acute or obtuse angle curves of the very fat or thin (or the very large- or small-boned) can strum out tension/release rhythms that are unerotic.[15] Asymmetry or misshapenness— from microlevel deviated septums to macrolevel hunchbacks—can interfere with the erotic coherence of physical curves. Their harmonic continuation can also be interrupted by bodily tumors, atrophications, or amputations, and by facial scars, pimples, or other blemishes.[16] Kinesics too can undercut the beat of erotic tempos, reducing the sexual sonority of the "uptight" who tense their muscles too tauntly and the "awkward" who relax them too loosely. Unsexy smells and sallow complexions as well as gender-inappropriate voices, densities, and textures (caused by faulty hair distribution) can all inhibit the formation of erotic reality. It is difficult to say what can make genitals unarousing because it is not easy to say what makes them arousing, the aesthetics of the pubis being an underdeveloped science. But if erotic male genitals are said to be "well hung," unerotic ones must be "poorly hung"—although it is unclear what these terms mean beyond size. (Presumably the female equivalents would be "well folded " and "poorly folded.")

All sexual features of the body lose their ability to generate erotic reality under perceived size transformations. Viewed from afar, facial microcurves and small segments of the torso such as breasts and genitals disappear, and even bodily macrocurves, skin texture, and hair distribution become difficult to determine. Viewed from close up, facial microcurves become macro, bodily macrocurves cease to seem curves at all (for only a narrow arc is now visible), skin texture coarsens as pores become craters and hair a jungle. Through the eyepiece of poetic whimsy, Kenneth Koch observes how these modulations in magnitude affect erotic experience:

Take a microscope to
Many varieties of beauty and they are gone. A young girl's
Lovely complexion, for example, reveals gigantic pores,
hideously, gapingly,
Embedded in her, as Gulliver among the Brobdingnagians
observed. . . .
Who would want microscopic eyes at
Such a moment? or macroscopic ones, for that matter, which
would make
Your girl look extremely tiny, almost invisible, like an insect
You might swat, if you weren't careful; and you would feel
Funny, wondering how someone so small
Could make you feel so happy. . . .
I think
The proportion between eye and nature, then, is, as
Far as Beauty goes, the most important proportion of all.

[1975, pp. 52–54]

Size transformations of the genitals produce the most
starting change in erotic generating power. As the genitals
become larger, they become more erotic (at least in our
society); but beyond a certain length or width, their erotic
power declines dramatically. Ask any porno movie fan who
has seen intercourse between what appear to be twenty-foot
genitals. Twenty-foot genitals are as erotic as a sonata played
at one hundred decibels is musical.[17] Since physical features
attractive at normal interaction distance may become repulsive during the close-up of intercourse, many people dislike
"lights on" sex or oral sex because it seems to fill their visual
field with giant genitalia.

One person's ugly duckling may be another person's
swan. There have always been those sexually aroused by the
very fat or lean, by the misshapen, by the curveless young or
the wrinkled old, by the blemished, the smelly, or the sallow. In the nineteenth century Flaubert reported that
"hunchbacks" were "much sought after by lascivious
women" (1968, p. 49). Thus physical abnormalities increase
erotic tension for some just as temporal, spatial, or social
abnormalities increase it for others. (All these norm-
negating intensifiers of erotic reality seem to be becoming

more prevalent today as phenomenological inflation forces everyone to intensify all his experiences.)

But the physically flawed need not wait for someone with minority tastes to come along. There are available many beautification kits and techniques designed specifically to turn toads into princes or princesses. Much of the industrial capacity of our society, in fact, is devoted to this task, as if increasing the generation of erotic reality for others were our prime task in life.

Take fashion, for example. Since the power of each bodily curve or area of skin to generate erotic reality can wear out through overexposure, fashion in women's clothing continually circulates these sexy spots around the body by alternately or sequentially baring shoulders, back, midriff, and thighs. This technique of flesh rotation is supposed to restore vitality to sexiness in the same way that the technique of crop rotation is supposed to restore it to soil.

All beautification techniques, however, are ultimately doomed to fail; at best they can only slow the intractable transformation of the sexy into the unsexy that comes with aging—at least in our society.[18] Aging switches off the physical features that generate erotic reality one by one, though it may increase the erotic power of personality and social generators almost enough to compensate for their loss. If personality and social characteristics may age like wine, bodies must always age like milk.[19]

Andy, a rich member of an over-forties singles club, describes how aging has improved his social attractions:

> I make a lot of money; my apartment is glamorous, so I was never sure that women wanted me for myself. That's the kind of problem young kids don't know anything about. When you're young you start out fairly even with all the other guys. You fall in love with some girl; she falls for you and you gamble. You might fail in life or make a million; she might keep her figure or become a sloppy mess.
>
> Now, though, the results are in. That gal who turned me on as a junior at C.C.N.Y. weights 180 pounds, and nobody

wants her. She can't give it away. But I'm a saleable commodity. I'm in a position to collect art and spend three months a year in the Caribbean. I'm just scared I'm going to be taken.

But Joyce, another member, observes that aging has not improved his physical and personality attractions:

Joyce took one look at Andy, noticed that he was wearing a toupee, and that was pretty much that. . . . "That rug is a sure sign of insecurity. Don't you agree? Andy What's-His-Face is typical of what's around . . . losers." [Blum 1976, pp. 11, 16]

The homely may be better off in the long run than the handsome or the beautiful, for the former are forced to enhance their personality and social status to become sexually attractive to all. These latter generators may be less erotic than physique at its peak, but their eroticism is more durable.

Aging is not quite so dismal a prospect as it seems, however, for though there is no justice in human existence, there is some mercy. The same aging process that increases the physical flaws of one sex partner can decrease the displeasure they cause the other. Since all aspects of the body do not age equally, focus may shift to those that stay young:

Covering all above with a basket and regarding only what is below the girdle, it is impossible of two women to know an old one from a young one. And as in the dark all cats are grey, the pleasure of corporal enjoyment with an old woman is at least equal, and frequently superior. [Benjamin Franklin, "On the Choice of a Mistress"]

Moreover, each partner in a long-term relationship may have a blurred image of the other, one composed of the other's appearances at various stages of life. Because past and present are so intermingled in their minds, each may find the other sexually attractive in the present for exactly the same physical features that sexually attracted them in the past: "I think you're still as beautiful as you were the day I married you." Finally, aging may decrease the frequency with which people experience erotic reality and consequently relate to each other solely on the sexual level. (This accounts for the continual complaint of the old that the young are "too preoccupied with sex.")

But note that much recent geriatric research has also pointed out that erotic experience does not disappear completely with age. Although geriatric researchers have rightly tried to demolish the popular stereotype of the aged as sexless beings, they have not investigated where this stereotype comes from. I suggest that it results from our society's antitragic view of life: from a belief that one cannot and should not be sexually *attracted* to others unless one is—at least to some degree—sexually *attractive* to them as well.

Conclusion

In this chapter I have tried to describe the nonphysiological factors responsible for sexual arousal. No doubt hormones in the brain can also produce horniness in the mind. But it is equally true that the temporal, spatial, social, and physical factors mentioned in this chapter can stimulate mental arousal,[20] which in turn can produce bodily arousal. Thus phenomenological horniness can precede physiological hormones as well as proceed from them (making the argument for Bishop Berkeley's famous pronouncement, "The brain is in the mind," at least as strong as the argument for its converse).

These nonphysiological factors are currently regarded merely as "releasers" for the physiological factors directly responsible for sexual arousal. But we can negate the biological determinism implicit in this position by instead regarding the latter merely as "releasers" for the former. Thus physiological fluctuations may increase or decrease a person's sensitivity to erotic transmissions from these nonphysiological factors. When many hormones make him hot, erotic transmissions weaker than normal will turn him on; when few hormones make him cold, erotic transmissions even stronger than normal will not turn him on. Both a person's own sensitivity to receive erotic transmissions and the power of temporal, spatial, social, and physical phenomena to send them are variable. Consequently, sexual arousal depends on the chance conjunction between these physiological and nonphysiological factors.

A person usually experiences the nonphysiological generators of erotic reality not singularly but rather combined into an overall effect. If this overall effect could ever be quantified—into, say, a "sexiness score"—we could analyze more precisely the relative contributions of physical, social, and situational (time and place) factors to a particular sexual experience and compare the erotic power of different sexual experiences, actual or fictional.[21]

The overall strength of an erotic experience depends not only on the objective power of each sexual generator but also on the perceiver's subjective weighting of each of them. Some persons are aroused more by particular physical features (e.g., leg-men), others by particular personalities and social types (e.g., women who prefer older men), still others by particular temporal moods and spatial settings (e.g., romantics). Some research (for instance, Byrne 1970) has confirmed the stereotype that men are more aroused by physical characteristics whereas women are more aroused by situational, social, and personality characteristics, but that has not stopped each gender from feeling that its concerns are superior to the other's.

The overall intensity of an erotic experience need not be merely the sum of its parts. Beyond a certain point, erotic generators begin to multiply each other's power synergistically, creating an *erotic resonance*. When all the particular erotic generators are in phase—when microcurves harmonize with macrocurves, when body harmonizes with personality, when social type harmonizes with setting, and so on—the intensity of erotic experience increases exponentially as each sexual wave begins to reinforce the others.

Laymen to this erotic resonance as "a matter of chemistry," implying that an unknown (and therefore "chemical") combination of causes produces their extreme experience. As scientists, however, our task is to analyze the components of this unknown compound. Like analytical chemists, we can proceed by elimination, observing instances when the absence of one factor hinders the hypothesized reaction. In the following example a homosexual decides that a potential partner does not resonate erotically, although his body is still sexy. What's missing, apparently, is a youthful demeanor.

> A man approached across the sand. He was almost sixty, but his body was still firm. He had a white goatee and wore a golfer's cap. He should have been wearing knickers.
> I calculated my measure of fleshy desire. Nothing came through. He didn't excite anything in me.
> "Don't you find me the least bit attractive?" he asked when I was forced to remove his hand from my breast.
> "With me," I said, "it's a matter of chemistry. It's nothing personal. If I had felt a spark I wouldn't care how old you were, or how ugly."
> "I'm only fifty-seven."
> "Please," I pouted, "do not make me sad." [Vassi 1976a, p. 87]

We can also better determine the contribution of each component to the overall erotic effect when it is out of phase rather than in phase. Instead of being dazzled by the erotic resonance when all generators are operating on full power, we can better see the effect of each when some are tuned to maximum while others are tuned to minimum. For instance, the cliché "What's a girl like you doing in a place like this?" implies that setting is out of phase with social type, allowing us to determine how and how much an unsexy spacial setting's unerotic energy can neutralize a sexy social type's erotic power.

Finally, the sexual wave reinforcement of erotic resonance can turn into *erotic overload* if it becomes too powerful for either its receivers or its senders to control, and consequently to appreciate.

On the one side, people may become so overwhelmed by erotic reality that they become incapable of interacting with those generating it. A common scene in comedy: a man encountering an extremely beautiful women is struck speechless, unable even to return her greeting let alone stammer out an attempt to seduce her however willing she appears. Technical competence in interaction belongs to everyday reality, out of which he has just been yanked too far too suddenly.

On the other side, people may feel that their ability to generate erotic reality is too high for their situation (given its norms) or their perceiver (given his personality or social type). A prurient woman, who believes herself so sexy that she incapacitates her admirers, may add a slight flaw (like a mole) to her face to make herself seem more human, more approachable. A prudish woman, who believes herself so sexy that she stimulates lustful thoughts in others, may wear unattractive clothing to muffle the erotic reality generated by her physical features. But if unerotic accoutrements do not reduce sexiness sufficiently, more extreme antierotic activities may have to be tried. New York women have come up with a new technique to break the erotic aura they generate on streets for creeps:

> Typically, the young woman is walking alone beside a construction site, or by a corner saloon where the fever of machismo runs high. To talk back is risky. What, then to do?
>
> A . . . teacher had an answer: "I pick my nose," she said.
>
> "It works every time," she contended. "They're disgusted. They don't even want to look. No whistles, nothing. I walk on by. . . ."
>
> Another wondered whether this tactical advice might be passed on to the public in, for instance, a newspaper article?
>
> "It couldn't hurt," said the teacher. "The creeps don't read."
>
> But, but . . . would this city be worth living in if all its beautiful young women walked around with their fingers in

their nose? [John Leonard: "About New York," *The New York Times* 8 August 1976, p. 30]

I can't answer that question, but certainly this city would be worth studying to determine what the attractions are of beautiful young women that nose picking undermines. In fact, they would become more apparent, just as the sun becomes more observable when its otherwise blinding brightness is dimmed by a partial eclipse.

2.

The Sensual Slide into Erotic Reality

Perhaps the most essential feature of sexual experience is its development.[1] Copulators experience each scene of the sex act not only in itself but also as a prelude to the next.

Other nonordinary realities, such as the theater or the game, are sharply cut off from everyday reality. Their beginnings are abrupt and well marked by transition gates, like an opening curtain or bell. But erotic reality is entered so gradually that the unwary may find themselves entering it against their will. If the transition from everyday to other nonordinary realities is marked by a perceptible "shock" (Schutz 1962, pp. 231, 343–44; 1973, p. 24), the transition from everyday to erotic reality is characterized by an imperceptible "drift."

Having begun to drift into erotic reality, the "horny" feel themselves being drawn increasingly toward the "sexy" as if by some gravitational force: the closer they get, the stronger the pull, as though the very space around the object of their desire were curved in an Einsteinian way.[2]

Everyday reality, then, is pitted with sinkholes through which most people are continually falling into erotic reality.[3] In this chapter we will examine their experience of this *sensual slide*: the stages of its progressive movement and the factors affecting its progress at each stage.

Before describing this sensual slide in detail, I should note that it feels more "stacatto"—more like a skid—to those whose consciousness is riding it for the first time with any-one (or even with a particular partner),[4] whereas it feels more "glissando"—each stage more smoothly slurring into the next—to those whose consciousness has ridden it often. Those unadjusted to each other's rhythms of progression are continually conscious that their sensual slide may be side-tracked at any moment, whereas those more fully adjusted are less conscious of where their sensual slide may go askew. In short, first fucks are more interesting than later ones, phenomenologically speaking, because novice copulators are more sensitive to their critical points. For this reason I will draw many of my illustrations from Karl and Anne Flemming's *The First Time* (1975), a popular book in which certain celebrities reminisce about their early sexual exper-iences.[5]

The phenomenology of "the last time" with anyone (or even with a particular partner) should also differ from that of middle times. The difficulty obtaining data on this topic, however, explains why no one has yet published a book called *The Last Time*. For one thing, last timers may not realize they are last timers, discovering it only in retrospect, as in this passage from Mary McCarthy's novel *The Group*:

> "I'll call you," he said. "Toward the end of the week. To see how you're doing. If you need anything, call me." It came to her that he was going to leave without making love to her.
>
> This would mean they had made love *for the last time* this morning. But that did not count: this morning they did not know it was for the last time. When the door shut behind him,

she still could not believe it. "It *can't* end like this," she said to herself over and over, drumming her knuckles on her mouth to keep from screaming. [1963, p. 289]

For another, those copulating for the last time—the terminally ill, soldiers going off to war, the condemned, those breaking up, and eroticides (murderers of spouses and lovers)—are usually not in the mood to be interviewed about it. We would expect, however, that if those copulating for the last time were aware it was for the last time, they would linger over its stages like lovers.

And then there are those having sex for both the first and last time—"one night stands." On the one hand, they may feel more free to experiment sexually with routes of progression off the beaten path because they may never see each other again. On the other hand, they may feel less free to explore sexual sidestreets because their temporary liaison may become more permanent. The choice hinges on how discrepant the sexual aspect of their identity is from the rest of it and how much each partner cares if the other finds out. Among the many reasons rape differs from ordinary intercourse is that rapist and rapee are usually encountering each other for both the first and last time.

Prelude

Although the slide into erotic reality is self-sustaining once it has begun, certain external factors may facilitate or hinder its beginning by weakening or strengthening the hold of everyday reality.

Daytime, living rooms, plain social types and neuter personalities, and commonly observed body parts have been mentioned as anchoring a person in everyday reality. The sensual slide is also inhibited by work, which focuses consciousness on everyday reality, and by illness—such as colds, headaches, and exhaustion ("Not tonight, dear, I'm too tired")—which disperses consciousness too much for it to focus on any coherent reality.

Conversely, nighttime, bedrooms, attractive social types and sexy personalities, and uncommonly observed body parts have been mentioned as weakening the grip on everyday reality. Certain psychoactive drugs—like marijuana, cocaine, amyl nitrite, and alcohol—also lead into erotic reality, although overuse may lead away from it.

In the 1970s several state liquor control boards tried to curb alcohol consumption in places that featured nude dancing,[6] apparently in the belief that the best way to retard people's progress into erotic reality is by controlling their access to what allows them to leave everyday reality in the first place. Drunkenness and horniness, they claim, form an explosive mixture, but it is actually our conception of everyday reality that is exploded.

Gambling loosens the hold of everyday reality on consciousness by offering the potential for rapid and extreme social mobility with relatively little effort. Like drugs and alcohol, gambling also undermines the stability of the self and other props of everyday reality. All three, consequently, are commonly associated with (illicit) sex, especially in Reno and Las Vegas. These four horsemen of "victimless crime" not only assail everyday reality individually but also reinforce one another's assaults.

First Movement

Upon entering erotic reality, potential sex partners begin to interact as *embodied wholes*. In everyday reality one must relate to others as abstract nexuses of social and personal characteristics, obscuring the connection between one's intents and others' responses. The concretely embodied selves of erotic reality, however, establish a much closer and clearer connection between cause and effect. The responses to pushing sexual buttons or pulling sexual levers are direct, immediate, and visible. Thus erotic reality renews self-confidence in social interaction, for what is often too amorphous to be tractable in ordinary social life—identity—is given a more manipulable material form in sex.

But it is one thing to embody others in imagination and another to do so in actuality. For the complete sex act to occur, a person must not only wish his potential sex partners to be embodied, he must engage in practical action to make them so. (Masturbatory fantasies consist of imagining this practical action.)

Sartre refers to the attempt of one sex partner to embody the other's self as a "double reciprocal incarnation":[7]

> I make myself flesh in order to impel the Other to realize *for herself* and *for me* her own flesh, and my caresses cause my flesh to be born for me insofar as it is for the Other *flesh causing her to be born as flesh*. I make her enjoy my flesh through her flesh in order to compel her to feel herself flesh. [1956, p. 391]

Besides its asymmetrical sexism,[8] however, Sartre's analysis of sex fails to elaborate the details of the process through which selves become identified with bodies—to which I now turn.

People do not always undergo this self-embodiment easily or willingly. Theologians have long observed that the ethereal essence of the soul may be contaminated by the grosser propensities of matter. Many people fear that sexual incarnation involves a similar risk: their psychological identity may be polluted by contact with the flesh. In both cases, becoming coextensive with a less flexible substance entails a dangerous loss of freedom.

But one cannot move very far into erotic reality without this double incarnation. Consequently, a person must take steps to overcome his partners' resistance to it. If his sex partners refuse to "yield," he must employ specific seduction techniques to make them "willing" to undergo further stages of self-embodiment.

Seduction techniques may be, in order of increasing power, verbal, visual, or tactile. In theory, one could draw his sex partner's consciousness from everyday to erotic reality at an accelerating rate by turning up his own seductive power: first verbally, from "off" to "low"; then visually, from "low" to "medium"; and finally tactilely, from "medium" to "high." In practice, seduction seldom follows this sequence exactly. A woman often begins it with visual techniques, such as wearing sexy clothing; a man often begins it with verbal ones, such as assuring his partner that he is serious about the relationship, and moves on directly to tactility without the intervening visual step. Both visual and verbal techniques are designed to shorten the interaction distance to allow the seducer to bring into play more powerful tactile tactics. The sexually experienced often dispense with verbal and visual preliminaries, and move on immediately to the tactile main event. The sexually less experienced often start with the former, and move on to the latter only if they encounter no resistance. But sexual novices sometimes try tactile techniques first, being prepared—if these are rejected, as they usually are—to return to verbal ones ("But why not?").

Potential partners may resist self-embodiment because of a desire to avoid sex. In this case, a seducer must convince them that its commission will *not* lead to bad consequences:

Physically: "The chances of getting pregnant are 1 in 100."

Psychologically: "How can a physical act affect your mental health?"

Socially: "How can they call you a 'fallen women' if they never find out about it?"

Relationally: "It's not true that I won't love or respect you any more."

Metaphysically: "But millions of girls lose their virginity every year without the sky falling on them."

Or that its omission *will* lead to bad consequences:

Physically: "It makes boys sick if they don't come when they're horny."

Psychologically: "First you turn me on, then you turn me off. It drives me crazy!"

Socially: "But what'll the guys say if they found out I
   didn't make it with you?"
Relationally: "I just can't keep going out with you if
   you're not going to sleep with me."
Metaphysically: "Had we but world enough, and time,
   This coyness, lady, were no crime. . . ."

Potential partners may also resist self-embodiment because their desire for sex is lacking. In this case, a seducer
must convince them that they will enjoy the sex act's later
stages, even though its early stages may seen pointless.[9]
Modern sexual ideology, which assumes that everyone is
capable of being aroused by everyone else, allows a seducer
to interpret potential partners' indifference to him as nothing more than a symptom of their inhibition against sex in
general. Therefore, he is more likely to deny that sex with
anyone will lead to bad consequences than to demonstrate
that sex with him in particular will lead to good ones, which
would probably be a more effective rhetorical strategy.

Finally, potential partners may resist self-embodiment to
enhance the seducer's sexual desire:

> O gentle Romeo,
> If thou dost love, pronounce it faithfully:
> Or if thou think'st I am too quickly won,
> I'll frown and be perverse and say thee nay,
> So thou wilt woo; but else, not for the world.
> [*Romeo and Juliet* 2.2.93–97]

If sexual desire is the swelling need to break through identity
boundaries, resistance indicates that these boundaries are
still intact. Since one can sustain erotic enthusiasm only so
long as this resistance is being overcome, too little may
dampen desire as quickly as too much, as Al Capp remarks:

> if it isn't a contest then you don't want it. Even in your
> marriage, if things are handed to you, you don't want them. I
> want to earn it. . . . I never went out with pushovers. [Fleming
> and Fleming 1975, p. 37]

To increase resistance one potential partner may try to hang on to everyday reality while the other tries to seduce him or her away from it ("What are you doing to me? I'm trying to read"). When the former finally lets go, both will be accelerated into erotic reality with increased momentum, like a stretched spring suddenly released. Sighs the Roman poet Ovid:

All my ambition breaks down under the pressure of Love.
Often I've said to my girl: "Go away now! I ought to be writing."
What does she do, right away? Comes and sits on my lap. . . .
Then she'll be throwing her arms around me, and giving me kisses,
Thousands, I guess, I lose track, I am a poet undone. [1966, p. 64]

Unfortunately, during the early stage of sex, very similar behaviors may stem from very different motivations. A suitor often finds it very difficult to decide whether his potential sex partners' resistance indicates their desire to increase sexual tension, their lack of sexual desire, or their fear of sex—similarities that encourage the rapist[10] as much as they discourage the diffident. Reminiscing about his adolescence, the columnist Art Buchwald regretted his inability to distinguish the "no" that means "no" from the "no" that means "yes":

Another time, I was in a trailer with this gal who lived off the base at Cherry Point. She was putting up only token resistance, but like an ass I backed off. Then when I stopped, she got pissed off. And when I tried again, it was too late. . . .
I spent a lot of time going over the game plan, trying to figure out where I went wrong with girls. When I didn't make it, I'd spend hours saying, "Jesus Christ, why did I take no for an answer when she really wanted yes?" [Fleming and Fleming 1975, pp. 22–23]

On the other hand, no approach is less likely to succeed

than the direct approach. Why should those who suggest, "Let's join our genital organs and wiggle them around"— perhaps the most precise and concise behaviorist description of the sex act—be less likely to achieve their ends than those who, even after much preliminary verbal foreplay, are still reticent enough to suggest only a peripheral activity, such as "Let's make love" or "Let's go to bed"?

Lenny Bruce once planned to compile a manual of seduction techniques that were certain to fail, such as the following:

> "Oh boy, I wonder who'd gimme some nookie? Boy, I wonder." And they just think that's so cute, you'll get it right away. Just say extra things, like
> "Boy, would I *appreciate* it! Boy, I'd appreciate that. I'd tell *everybody* what a nice person you were, too."
> [Cohen 1967, pp. 192–93]

By demonstrating how seduction can fail, Bruce reveals what is necessary for it to succeed. The direct approach implies that the seducer does not regard his potential partner as a total human being with many different attributes, but only as "nookie." Although people realize that they must be embodied temporarily for sex to occur, they usually want assurances that their partners will return them to their previous state—reexpand their condensed identity to its original human magnitude and complexity—after the sex act is over.

Second Movement

In the middle stages of the sensual slide, incarnation becomes more localized. The self is now perceived as corporialized in certain bodily segments. After becoming coextensive with the body as a whole, the self appears to defuse into breast and chest, buttocks and thighs, before it finally refuses around the genitals. In erotic reality, in short, the exact locus of identity seems to travel around the body, migrating

from general embodiment throught partial embodiments to
a specific embodiment. This movement takes place in partially overlapping sequences, especially in the visual dimension in which the sex partners are distant and in the tactile
dimension in which they are close.

* Visual Phase—Distant

Along the visual dimension, a person experiences his sex
partners differently when he sees them (1) clothed, (2) partially naked, and (3) completely naked. At each point, new
generators of the body's erotic field begin to operate—rang-
ing from the textures and macrocurves of the clothed body,
through the textures and middling curves of the normally
concealed breast and buttocks of the partially naked body, to
the unexpected textures and microforms of the genitals.
Each specific generator entices the observer on to the next,
although other factors can accelerate or retard their progressive effect.

In general, the fall into erotic reality is retarded by clothing, which minimizes curves and conceals bodily textures,
hair, and genitals. Conversely, it is accelerated as the clothing that muffles these erotic generators is removed. "Partial
nudity" uncovers part of the body or covers it only with a
translucent or transparent material. The "swelling bosom"
fashion of the eighteenth century sped up the slide into
erotic reality down the bare top of the breast, before the
covered nipple at the end brought the slide to an abrupt halt.
"Quasi nudity" sets up a cycle of covered and bare. Any
chance breeze or movement that opens a slitted dress or
unbuttoned shirt unleashes erotic generators until they are
recaged by the next. Both partial and quasi nudity are combined in women's fashion today, ironically impeding the
aims of "Women's Liberation," as Art Buchwald perceptively points out:

> The other night I went to a dinner party in Washington
> prepared to behave as the perfect liberated male. I was going
> to treat my dinner partners as human beings who had minds

of their own and opinions on the subjects of the day that should be listened to. Unfortunately, the person on my right was wearing a black net pajama top with a neckline that plunged down to heaven knows where. The blouse was held up by two tiny straps that looked as if they would break any moment. . . .

God knows we've been sinners and most men are trying to change their attitudes toward women. But when you have nothing but bare backs and cleavage to stare at during dinner, how on earth can any man keep his mind on Henry Kissinger? [Art Buchwald's column in the *New York Post*, 23 March 1976]

"Sexy clothing," in fact, may be even more arousing than total nudity.[11] By mixing dress and undress in the proper proportions, it pulls its viewers into the early stages of erotic reality but continually frustrates their attempts to get beyond them. By revealing curves but concealing their continuation, sexy clothing swells the tension that enhances sexual arousal.

The transition between the fully clothed body's low-power erotic field and the fully unclothed body's high-power erotic field is accomplished by undressing, which gradually lays bare the entire body in time (rather than in space or in cycles). The French essayist Roland Barthes observes that stripping generates erotic reality more effectively than total nudity itself, indicating that the sexual process is more provacative than its goal:

Striptease—at least Parisian striptease—is based on a contradiction: Woman is desexualized at the very moment when she is stripped naked. . . .

It is only the time taken in shedding clothes which makes voyeurs of the public. . . .

There will therefore be in striptease a whole series of coverings placed upon the body of the woman in proportion as she pretends to strip it bare . . . all aim at establishing the woman *right from the start* as an object in disguise. The end of the striptease is then no longer to drag into the light a hidden depth, but to signify, through the shedding of an incon-

gruous and artificial clothing, nakedness as a *natural* vesture
of woman, which amounts in the end to regaining a perfectly
chaste state of the flesh. [1972, pp. 84–85]

Even magazines like *Playboy* and *Playgirl* usually give the
illusion of stripping by presenting pictures of their models in
sequence from clothed to nude, thereby thrusting their
viewers into erotic reality more powerfully than would an
unforeshadowed centerfold by itself. Several sociologists
have found that settings whose inhabitants suddenly appear
(rather than slowly become) completely nude—nudist
camps (Weinberg 1965), art modeling classes (Jesser and
Donovan 1969), and gynecological exams (Emerson 1970)—
are not as sexually arousing as we might expect because this
transitional devestment process in concealed.[12]

Why should stripping be so erotic? Besides exposing the
body's erotic generators, stripping is a form of role removal.
Since most social roles are permanently woven into the
clothing worn to play them, whoever undresses casts off
these other, sexually irrelevant, social roles—paring himself
or herself down to his or her gender role alone. The movement of one's consciousness into erotic reality, then, parallels the increasing revelation of the essential self of one's
sex partner, a self now identified with his or her body per se
without the usual overlay of extraneous roles that ordinarily
dissipate arousal.

It is not surprising, therefore, that a society which invests
social roles with great significance will discourage disrobing
(or "disroling"). In nineteenth-century Europe clothing was
so cumbrous that disrobing was a project in itself, as one of
the characters in Huysmans's novel *Là-Bas* complains:

"And I had better not wear suspenders, for they often cause
ridiculous delays." He took them off and put on a belt. "But
then there is that damned question of the skirts! I admire the
novelists who can get a virgin unharnessed from her corsets
and deflowered in the winking of an eye—as if it were possible! How annoying to have to fight one's way through all

those starched entanglements! I do hope Mme. Chantelouve
will be considerate and avoid those ridiculous difficulties as
much as possible—for her own sake." [1972, p. 146]

Although social custom may dictate whether one should
undress oneself or be undressed by one's sex partner, auto-
divestment is much easier. Most clothes are designed to be
taken off by the person inside them; most people have more
practice taking off their own clothes than others'; and each
gender is often confounded by the different sorts of fasten-
ers found in the other's clothes. In a recent short story by
Lynda Schor, a virgin cat, watching two lovers disrobe from
the perspective of everyday reality, scoffs at what appears to
be the inefficiency of such alterdivestment:

> They are tearing off their own clothes and each other's. He
> begins to take off his own pants, yet before he has succeeded
> he's begun tugging at Judy's shirt, trying to pull it over her
> head. As soon as it's covering her face, but before pulling it
> off, he's back pulling off his own pants again. All this activity
> seems ridiculous to me, as I sit, my front paws crossed,
> moving only my eyes, observing these harmless fools. If they
> just went about it in a rational manner, each one undressing
> either himself or the other, they could be done in half the
> time. . . . [1975, p. 14]

Of course, one may volunteer to remove one's own clothes
to prevent the technical problems of being disrobed from
interrupting progress into erotic reality. Encountering unexpected and unexplained undressing, however, may alarm
recent acquaintances. The clichéd pretext, "It's so hot. I
think I'll slip into something more comfortable,"[13] at least
permits potential sex partners to respond deliberately to the
anticipated unshielding of erotic generators, whereas the
direct "I'm going to take off my clothes now" may prompt
them suddenly to depart.

Since nudity can produce erotic reality, situations in
which people are totally, partially, or quasi nude for utilitarian reasons in everyday reality constitute *overlap points* be-

tween the two realms. These points of overlap are "bypass routes" around the resistances that normally prevent people's consciousness from falling out of everyday reality, allowing it to switch to erotic reality easily or even accidentally. Such switching situations include sports that require little clothing like basketball, tennis, jogging, or swimming;[14] leisure pursuits like lounging in robes or sleeping in nightees; nude art or modeling; and bathing. Pornographers, publicity agents, and others who want to generate erotic reality without acknowledging their intentions often portray these activities. Until the recent easing of film censorship, for instance, movie directors had their stars take showers and bubble baths with abnormal frequency. If accused of lewdness, they could always fall back on the excuse that the main purpose of the apparel—or the lack of it—was to propel its wearer more efficiently toward an everyday objective, even if a side thrust propelled its viewer toward an erotic destination.

The nude body's hair and curves draw its observer's attention down to its genitals, the former through replication of appearance (head hair, pubic hair), the latter through continuation of curve. On the body, it might be said, all roads lead to genitalia.

But such a destination is never fully expected nor easily arrived at. On the one hand, erotic momentum increases through each stage of undressing. On the other hand, the difficulty of integrating new experience with old also increases as visual attention shifts from the fully dressed façade to secondary sex characteristics to the genitals.[15] In short, it comes as a shock for someone to experience the sudden intrusion of other people's sex organs into his or her visual field. The abrupt appearance of the chaotic gentials in the context of a body that otherwise looks ordinary produces a reaction that could be called "genital surprise."

If it is startling to see the genitals after having seen the rest of the body, it is even more startling to see them suddenly without having seen the rest of the body. Genitalia contrast with the clothed, socially draped body even more than with

the naked unsocialized body, which explains why exhibitionism can be so disconcerting.

Nudity so accelerates the sensual slide for some persons
that they are whipped into erotic reality as though over a
roller coaster dip. Since they suspect that nudity affects their
partners in the same way, they try to slow their partners' fall
by demurely concealing their own breasts and genitals behind blankets, towels, or hands. Darkness too dims the
power of these visual sexual generators, though—as Al
Capp points out—it may actually facilitate the transition into
erotic reality by also obscuring phenomena and activities
that properly belong to everyday reality:

> And the girls at that time wore all sorts of armor, all sorts of
> buttons and girdles and things. I was absolutely horrified.
> Once you got it all disengaged, you rolled the hose down, you
> rolled that cast-iron girdle up around her waist, and there was
> this unsightly bulge. I never saw the girl with her clothes off,
> only flashes of her body in the dark. Thank heaven the lights
> were out! It was incredibly ugly, the whole thing, but that's
> that way it was. [Fleming and Fleming 1975, p. 38]

Those who have modestly omitted the visual phase of
copulation entirely move directly into its tactile phase without the preamplification of consciousness that the seeable
erotic transmitters provide.

* Tactile Phase—Close

Potention sex partners must halt at this point if they do not
wish to surrender themselves fully to erotic reality, for tactile
stimulators will accelerate their sensual slide even more
rapidly than visual ones.

> may i feel said he
> (i'll squeal said she
> just once said he)
> it's fun said she. . . .
> [E. E. Cummings (untitled) 1968, p. 399]

This transition between the visual and the tactile is also a major resistance point in commercial sexual arousal: burlesque, topless and/or bottomless dancing, and pornography are all restrained by this "museum model" of the erotic—look, but don't touch. Although this curb on contact frustrates most of the audience, exploring only the visual dimension of erotic reality is sufficient for the few who prefer the ease of the travelogue to the rigors of the actual tour.

The visual and tactile phases of the sensual slide often overlap. Physical contact usually begins while partners are fully clothed. And even when they are partially nude and touching, they often draw back to admire their handiwork visually. Only during the early stages is the crossover between visual and tactile interaction a major resistance point. By merely becoming nude one gives implicit permission for further physical contact.

In the tactile phase, according to Sartre, the process of self-embodiment commences with a *caress*:[16]

> In caressing the Other I cause her flesh to be born beneath my caress, under my fingers. The caress is the ensemble of those rituals which *incarnate* the other. [1956, p. 390]

The *embrace* or total caress assures that the self is now fully fastened to the body. Sartre continues:

> It is not by chance that desire while aiming at the body as a whole attains it especially through masses of flesh which are very little differentiated, grossly nerveless, hardly capable of spontaneous movement, through breasts, buttocks, thighs, stomach. . . . The true caress [i.e., the embrace] is the contact of two bodies in their mostly fleshy parts, the contact of stomachs and breasts; the caressing hand is too delicate, too much like a perfected instrument. But the full pressing together of the flesh of two people against one another is the true goal of desire. [1956, p. 396]

If the hugging of the embrace embodies the self generally throughout the entire body, the fondling of the caress diffuses it specifically into particular bodily segments. By touching or kissing each organ in turn, sex partners nudge the self into motion again should it become stuck in one place.

As the tactile phase of intercourse begins, one partner may attempt to determine its overall style and tone by signaling the "key" he or she desires for it. This key signature tells the other partner to sharpen (exaggerate) some sexual activities ("Be cruel!") or to flatten (minimize) others ("Please be gentle with me"). The copulators may also modulate to a different key during a later phase of intercourse with an internal metacommunication ("Oh! Harder! Fuck me harder!").

After working its way through the body once, the self can more easily traverse that way again. But a first-time copulator will often strongly resist the initial clearing of the path along which his self is to travel:

> (let's go said he
> not too far said she
> what's too far said he
> where you are said she). . . .
> [E. E. Cummings (untitled) 1968, p. 399]

When one potential sex partner resists this self-channeling, the other must tug the former's self forward inch by inch. The actress Victoria Principal describes the difficulty of deciding continually how much to hinder her boyfriend's attempt to construct the conduit along which her self is to flow:

> After kissing came touching. First we'd touch through the clothes. You'd let a boy hold your ribs and maybe his thumb would be touching the edge of your breast and you'd think, "Well, okay, tonight I'll let him." Then the next night his hand would go higher. When he reached your nipple you knew you had to make a decision. He'd either have to stop and start all over again at the ribs, or the next thing was to lift the shirt up and let him work through your bra. [Fleming and Fleming 1975, pp. 182–83]

Many female adolescents have adopted ground rules concerning how far tactile foreplay may go, changing it in fact from being "fore-" anything to being an end in itself (called "necking," "petting," or "making out"). But many male adolescents have always tried to stretch these rules as far as possible, usually describing their progress in terms of a stage-by-stage baseball metaphor (first base, second base, home run, etc.).

Yet if one partner's seduction techniques are not weakening the other's physical points of resistance sufficiently for both to move on to the next erotic stage, the first partner might be tempted to blast through them. One form of rape—sometimes called "acquaintance rape"—results when one partner decides to maintain the momentum of his own sensual slide regardless of the other's continued resistance ("Please don't. No. Stop!"). (Therefore, those not wishing to go "all the way" would be wise to go as short a distance as possible; for the farther they go, the faster their partner's sensual slide accelerates, and the less likely their partner will willingly acquiesce to any last minute blockade.) The journey to the erotic was especially erratic in the nineteenth century, when many people oscillated between Victorian prudishness and Romantic passion. In the following passage from Huysmans's novel *Là-Bas*, Durtal is so disconcerted by Hyacinthe's intermittent resistance that he ponders modulating his ineffective gentle seductions into brute force:

> He took her gently by the arms, drew her to him and abruptly kissed her mouth.
> She rebounded as if she had had an electric shock. . . . He . . . embraced her furiously, then with a strange gurgling cry she . . . caught his leg between both of hers.
> He emitted a howl of rage, for he felt her haunches move. He understood now—or thought he understood! She wanted a miserly pleasure, a sort of solitary vice. . . .
> He pushed her away. . . . Then Durtal's wrath vanished. With a little cry he . . . caught her again, but she struggled, crying, "No! I beseech you, let me go. . . ."

Her accent was so despairing that he relinquished her. Then he debated with himself whether to throw her brutally on the floor and violate her. [1972, pp. 149–50]

The progressive embodiment of the self in various sections of the body is facilitated by activities designed to soften it up and make it more malleable: massaging,[17] kneading, pressing. Through these manipulations the self is first dispersed throughout the various bodily sections, then drawn from these peripheral parts and concentrated inward and downward toward the bottom center of the body, and finally (for conventional sex) refocused in the genitals—much as one might squeeze a partially used tube to work the toothpaste down toward its tip. In *Lady Chatterley's Lover*, Lawrence describes the caresses with which Mellors seduced Connie:

And softly, with that marvellous swoon-like caress of his hand in pure soft desire, softly he stroked the silky slope of her loins, down, down between her soft warm buttocks, coming nearer and nearer to the very quick of her. [1968, p. 186]

And in *The Group* Mary McCarthy describes subjectively the refocusing of Dottie's consciousness by Dick:

She struggled against the excitement his tickling thumb was producing in her own external part; but as she felt him watching her, her eyes closed and her thighs spread open. He disengaged her hand, and she fell back on the bed, gasping. His thumb continued its play and she let herself yield to what it was doing, her whole attention concentrated on a tense pinpoint of sensation. . . . [1964, p. 44]

Both men and women sometimes complain that their partners attempt to move on to the next stage of intercourse before fully relocating their identity in their genitals: "Wait, do it some more, I'm not ready yet." The physical concentration of the self in the genitals is an necessary prerequisite for the ultimate psychological interchange of identity, for the genitals are the point at which that interchange occurs.[18]

Third Movement

In ordinary sex, the coupling of genitals is the concrete embodiment of the interpenetration of selves. Sexual experience becomes even more intense at this juncture, marking it as another potential resistance point along the road to erotic reality—the last exit, in fact, before "going all the way."

> Then there's another great classification—the promiscuous virgin:
> "I don't go all the way. That's all—I don't go all the way." And these chicks better be careful. Because when they're gonna go, that may not be the way any more. [Lenny Bruce, quoted in Cohen 1967, pp. 191–92]

There are many reasons for resistance at this point. Alcohol, for instance, facilitates leaving everyday reality but may impede entering erotic reality.

> *Macduff*:   What three things does drink especially provoke?
> *Porter*: Marry, sir, nose-painting, sleep, and urine. Lechery, sir, it provokes and unprovokes. It provokes the desire, but it takes away the performance. Therefore much drink may be said to be an equivocator with lechery. It makes him and it mars him, it set him on and it takes him off, it persuades him and disheartens him, makes him stand to and not stand to; in conclusion, equivocates him in a sleep and giving him the lie, leaves him.
> [Shakespeare, *Macbeth* 2.3 29–40]

Birth control may also cause resistance. Since its benefits properly belong to the concerns of everyday reality and its devices usually require a "time-out" from erotic reality for their insertion or application, it may halt the sensual slide after it has begun to accelerate. If birth control is necessary for sex, some people would rather forget the whole thing.

On the other hand, the sociologist Kristin Luker (1976) found that many women would rather forego contraception than coitus because it interferes with the "spontaneity" of sex, the ideal currently in vogue.

After genital insertion, the temporal focus of intercourse shifts from progression to rhythm. The rhythm of muscular contraction and relaxation that softens the self becomes the dominant motif whereas in the earlier stages it remains subordinate to simple tactility. The partners now try to coordinate their rhythms of tension and release to propel their consciousness farther into erotic reality while compressing themselves deeper into their bodies. Copulators new to each other must learn each other's erotic rhythm, just as a musician must learn the rhythm of a new piece.[19] Of course, they may apply standard patterns, already observed in previous copulations (both actual and imagined), applying fine turning at those points where the partner's unique variations diverge from this norm.

Both sex manuals and pornography, however, overemphasize these standard patterns, obscuring the need to make these microadjustments frequently to suit the partner's idiosyncrasies. Indeed, overly technical foreplay is self-negating (See May 1969, esp. pp. 43, 54–55). The very techniques that should facilitate the transition between everyday and erotic reality impede it when done for their own sake. By overstressing technique one becomes too "mechanical," too deaf to the feedback cues that tell a person how to synchronize his rhythm with his partner's. And since the techniques of sex belong to everyday reality, whoever is preoccupied with them may find it difficult to become aroused himself. In another short story Lynda Schor parodies those whose means make them lose sight of their ends:

> I picture us in bed. He has prepared for it by finding time to study a new sexual manual. We kiss and do foreplay. He does everything the manual specifies to excite me, including fondling and kissing my erogenous zones: a. lips; b. nipples; c. tongue in ear. Unable to recall with certainty about my navel,

he gives it a quick feel and semiperforates it with an instant index finger. . . . I press more and more closely until we're lying on our sides. He wonders what to do next. According to the book I'm not on my side at all. . . . He decides to push me onto my back, props my legs up, and throws a pillow under my ass. He seems to measure the distance between my two raised knees, and, slightly doubtful without immediate access to a compass and ruler, he studies me closely in the correctly dim light to ascertain whether I've broken out in the sex flush, those hivelike red blotches indicative of readiness. . . . He feels my vagina to test the lubrication and, after a moment of indecision, decides that I'm ready. It isn't until then that he notices that he isn't. [1975, pp. 241–42]

Even at this point there may be resistance if one's partner is unwilling or unable to advance his or her rhythmic progresssion to its climax. In this event, instead of adjusting one's rhythm to one's partner's, it may be more effective to adjust one's partner's rhythm to one's own. The dominant partner can shift into *rhythmic override*, first getting into the submissive partner's muscle tension/release cycle and then, when both are vibrating together, suddenly changing the tempo, compelling the submissive partner to follow. Norman Mailer's short story "The Time of Her Time" contains a classic description of an attempt at rhythmic override— albeit an unsuccessful one:

She hammered her rhythm at me, a hard driving rhythm, an all but monotonous drum, pound into pound against pound into pound . . . my rhythm no longer depended upon her drive, but found its own life, and we made love like two club fighters in an open exchange, neither giving ground, rhythm to rhythm, even to even, hypnotic, knowing neither the pain of punishment nor the pride of pleasure, and the equality of this, as hollow as the beat of the drum, seemed to carry her into some better deep of desire, and I had broken through, she was following me . . . my hand came up and clipped her mean and openhanded across the face which brought a cry from her and broke the piston of her hard speed into something softer, wetter, more sly, more warm, I felt as if her belly

were opening finally to receive me, and when . . . her body
sweetened into some feminine embrace of my determination
driving its way into her, well, I was gone, it was too late, I had
driven right past her in that moment she turned, and I had
begun to come . . . and for a moment she was making it, she
was a move back and surging to overtake me, and then it was
gone, she made a mistake, her will ordered all temptings and
rhythms to mobilize their march . . . and as I was going off in
the best for many a month, she was merely going away, she
had lost it again. [1960, pp. 438–39]

The difficulty of synchronization increases with the number who must be syncronized. Many people prefer masturbation to intercourse because coordinating one's own
rhythms to achieve orgasm is so unproblematic. Two-person
sex was easier to coordinate in the past than it is today since
the norm then was that the female partner should not satisfy
herself directly but rather help the male partner satisfy himself while participating vicariously in his pleasure. The current movement toward equal rights to sexual satisfaction is
an instance of a more general trend toward participatory
rather than representative democracy. This trend un-
doubtedly increases one participant's satisfaction in sex as in
other areas, though it may decrease the total amount of
satisfaction available to all participants, if efficiency is reduced by the friction involved in coordinating disparate
wills. Three or more persons face still more complications in
harmonizing their behavior, as Marco Vassi observes:

Amateurs that we were, we had no sense of the complexity of
rhythm involved in a threesome, nor of how to keep the
tension-relaxation cycle flowing smoothly. [1967a, p. 53]

Moreover, if one partner is too intense—shouting, tearing
flesh, bouncing erratically—the other may be unable to
accommodate. The choppier rhythms of intercourse may
even inadvertently uproot a penis from a vagina, plucking
consciousness out of erotic reality until the genitals are re-
planted. Conversely, too little response from one partner—

passivity, frigidity— may also disconcert the other; unless the first partner slows, catches, and returns the second partner's every push, the latter may push too far, losing balance and breaking tempo.

Of course, some people find it easy to syncronize their rhythms because they are naturally compatible. Victoria Principal contrasts this experience with one less satisfying produced by an incompatible partner:

> Whereas my original lover had many hang-ups and guilts and reservations, this man—he was twenty-seven—was so natural and encouraging. In fact, the relationship was based on pure chemistry. It was just like finding your perfect tennis partner. . . . I fell in love with another big blond Adonis, a sports hero, and this was another disaster. His problems and my problems just didn't mesh. The sex was very confusing.
> [Fleming and Fleming 1975, pp. 188, 189]

The sexually compatible usually synchronize their behavior silently, afterward perhaps referring to their harmony with phrases such as "Mmmmm. You know just what I like" or "You know just what to do." Sexual incompatability occurs when one partner wants to do what the other doesn't. The first must then distinguish the sexual activities that the second (1) will eventually find desirable, (2) will eventually find tolerable, and (3) will continue to find repulsive. If the benefits of other aspects of their relation outweigh the costs of its sexual side, naturally incompatible couples may attempt to coordinate their coupling artificially through bilateral "talks" or trilateral counseling in the hope that their conflicts over (3) will diminish relative to their compromises over (1) and (2).

Ideally, copulators are able to coordinate their rhythms enough to reach orgasm simultaneously:

> Neither go too fast, nor let her get there before you;
> Pleasure is best when both come at one time to the goal.
> [Ovid 1957, p. 152]

But gender differences in erotic rhythms make it difficult to reach this ideal. Whether for cultural or biological reasons, men in Western society have long moved into, through, and out of erotic reality faster than woman. The seventeenth-century poet and playwright John Dryden describes their temporal disparity, though noting that repetition can reverse it:

> While Alexis lay pressed
> In her arms he loved best,
> With his hands round her neck,
> And his head on her breast,
> He found the fierce pleasure too hasty to stay,
> And his soul in the tempest just flying away.
>
> When Celia saw this,
> When a sigh and a kiss,
> She cried, Oh my dear, I am robbed of my bliss;
> 'Tis unkind to your love, and unfaithfully done,
> To leave me behind you, and die all alone.
>
> The youth, though in haste
> And breathing his last,
> In pity died slowly while she died more fast,
> Till at length she cried, 'Now, my dear, now let us go!
> Now die, my Alexis, and I will die too.'
>
> Thus entranced they did lie,
> Till Alexis did try
> To recover new breath that again he might die:
> Then often they died; but the more they did so,
> The nymph died more quick and the shepherd more slow.
> [Marriage a-la-Mode 4.2.47–67]

Sexually "carnivorous" women continually complain that sexually "herbivorous" men race through intercourse much too fast ("Slam, bam, thank you, ma'am").[20] The "ass grabbing" of dirty old (and young) men especially annoys women because it caricatures men's ability to move through erotic reality more rapidly than they can. As far as sex is concerned, most women prefer men who beat around the bush rather than coming straight to the point.

The length of time people want to remain in erotic reality varies not only with their gender and social class (Kinsey 1948, p. 580), but also with their personality and even with their mood, greatly complicating the copulators' task of synchronizing a simultaneous exit. To sustain consciousness of erotic reality until both are ready to leave it together each partner must maintain a gradually increasing amount of sexual tension. Should one begin to go too slow or too fast, the other must moderate his or her speed:

> (tiptop said he
> don't stop said she
> oh no said he)
> go slow said she. . . .
> [E. E. Cummings (untitled), 1968, p. 399]

Sexual tension that increases too rapidly leads to premature orgasm, blasting one partner out of erotic reality long before the other is ready to let go. Sexual tension that increases too slowly leads to postmature orgasm, leaving one partner still exploring the outskirts of erotic reality long after the other wants to go home.

Given the difficulties in bringing their sexual encounter to a mutually agreeable conclusion by natural means, copulators may try to synchronize their climax by controlling the accumulation of sexual tension with artificial devices such as anesthetic ointment or rubber bands. Psychological techniques for adjusting the timing of orgasm involve imagining situations containing erotic generators that are more or less powerful than those in the present situation. A person can hasten orgasm by imagining a sex partner or activity more appealing than the current one, or retard orgasm by imagining everyday events like doing the dishes. Should orgasm be too close, however, one may have to fanatasize about extraordinary events that undercut erotic reality even more deeply than everyday events: being in antierotic settings (e.g., mother's funeral), being with antierotic partners (e.g., a repulsive), performing antierotic activities (e.g., wallowing in feces), or being off in another realm, like Kay's husband Harald in *The Group*:

> Even in bed he kept his *sang-froid*; he did the multiplication tables to postpone ejaculating—an old Arab recipe he had learned from an Englishman. [McCarthy 1964, p. 91][21]

The most precise control over the timing of orgasm results from alternating these artificial techniques of speeding up and slowing down,[22] much as the thermostat on a refrigerator or heater maintains the correct amount of coldness or heat by alternately switching on or off. Developing such an exact *erotostat*, however, is a difficult skill to perfect. Even after mastering the mental and physical oscillations necessary to control arousal, a person must also take into account his partner's gyrations, which can easily unbalance his own.

Certain extreme forms of sex—especially bondage and discipline, sadism and masochism, transvestism and fetishism—present unique difficulties in sustaining a sense of erotic reality. They require more cooperation and equipment than commonplace sex, increasing the probability that something will go wrong. In a well-known *Playboy* article, Dan Greenberg recounts some of the prop problems he encountered in his attempt to get into the S and M scene:

> Knowing that a homely length of clothesline is never going to be enough for Edith, I lay out eight dollars for handcuffs and $25 each for two sets of wrist and ankle shackles. I suppose that going into an S/M store to buy chain shackles in the Seventies in equivalent to going into a drugstore for a box of condoms in the Fifties. I've done both with an equal amount of aplomb.
>
> Back home, it occurs to me for the first time that I have no place to attach the swivel snaps on the ends of the shackles. If only I owned a four-poster bed. Luckily, I am handy with tools, and without much hassle I attach four screw eyes at strategic locations in the platform of the bed to anchor the swivel snaps. I practice snapping the snaps to the shackles

and buckling and unbuckling the heavy leather straps so it
will look like I've been doing it all my life. . . .

[*Playboy*, (January 1976, p. 197)]

Even after assembly, this equipment presents many technical problems,[23] for nonordinary sex often requires that ordinary paraphernalia be put to extraordinary uses:

> "Lie down on the bed," I growl.
> She does. I pull off her panties, attach straps to both her
> ankles and snap the ends of the chains to the screw eyes. I
> start to untie the tie from around her wrists and realize it'll be
> hopeless with my shades on. I take them off and struggle
> myopically with the knot. I'm sweaty and hot and in a terrible
> mood. I pull off my boots and my sweaty leather jeans and
> again attack the knot, but it's still hopeless. I sigh and get a
> scissors and cut it apart.
> "I'm ruining a perfectly good tie because of you," I mutter.
>
> [*Playboy*, January 1976, p. 200]

The need to return to everyday consciousness to rearrange
people and props continually interrupts the progression of
erotic rhythm.

Finale

During orgasm, the barrier enclosing one's self falls away
completely, merging it totally (if temporarily) with the self of
one's sex partner. Most people can talk concretely about
such an ontological transformation in their basic being in
terms of the only equivalent model they know: a natural
environment undergoing upheaval—"It felt like an earth-
quake," "The sky moved"—or one so completely structure-
less as to be fluid, like water or air. *Penthouse* Pet of the
Month Joann Witty describes it thus:

> The best moments in sex come when both lovers really seem
> to merge into one. You know, those moments that seem to go
> on forever when the sheer pleasure of loving just wipes out

the inhibitions and the egos. That release . . . just like flying
. . . is the most exhilarating feeling in the world.
[*Penthouse*, March 1976, p. 85]

But this same softening of the self in erotic reality makes a person extremely vulnerable. Fear of ontological contamination may restrain one from letting oneself (rather, one's self) go. Long after physical resistance to embodying the self has been overcome, psychological resistance to merging it with another's self at orgasm may remain. Marco Vassi describes this psychological resistance from the male perspective:

> In all the times we had had sex, I had never let go in her arms. I always performed, not in the adolescent sense of trying to be the best fuck she ever had, but in the more insidious way of never losing my self-consciousness. Both in and out of bed I kept my distance, and we shared no existential rushes. [1976a, p. 8]

D. H. Lawrence describes it from the female perspective:

> And when [Mellors] said, with a sort of little sigh: "Eh, that'rt nice!" something in [Connie Chatterley] quivered, and something in her spirit stiffened in resistance: stiffened from the terribly physical intimacy, and from the peculiar haste of his possession. . . . "Ay!" he said. "It was no good that time. You wasn't there." So he knew! Her sobs became violent. . . . It was from herself she wanted to be saved, from her own inward anger and resistance. Yet how powerful was that inward resistance that possessed her [1968, pp. 184, 185, 186]

Those well versed in the ways of sex can overcome even this last stronghold of their partner's resistance to self-merger. Most sex therapists recommend tranquilizing it with tenderness. One of Norman Mailer's fictional personae, however, touts the effectiveness of force:

> And so I took her with a cold calculation, . . . I worked on her like a riveter, knowing her resistances were made of steel, I

threw her a fuck the equivalent of a fifteen-round fight, I
wearied her, . . . and I took her mouth and kissed it, but she
was away, following the wake of her own waves which
mounted, fell back, and in my new momentum mounted
higher and should have gone over, and then she was about to
hang again, I could feel it, that moment of hesitation between
the past and the present, the habit and the adventure, and I
said into her ear, "You dirty little Jew."
   That whipped her over. A first wave kissed, a second
spilled, and a third and a fourth and a fifth came breaking
over, and finally she was away, she was loose in the water for
the first time in her life. . . . [1960, pp. 449–50]

There is, of course, much more to be said about this orgasmic merger of selves, but since this process is what sets off
the extreme emotional and religious reaction that has colored our view of sex for the last several thousand years, I will
postpone further discussion of this topic until part two.

Postlude

The crack between everyday reality and erotic reality,
which opens imperceptibly, widens gradually until (at the
point of maximum separation) orgasm suddenly snaps it
shut again—hurling consciousness back into everyday reality. (This may be the paradigm human experience for Martin
Heidegger's notion of *Geworfenheit*, being-flung-down-into-
the-world-that-is-there.)
   As the individual descends into everyday reality after
orgasm, the world appears to undergo a rapid transformation: time and space reexpand to their previous dimensions,
objects and people (as well as their components) reestablish
their original hierarchies of importance, and selves disen-
gage from bodies and disentangle from each other. Lawrence provides one of the best descriptions of this last experience:

   And yet when he had finished, soon over, and lay very very

still, receding into silence, and a strange, motionless distance, far, farther than the horizon of her awareness, her heart began to weep. She could feel him ebbing away, ebbing away, leaving her there like a stone on a shore. He was withdrawing, his spirit was leaving her. [1968, p. 185]

But everyday reality does not look quite the same after orgasm. For a time it retains a certain phenomenological coloring conferred by the erotic reality that preceded it, though there is some dispute whether the postcoital world seems more dingy or more dazzling than the precoital world. According to Tristram Shandy [Sterne 1967, p. 38], Aristotle once observed, "Quod omne animal post coitum est triste" ("After coitus, every animal is sad.") But a more recent observer claims the opposite is true:

Far, far more closely than even the rapture of mutual orgasm does the bliss and content of the *after-glow* unite true lovers, as they lie embraced, side by side, while nature recuperates. . . . [Van de Velde 1965, p. 229]

Regardless of whether its coloring is dim or bright, the period immediately following orgasm acts as a temporal decompression chamber, smoothing out the shock of transition and preventing the aftershocks of phenomenological disorientation. Many people go to sleep after sex because sleep provides the most regular, if not the most rapid, transit from other realities to everyday reality, for we have all had plenty of practice putting our ordinary world together when we wake. But those who do not resort to sleep must resolve two sets of technical problems in order to switch from one reality to the other.

A person must reorient himself to the erotic reality he has just left. One may have enjoyed one's stay there so much that revisiting it immediately is appealing psychologically, though physiology may delay the return trip—especially for the male. A poem from an anonymous eighteenth-century play illustrates:

Do not thy——, Nature's best gift, despise,
That girl that made it fall, will make it rise;
Though it awhile the amorous combat shun
And seems from mine into thy belly run,
Yet 'twill return more vigorous and more fierce
Than flaming drunkard, when he's died in tierce.
It but retires, as losing gamsters do,
Till they have raised a stock to play anew.

[*The Cabinet of Love*, act 1 scene 1]

It usually exasperates those whose spirit is willing to find that their flesh is weak. But in his novel *Cockpit*, Jerzy Kosinski describes a character so mercenary that he tries to turn even this physiological deficiency to pecuniary advantage:

The man was proud of the hard bargain he drove with every woman. Since a whore usually demanded more money for each successive climax, he had developed a sexual con. He turned off everything but a night light while she undressed. As she smoked or drank, he caressed her until he climaxed without her noticing it. She would have to work twice as hard, not knowing it would be his second orgasm. . . . No woman, he bragged, had ever suspected how many orgasms he managed to get for the price of one. [1976, p. 231]

Barring a return journey, a person must also reorient himself to the everyday reality just reentered. Upon landing, one must decide if, when, and how to carry out physical maintenance on oneself: go to the bathroom? wash genitals? douche? shower? (see Gagnon and Simon 1973, p. 79). A related concern is to reestablish one's customary connection with outside role partners uninvolved in the intercourse. Ovid cautions women to restore their familiar appearance, demeanor, and surroundings in order to present no direct evidence of being freshly fucked:

But, when you put on your dress, put on a decent appearance:

> Try not to look like a girl who has been recently—
> loved. . . .
> Why must I see, in the bed, signs it was slept in by two?
> Why must I see your hair disordered, not simply by slumber?
> Why must I see, on your neck, marks of another man's bite?
>
> [1966, p. 94]

One can retain the status of a full participant in everyday reality only by giving nonsexual associates no cause to suspect that one takes off for other realms as soon as they are out of sight.

Preoccupation with self and others after sex would not present much difficulty were it not an implicitly negative comment on one's relationship with one's erstwhile partner. Washing implies an attempt to remove all of the material traces of the relationship; straightening up implies a reorientation of concern away from it and toward other significant relationships. Everyone is aware of the long-lamented lack of correlation between those appealing in erotic reality and those appealing in everyday reality. Even those who go to sleep immediately after making love may discover this discrepancy when waking up the next morning by finding that they cannot now stand their bedmates. Because such repulsion is possible, each sex partner may have to reassure the other that he or she values their postcoital relationship as much as their coital relationship. Such reassurances are given nonverbally through touching various parts of the partner[24] or verbally through expressions of delight with one's own erotic experience, interest in the quality of one's partner's erotic experience, and general reaffirmation of their relationship.[25] An all-purpose after-orgasm oration that speaks to all these issues might go something like: "That was wonderful! You're really great in bed. Was it good for you too? I love you more than ever now." In sum, each copulator's prime postcoital task is to reassure the other that the latter's image in erotic reality has been favorably integrated with the latter's image in everyday reality, restoring and perhaps even enhancing the relationship.

Conclusion

I have tried to develop a dynamic phenomenology of
sexual experience in this chapter to describe the circuit of
consciousness from everyday to erotic reality and back
again. During this journey consciousness travels through a
series of stages, experiencing each one differently from the
others. (Since consciousness moves simultaneously through
different dimensions—e.g., visual and tactile—at different
rates, this qualitative distinction between the stages may be
somewhat blurred.) Progress is sporadic because the mind's
advance from one stage to the next encounters, and must
stop to overcome, resistance.

This sensual slide is directional. Whereas everyday reality
seems to go nowhere (except for a slight trend imposed by
various social rhythms and cycles: work-leisure, weekdays-
weekends, promotions within and graduations from educa-
tional institutions, etc.), erotic reality seems to have a defi-
nite direction: a thrust toward the finality of orgasm. The
goal-oriented ideology of Western culture, however, must
greatly reinforce this physiologically induced directionality,
for sex may take a different direction in other societies:

> It is not necessary that for either sexual excitement or
> orgasm to occur that the movement be from the lips to the
> genitals, nor is it necessary that orgasm culminate from these
> acts. In other cultures, coitus occurs first and then what we
> consider precoital behavior occurs after coitus. [Gagnon and
> Simon 1973, p. 80]

How "running sex backwards" from orgasm to foreplay
affects the phenomenology of erotic reality remains to be
explored.

This directionality involves a paradox. On the one hand,
erotic reality is more pleasureable than everyday reality *phenomenologically* because of its freedom from ordinary constraints. On the other hand, sexual arousal is less pleasur-

able than unarousal *physiologically* because of its "itch" of sexual tension (Freud 1972, pp. 80, 109). A person wants therefore both to prolong this state and to terminate it. This paradox is one source of the social taboos that surround sex, for the internal contradiction in sexual desire between wanting it to continue and wanting it to cease synecdochically objectifies—and therefore concentrates and intensifies—the pleasureable-painful paradox of life itself.

This sensual slide is not only directional but also accelerating. (This characteristic suggests why sex is often symbolized in dreams by falling. As a would-be copulator's consciousness moves into erotic reality, the locus of his or her self seems to descend from head to genitals with increasing rapidity.) Compared with Indian civilization, which has developed sophisticated techniques for amplifying and controlling the acceleration of the sensual slide, and Chinese civilization, which has developed ingenious gadgets for this purpose, Western civilization has until recently been primitive indeed (Atkins 1972, p. 335).

This acceleration of the sensual slide accounts for the extreme displeasure one feels should it suddenly be brought to a halt—especially during the later phases of sexual activity. Some "masseuses" and other prostitutes take advantage of this increasing desire to continue a sensual slide by demanding a "toll" before switching on the erotic generators that will carry a person on to its next stage ("Wait a minute! It'll cost you another $5 if you want me to take off my panties and another $10 if you want to touch my tits too"). If physiological frustration were the only effect of coitus interruptus, the psychological jolt it produces would not be so severe. But coitus interruptus is so shocking because it abruptly collapses one's entire conception of reality.[26]

The following are some of the factors that produce these "reality blowouts," roughly in order of increasing intensity:
1. Behaviors regarded as having low status in everyday reality.
   A. Generally (from *The Unexpergated Code* by J. P. Donleavy):

There are however awkward environs for the sounding and the fuming of the fart. Namely during lectures on art, largo passages in symphonies, high points of religious ceremony, or when another is spiritually transported in the rapturous delirium of orgasm. [1976, p. 107][27]

B. Idiosyncratically (from an interview with Clifford Irving):

I started kissing her, then peeling off her clothes and she didn't protest and I thought, "God, you've answered my prayers." But God is ever a joker. When we got into bed—the big moment, I've finally found a girl who wants to fuck and there's no bullshit—I said, "Would you mind stopping chewing that gum." And she said, "What for? I always chew gum in bed." What a disaster. I can smell it now. That girl smelled of chewing gum the whole time. [Fleming and Fleming 1975, pp. 91–92]

2. Prop failures. Copulators may fall off their pedestal or it may fall down. An anonymous limerick:

There was a young man of Kildare,
Who was having a girl in a chair.
    At the sixty-third stroke
    The furniture broke,
And his rifle went off in the air.
                              Quoted in Atkins 1972, p. 354]

3. The intrusion of others.
    A. Via the telephone. Even if unanswered, a telephone continues to ring out of rhythm with erotic tempi (from Dan Greenberg, the simulated sadist):

Just then the phone rings. When I am making love, I never answer the phone. But when I'm spanking? I pick up the phone. . . . It's my next door neighbor, Fred. . . .

"I was wondering if you'd like to go grab a bite to
eat," he says.
"I can't right now, I'm busy," I say.
"What're you doing?"
"You wouldn't believe me if I told you," I say.
"Try me."
"I'm spanking someone," I say.
"I don't believe you," he says.
"Suit yourself. Fred. I'll talk to you later," I say and
hang up the phone."

[*Playboy*, January 1976, p. 200]

B. In person. Freud and his followers have asserted that
the child who walks into the bedroom while his parents are performing their marital rites experiences the
most emotionally charged scene of the human drama.
(Although this scene may traumatize the child, it certainly traumatized the parents when Freudian theory
was popular; they came to believe that it would warp
their child for life.) Today, however, a more common
traumatic scene occurs when the parents stumble in
upon their copulating child. Leonard Michaels vividly
portrays this scene in his short story "City Boy":

It was nearly three in the morning. . . . We were on
the living-room floor. . . . She was underneath me
and warm. . . . This was crazy, dangerous. . . . The
maid might arrive, her parents might wake. . . . A
voice, "Veronica, don't you think it's time you send
Phillip home?" . . . Mr. Cohen had spoken. He stood
ten inches from our legs. . . . His foot came down on
my ass. He drove me into his daughter. I drove her into
his rug. "I don't believe it," he said. . . . Veronica
squealed, had a contraction, fluttered, gagged a
shriek, squeezed, and up like a frog out of the hand of a
child I stood. . . . Veronica wailed, "Phillip." Mr.
Cohen screamed, "I'll kill him." . . . The door
slammed. I was outside, naked as a wolf. [1969, pp.
13–18]

Erotic reality can be exploded by the unexpected arrival of
any authority figure, e.g., the cops.

4. The intrusion of the environment. Earthquakes, explo-
   sions, and fires may bring down the entire bedroom on
   the copulating couple's heads.
5. The sudden transformation of one of the copulators
   themselves.
   A. From a disabling biological breakdown that results in
      cardiac arrest, stroke, or worse:

> Mayor Edward Koch dismissed New York City's
> chief medical examiner Tuesday following . . . allega-
> tions that during a hospital lecture the physician pre-
> sented details about Nelson Rockefeller's death so as
> to indicate that the former Vice President had died
> during sexual intercourse. . . . Rockefeller has suf-
> fered his heart attack while with Megan Marshack, a
> 25-year-old aide, in a townhouse he owned. . . . [Los
> Angeles Times 1 August 1979, part I, p. 4].[28]

   B. From a violent psychological mania that results in
      attack from a completely unsuspected source (hence
      the fear of vampires). Jerzy Kosinski describes an even
      worse fear in his novel Cockpit:

> His only fear in the peepshows, he confessed to me,
> was that he might encounter the Snapper, a well-built
> blond youth who prowled the porn houses. . . . Like
> everyone else, the Snapper would stand in front of the
> booth and nod at an older man, who would promptly
> follow him into the booth. The young man would
> squat on the floor while the older one dropped a quar-
> ter in the slot and unzipped his pants. The boy would
> take the man's flesh into his mouth, easing it gently
> into his throat, then suddenly bite down. With one
> bite, the victim's organ was severed. . . . With blood
> oozing through his pants, the victim would clutch his
> groin and beg the peepshow manager not to summon
> the police. [1976, pp. 234–35]

All these unexpected events suddenly jolt the sexually
aroused back to everyday reality, sometimes before they

even know what has hit them. After one's sensual slide has been derailed by any of these sudden and serious smash-ups, it is almost impossible to recover enough to resume one's journey into erotic reality. Yet it is certainly possible to recover from less momentous mishaps and be on one's way again. Unfortunately, whoever employs the techniques necessary to make even these minor repairs may become still more embedded in everyday reality, for, as noted, these techniques belong to the workaday world. Thus it may be self-defeating to attempt to remove obstacles to erotic pro-gress oneself, for the act of doing so often hinders the forma-tion of the very reality it is supposed to facilitate.

It is more efficient to travel into erotic reality with those who will eliminate all impediments for one, especially with partners who do not require in return any aid that might interfere with one's own trip. These partners agree to remain in everyday reality in order to handle all the difficulties a copulator might encounter en route to erotic reality, just as travel agents are supposed to handle all the difficulties a tourist might encounter on a tour without actually going on it themselves. Marco Vassi describes the one-sided satisfac-tion produced by this asymmetrical acceleration into erotic reality. One of his existentially bored characters proposes:

> "If we had a closed car, you would kneel before me and take my limp warm penis in your mouth . . . and then suck until I sprayed your mouth with sperm. And all the while I should continue to smoke, and gaze out the window, gently comtem-plating the destruction of a civilization, the end of the culture, the curtains on history." [Vassi 1976a, p. 119]

Of course, it is not easy to find partners willing to remain at home mentally while one wanders off to other realities. A way to procure them is through physical persuasion, or rape. The rapist compels a partner to go through the physical motions of sex while remaining in everyday reality[29] in order to forward the rapist's own phenomenological progression. But since the rapist must continually monitor the rapee, who is usually looking for a means of escape, the rapist is often distracted from devoting his full attention to erotic pleasures.

A more effective way to procure partners less likely to flee when one's back is turned is through economic persuasion, or prostitution. Unlike rapees, prostitutes often help their partners progress through erotic reality by pretending to do so themselves, exhibiting its physical symptoms (e.g., by faking orgasm) to help their partners experience its mental processes. Prostitutes can be careless, however, for their everyday concerns—time and money—often clash with their customers' erotic concerns. An ex-masseuse once reported that she never "got off" with her customers, but treated her hand-jobs "like ironing." Conceiving of sexual activity as one of the dull, repetitious, mechanical task of everyday reality lessens the enthusiasm necessary to give a good tour of erotic reality.

The most effective way to procure partners willing to satisfy one sexually at all costs is through psychological persuasion, or charisma. Charm is more certain than money or fear to ensure sensitivity to the subtle cues, and agreeability to the expressed desires, that will make one's erotic journey a success. Unfortunately, few possess this charismatic attraction naturally and—commercial advertisements to the contrary—it is almost impossible to acquire by effort or purchase.

All sexual fantasies, in fact, either minimize the technical problems involved in an erotic journey or provide imaginary partners selflessly willing to resolve them.[30] In her novel *Fear of Flying*, Erica Jong called her fantasy of intercourse without these technical problems the "zipless fuck":

> The zipless fuck was more than a fuck. It was a platonic ideal. Zipless because when you came together zippers fell away like rose petals, underwear blew off in one breath like dandelion fluff. Tongues intertwined and turned liquid. Your whole soul flowed out through your tongue and into the mouth of your lover. [1974, p. 11]

(The extremely important implications of the last sentence will be explored in part two.) This idealization of intercourse is the reason sexual fantasies usually remain merely fantasies. Only after acquiring some real sexual experience does one realize the effort required to remain in erotic reality while overcoming the technical difficulties that continually return one to everyday reality, as a character in Edward Albee's play *The Zoo Story* points out:

> What I wanted to get at is the value difference between pornographic playing cards when you're a kid, and pornographic playing cards when you're older. It's that when you're a kid you use cards as a substitute for the real experience, and when you're older you use real experience as a substitute for the fantasy. [1958, p. 27]

It is one of the peculiar characteristics of the human condition that a person can be knocked out of erotic reality by the actual activities of sex itself.

Part Two
Smut Structure

Sex and Dirt

"In the lore of love," writes Van de Velde (1965, p. 15), whose influential marriage manual lay beside many a bed during the middle of the twentieth century, "supreme beauty and hideous ugliness are separated by a border-line so slight that our minds may transgress it, unawares!" Van de Velde was referring specifically to his qualms about what he delicately calls the "genital kiss," but his observation applies more generally to other aspects of sex as well. Sex is an either/or phenomenon—appealing or appalling, rarely inbetween. Ambivalence toward sex occurs at every social level. An individual may like or dislike it at different times or even at the same time. Some groups delight in it, others detest it. Society as a whole may encourage or repress it alternately during different historical periods or—like America today—simultaneously during the same historical period.

What is responsible for the slight shift in cognition that transforms sex into smut? To answer this question we must ascend a cognitive level from experience to interpretation.[1] Experience, in itself, is neither good nor bad; it simply is. One can evaluate an experience only by interpreting it in terms of a scheme that is posited as an ideal. Our discussion of sex, therefore, must now shift from phenomenology to ideology, from describing sexual experience to analyzing an interpretation of sexual experience that measures it against an ideal.

An interpretation is less general than an experience, for each group within a society will interpret the same experience in terms of its own unique criteria. In this part we shall examine the ideology of the group that interprets sexual experience through a scheme that judges it as evil. Of course, this is not the only way to look at it. In part three we shall examine the ideologies of two other groups that interpret sexual experience through quite different schemes, thereby evaluating it as good or, at worst, neutral. A society is hostile toward sex to the extent that it is controlled by proponents of the negative interpretation. The current ambivalence toward sex in America today results from this group's struggle to retain its dominance over groups that interpret sex more positively.

Sex is interpreted negatively because of its connection with dirt, a linkage manifested in the word *obscene*. One etymology derives this term from the Latin *obscenus*, meaning "from or with filth" (another traces it to *obscaena*, meaning "off stage," i.e., what was not fit to be seen on stage). In the early centuries of Christianity, the Latin Fathers of the Church used this root sense of obscene to describe the gender that enticed men to experience sexual desire. Jerome referred to woman as "a sack of filth," Tertullian called her "a temple on top of a sewer," and Augustine pointed out that she gave birth "between urine and feces." Even now, Church representatives still use metaphors for sex that imply it is somehow involved with dirt:

> "We live at a time when man's animal side often degenerates into unchecked *corruption*. We walk in the *mud*," Pope Paul

told 3,000 visitors in his weekly public audience. He linked psychoanalysis and sexual education with porno magazines and sex shows for contributing to what he called the *"pollution"* of environmental immorality.

> [*Chicago Sun-Times* 14 September 1972, p. 33; emphasis added]

Spokesmen for this moral ecology movement often characterize sexual activity, the sexually active, and pornography in terms used to describe dirt—"pollution," "filth," "garbage," "trash," "slime," "smut," "dregs" (as in the "dregs of society"):

> I am convinced that this traffic in hard-core pornography is . . . *pollution* as surely as *sewage*, and it ought to be equally subject to Federal control through the commerce clause. [J. J. Kilpatrick 1967, quoted in *The Report of the Commission on Obscenity and Pornography, 1970*, p. 50; emphasis added]

Alternatively, these terms refer to places where dirt is found—"gutter," "sewer," "toilet," "outhouse," "dunghill," "barnyard," "pigsty":

> Dean Burch, chairman of the Federal Communications Commission, said today that . . . it had been forced to begin an investigation of obscene sex-oriented radio talk shows. . . . "Halfway between here and the bank," he said, "they may just find themselves in the *gutter*. . . ."
>
> A relatively few broadcasters are involved in "this new breed of *air pollution*," Mr. Burch said, but they have made Congress aware in the last few months of "the prurient *trash* that is the stock-in-trade of the sex-oriented radio talk show, complete with the suggestive, coaxing, pear-shaped tones of the *smut*-hustling host."
>
> "This is *garbage* pure and simple," he said. . . . [*The New York Times* 29 March 1973; emphasis added]

Finally, sex is also equated with creatures who live with dirt—"animals," "pigs," "vermin":

Movies appealing to homosexuals are now being shown in a
theater directly across 44th Street from Shubert Alley. . . .
Alexander H. Cohen, the Broadway producer, promised:
"We will drive the *vermin* away." [*The New York Times* 18
September 1973, p. 43; emphasis added]

Community leaders often launch what they call a "clean-
up drive" to banish prostitution or pornography from their
town:

City Attorney Burt Pines, who had promised in his recent
election campaign to de-emphasize prosecution of victimless
crimes—but who had excepted prostitution and gambling
from that list . . . pledg[ed] to assist the LAPD in *"cleaning up*
the streets of Los Angeles." [*Los Angeles Times* 8 October 1973,
part II, p. 3; emphasis added]

Although such sanitation of illicit sexual activity is usually
meant only figuratively, sometimes it is put into literal practice:

In Russia, the punishment for lewd exhibitionism is two
weeks of *street cleaning*. [TV news bulletin, 15 August 1974;
emphasis added]

Why do so many people associate sex with dirt? Biologists
and psychologists presume that it is because the sex organs
happen to be located near the excretory organs in human
beings.[2] "Excremental things," Freud wrote (1963, p. 69),
"are all too intimately and inseparably bound up with sexual
things; the position of the genital organs—*inter urinas et
faeces*—remains the decisive and unchangeable factor." (For
an extreme elaboration of the consequences of this conception of sex, see Norman O. Brown 1959, pp. 179–304.)

This bio-psychological explanation proves inadequate,
however, when we contrast sexual "perversions" with "normal" sex. Certain sexual activities (e.g., fetishism, sadism,
voyeurism) are regarded as "dirtier" than ordinary intercourse even when—perhaps especially when—they scarcely

involve the sexual organs, let alone the excretory organs. Plainly, then, the association between sex and dirt must involve a more profound connection than the chance proximity of the organs of copulation and excretion. Let us look for this deeper tie in higher realms.

"Dirt," writes the English anthropologist Mary Douglas (1970, p. 12), "is essentially disorder"; even further it "offends against order." Those who call sex dirty, then, imply that it somehow goes against their conception of order. In fact, the word "vice," often used in conjunction with "dirty" sex, stems from the Latin *vitium*, meaning "fault," "blemish," "imperfection"—all characteristics that describe a flaw in an otherwise faultless, unblemished, perfect order. "Where there is dirt," Mary Douglas concludes, "there is system":

> Dirt is the by-product of a systematic ordering and classification of matter, in so far as ordering involves rejecting inappropriate elements. . . . Dirt . . . appears as a residual category, rejected from our normal scheme of classification. [1970, p. 48]

Where there is dirty sex, I want to demonstrate, there is also a system. In this part, I will try to discover the system that is violated by "smut."

I will define a cognitive system as the total logical interrelation of categories by which people organize their view of the world. There have been only scattered inquiries into the way people are affected by violations of their cognitive systems.[3] But brought together, these inquiries form an intellectual tradition in themselves, and provide the foundation for a science that focuses on the relation between formal logic and what might be called "psychologic". Formal logic is the logic of cognitive systems; psychologic is the logic of affective systems, of emotions and their physiological manifestations. By investigating the relation between these two systems, I will try to discover why people react with affect to something that disorders their cognitive system, why experiences that do not fit the patterns in their heads may adversely affect their hearts, or even their stomachs.

The earliest modern theorist to consider this relation between formal logic and psychologic was Sartre. In his first book, he pointed out that everything that exists overflows the neat logical categories in which man has tried to locate it. The human reaction to this "absurdity" of existence is what he calls *nausea* (1964).

More recently, Gregory Bateson and his associates have presented a clue to the origin of certain mental illnesses in the relation between cognitive and affective systems. The Bateson group examined contradictions in patients' external experiences that undermined their ability to categorize phenomena logically. Under certain conditions, these "double binds" led to the relatively permanent physioemotional reaction of *schizophrenia* (1956).

The ethnomethodologist Harold Garfinkel has also explored the connection between the cognitive and the affective. In a study of transsexuals, he found that the boundary between certain social categories—especially between male and female—has acquired a moral character. The public reacts with *moral revulsion* to whoever transgress this boundary, stigmatizing them as "incompetent, criminal, sick, and sinful." Consequently, at least at the time of his study, most transsexuals would rather "pass" as a member of one gender category or the other than be seen as inbetween (1967).

Erving Goffman has discussed another affective reaction to cognitive disorientation. What he calls *negative experience* occurs when an ongoing activity or "frame" is disrupted by the sudden intrusion of logically incongruous elements—as when a fight erupts at a hockey game. The experience is negative because it takes its character from what it is not (1974).

Finally, and most important for my purpose, are the findings of Edmund Leach and Mary Douglas. Leach has determined that intermediate categories in a logically exhaustive system are *taboo*, provoking both "special interest" and "anxiety" (1964). Douglas has determined that "any

object or idea likely to confuse or contradict cherished clas-
sifications" is *polluted* (1966). Leach and Douglas draw these
broader conclusions from their analysis of what causes certain primitive peoples to react negatively to animals they
regard as taboo or polluted. I will be looking for what causes
certain members of modern society to react negatively to
sexual practices they regard as "obscene." I want to find out
why, in other words, those suddenly confronted with the
existence of what they consider smut may be moved to
exclaim: "It makes me sick!"

As the survey above has shown, anything that undermines confidence in the scheme of classification on which
people base their lives sickens them as though the very
ground on which they stood precipitiously dropped away.
The vertigo produced by the loss of cognitive orientation is
similar to that produced by the loss of physical orientation.
Philosophic nausea, certain forms of schizophrenia, moral
revulsion, negative experience, the horror of having violated
a taboo, and the feeling of having been polluted are all
manifestations of this mental *mal de mer*, occasioned by the
sudden shipwreck of cognitive orientation which casts one
adrift in a world without structure.

People will regard any phenomenon that produces this
disorientation as "disgusting" or "dirty."[4] To be so regarded, however, the phenomenon must threaten to destroy not only one of their fundamental cognitive categories
but their whole cognitive system. Because of its intrinsic
properties, dirt is the most appropriate metaphor. For dirt is
not merely chaotic: it clings insidiously to those whom it
touches, quickly spreading its poison from one cognitive
category to another until the entire structure of their universe has been corroded.[5]

It is not, therefore, the physical proximity of Eros to anus
that gives rise to the feeling that sex is dirty. On the contrary,
people regard *both* sexuality and anality as dirty for the same
reason: both disorganize their ordering of the world. Sex
makes people sick by threatening to overturn their whole
cognitive system. If their sudden loss of orientation is mild,

they will react with a blush or other signs of embarrassment; if extreme, with shock, nausea, or revulsion.

A subgroup in a society may assume that its common category system is both "natural" (i.e., true) and "moral" (i.e., good). Since, as we shall see, sex subverts the validity and morality of the category system of the subgroup we are concerned with here, this subgroup will regard it as both "unnatural" (i.e., false) and "immoral" (i.e., bad). If this subgroup also assumes that it speaks for their society as a whole, it will regard those who engage in these forbidden sexual activities as forfeiting their status as social, or even human, beings. It will brand them as degenerates, as having dropped below the minimum level of adherence to the classification scheme in which all "civilized" beings are required to believe. As "barbarians," "animals," or even "miscreants," they live outside and beneath the category system that is supposed to define the essence of the human. "Degraded," "depraved," and "decadent," they dwell in the evil land of chaos and disorder.

We can now begin to examine the system of cognitive categories that sex attacks. The best way to identify this system is first to locate the precise points where it conflicts with sexual activities and then to work backward to infer the abstract categories of the system itself. Thus the particular features of sex considered dangerous can reveal the general features of the world view they threaten. These aspects of sex must confute a category in a classification scheme if those who believe in this scheme are disgusted enough to proscribe them. Their nausea, then, must be a physioemotional reaction to the conjunction between the unnatural and immoral category exemplified in the proscribed aspects of sex and the confuted natural and moral category called to mind.

By analyzing each proscribed aspect of sex into its unnatural and immoral components and its natural and moral component, we can determine the precise conjunction of actual and implied categories that produces a sickening cognitive disorientation, as well as the common dimension in which both of these opposite categories lie. The systematic inter-

relation of these primary dimensions constitutes the sanc-
tified substructure of a cosmos.[6] In short, the system of the
sacred can be derived from the chaos of the obscene.

In this part, I will use this procedure to work out the world
view of those in our society who are opposed in principle to
most aspects of sex.[7] It is useful to group together the many
proponents of this view because, whatever their surface
differences, their common hostility toward sex results from
the same underlying conceptual structure.[8] I will call these
sexphobes "Jehovanists,"[9] after the name for the God of the
Old Testament who becomes especially wrathful whenever
his lawful category system is violated by sex, or other
tabooed activities.[10] Although currently in decline, these
Jehovanists have dominated Western society for so long that
their sexual views have been practically synonymous with
those of the society itself. For this reason, I shall sometimes
write in this part as though everyone in our society has
accepted the Jehovanist world view, but I shall qualify the
extent of their influence in part three by discussing the world
views of competing groups.

Essential to the Jehovanist world view is the division of
sexual behavior into two types: (1) "normal" sex—which is
bad enough—and (2) "abnormal" ("perverted") sex—which
is even worse. Abnormal sex, then, must violate categories
in their cognitive system more fundamental than those normal sex violates. Chapter 3, which will deal with less
strongly held categories, will show how normal sexual activity punctures their conceptions of bodies and selves. Chapter 4, which will deal with more strongly held categories, will
show how abnormal (perverse) sexual activity pierces their
conceptions of social interaction and social structure. Only
those who carve up their cosmos in a particular way will find
that sex cross-cuts their categories obscenely.

3.

Normal Sex: The Destruction of the Individual

*I*f Jehovanists can denounce even normal sexual behavior as "obscene," it must possess certain characteristics that collapse part of their cosmos. In the following sections I will proceed inductively from the particular psychological, physical, and social aspects of normal sex that disturb Jehovanists to the general features of their world view that each aspect must negate. But before we can specify the intellectual structure that sex subverts, we must reconceptualize sex in a way that brings out its potential for causing cognitive chaos.

Why Sex Can Be Psychologically Frightening

Those who fear sex must believe that it will somehow change them—fundamentally—for the worse. But how can sex change their essential nature? According to Freudian psychology, it cannot. Freud conceived of sex as a biological instinct, and his model of man required a distinction between this sexual instinct and the person him- or herself. Although the instincts (the id) are part of the total system of mental life, they are basically alien to its existential core (the ego) (see Freud 1960, pp. xii ff). Freud pointed out that the sexual instinct influences people's activity much more than had been thought; nonetheless, people experience it as pressure from an *external* source.[1] Since the biological id is outside and different from the psychological ego, sex cannot change people essentially. (It may, of course, expose their body to danger, their status to shame, and their peace of mind to guilt.) In fact, Freud assumed that almost no external force could alter the ego (at least after childhood), for the ego is a homeostatic constant, continually defending its constancy under the ever-changing pressures of the sexual instinct, as well as other instinctual and environmental forces.

Yet many people feel that sex does transform them in some fundamental way. To explain this feeling we must turn to an alternative theory which posits that people can be psychologically reconstituted. This position has been developed extensively within the symbolic interactionist tradition by Mead (1934), Goffman (1959), and Berger and Luckmann (1967). Recently, a similar position has been developed within the Freudian tradition itself, particularly by Erikson (1968). Both the symbolic interactionists (who use the term "self") and Erikson (who uses the term "identity") assume that a person is capable of psychological change, even essential psychological change, under certain conditions.

Unlike Freud's biopsychological perspective, this "social" psychological perspective allows us to see sex as an activity that may actually reconstitute the self or identity (terms I will use interchangeably). Precisely how sex does so is unclear, and the description of this process I will offer in the next few pages is only tentative—but presupposing such a process has the incomparable virtue of explaining in terms of a single system a wide range of sexual phenomena that have not been pulled together previously.

From the vantage point of this social psychological perspective, we can observe how sexual arousal may result in
part from the need to remove one of the "waste products" of
ordinary interaction, the inconsistent identities produced
therein. During ordinary interaction, the inconsistent identities imposed by others and the latent identities unactualiz-
able with others may weaken the coherence of the self as a
whole. The accumulation of these imposed or unactualized
identities may eventually motivate a person to attempt the
self-work or self-maintenance necessary to achieve psychological reunification.

An effective way to reintegrate these inconsistent identities is through erotic fantasies or activities, for the self seems
to become more malleable, more open to alteration, during
sexual arousal. During this erotic interlude, the psychological energy that normally sustains identity boundaries
through internal integration and external defenses is suspended. Writers, like D. H. Lawrence, often describe this
softening of the self that occurs during sexual intercourse as
a "melting" or "disolving":

> It was gone, the resistance was gone, and she began to melt in
> a marvellous peace. . . . And she felt him like a flame of desire,
> yet tender, and she felt herself melting in the flame. She let
> herself go. . . . She dared to let go everything, all herself, and
> be gone in the flood. And it seemed she was like the sea,
> nothing but dark waves rising and heaving. . . . [1968,
> pp. 186–87]

In this state of heightened psychological susceptibility
produced by sexual arousal, one may consume (burn up, as
it were) the debilitating interactional waste products mentioned above by reversing the polarity of one's identity with
that of a real or fantasied partner—alternately looking at the
partner through one's own eyes and at oneself through the
partner's eyes. (One can also look at both through the
imagined eyes of some observing third party. Mirrors facilitate this last, omniscient point of view.) These oscillations of

identification (identity feedback) increase in frequency and intensity as orgasm approaches. When orgasm occurs the self is experienced as a mixture of both identities (identity fusion)—a precarious state that transforms itself almost immediately into a state of no identity. After entering this phase of amorphous unself-consciousness, one falls into unconsciousness, wakening momentarily to find oneself slowly recohering around one's original identity. Lawrence concludes his descriptions of Connie Chatterly's orgasms:

> She was gone, she was not, and she was born: a woman. . . . And this time his being within her was all soft and iridescent . . . such as no consciousness could seize. Her whole self quivered unconscious and alive, like plasm. . . . She could not remember what it had been. Only that it had been more lovely than anything ever could be. Only that. And afterwards, she was utterly still, utterly unknowing, she was not aware for how long. . . .
> When awareness of the outside began to come back. . . . [1968, pp. 187–88]

Sex, then, temporarily enfeebles the self in order to return it reaffirmed. After shifting the focus of identification to another during arousal and intercourse, one can reidentify with one's own self with renewed vigor. In this way sex functions as a recurrent personal ritual of self-renewal, just as certain social ceremonies function to renew the community periodically.[2]

It is this reversal of identification during the erotic interim that brings the other into the self—however temporarily—and consequently reconstitutes identity—however permanently. (Freud and his followers, of course, have also treated "identification" extensively, but they have focused on identification with parental figures of the past whereas I will focus on identification with social types in the present.) Let us look at this process more closely so that we may specify the components of a person's identity that are affected by having sex with particular kinds of people. This inquiry is extremely important because those whose identity components are altered by sex will be refashioned in essence and may even be reappraised in value as well.

Although identity is as significant a unit for social analysis as the atom is for physical analysis, a comprehensive catalog of its components has not been made. Unfortunately, it is not possible to "split the self" in the laboratory, as it is possible to split the atom. Nevertheless, we do not need a sophisticated methodology or technology to confirm that the gender component of identity is the most important one articulated during sex. Nearly everyone (except for bisexuals, perhaps) regards it as the prime criterion for choosing a sex partner. Since most people are unable to express attributes of the opposite gender during their ordinary interaction, they must reaffirm them by reversing this component during sexual interaction. Rollo May reached the same conclusion in the context of existential psychiatry:

> The sex act . . . is the drama of approach and entrance and full union, then partial separation (as though the lovers could not believe it were true and yearned to look at each other), then a complete reunion again. . . . We note that both of these persons happen to be identifying with someone of the opposite sex. This reminds us of Jung's idea that the shadow side of the self which is denied represents the opposite sex. . . .
> The love act can and ought to provide a sound and meaningful avenue to the sense of personal identity. We normally emerge from love-making with renewed vigor. . . .
> [1969, pp. 112, 113, 133, 313]

Normally, people strengthen the gender component of their identity during sex through contrast, through looking at themselves from the viewpoint of members of the opposite gender. They also clarify by contrast a penumbra of other components often linked to gender. After reviewing a large number of studies completed since 1954, the family sociologist Robert Winch (1974) found that mate selection is heterogamous for "complementary needs" such as nurturance-receptiveness, dominance-submissiveness, and achievement-vicariousness. (Mate selection is largely, but not fully, correlated with sexual selection.)

But all identity components are not clarified by contrast. People strengthen many other components during sex through similarity, through looking at themselves from the viewpoint of those who possess the same characteristics (sometimes to an even greater extent) as themselves. Winch also found in his review that mate selection is homogamous for age, race, religion, class, education, and residence.

According to Winch, then, mate selection is homogeneous for social characteristics other than gender, and heterogeneous for gender-linked psychological characteristics. But of course Winch's finding is too general to specify which identity components are delineated by contrast and which by similarity in every act of intercourse. If gender becomes subordinated to certain other identity components, it may be reaffirmed through likeness rather than difference, as in homosexuality. And, if certain other identity components become subordinated to gender, they may be reaffirmed through difference rather than likeness, as in miscegenation.

Take, for example, the duality of dominance and submission. Many of those dominant in social interaction are also dominant in sexual interaction; likewise with the submissive. But the opposite is also common. Those submissive in social interaction may feel the need to dominate sexual interaction. Marxist feminists complain about the male underlings in our society who relieve their own economic exploitation by oppressing women sexually. Conversely, some males who are dominant in the boardroom desire to be submissive in the bedroom. Xaviera Hollander found this to be true of the clients at her brothel:

> Marco Polo (a pseudonym) described to me a set of symptoms that were familiar with many successful and powerful men. As absolute ruler in his corporation, he manipulates the men beneath him like a puppeteer. However, this daytime

domineering makes him feel insecure, and as a balance to reality, he craves being submissive. These powerful men become slaves to release the tension of running other people's lives. [1972, p. 221][3]

Thus it is far from clear whether sexual interaction reinforces social interaction or compensates for it.[4]

Those who find it difficult to decide whether to clarify some of their identity components through similarity or through contrast may try to avoid these problematic attributes entirely. They may blot them out with blindfolds or disguise them with masks and costumes. In the pornographic novel *Story of O*, Pauline Reáge describes how these people may also focus exclusively on what is to them a less problematic component—gender per se:

> With them came a man dressed in a long purple robe. . . . Beneath his robe he had on some sort of tights which covered his legs and thighs but left his sex exposed. It was the sex that O saw first. . . . Then she saw that the man was masked by a black hood. . . . [1967, pp. 7–8]

Another way is to copulate with strangers, most of whose identity components are unknown. Erotic attraction to strangers has become an increasingly common theme in the culture of modern Western society,[5] from the mysterious apartment hunter (Marlon Brando) in the movie *Last Tango In Paris*, whose allure dissipates as soon as Maria Schneider learns his social attributes, to the "zipless fuck" in the novel *Fear of Flying*:

> For the true, ultimate zipless A-1 fuck, it was necessary that you never got to know the man very well. I had noticed, for example, how all my infatuations dissolved as soon as I really became friends with a man. . . . I no longer dreamed about him. He had a face.
>
> So another condition for the zipless fuck was brevity. And anonymity made it even better. [Jong 1974, p. 11]

If sexual intercourse can articulate the identity by shifting perspective on it to the partner's point of view, sex can weaken the self as well as strengthen it. The characteristics of some potential partners may be so different, so low status, or even so polluted that whoever attempts to reverse perspectives with them sexually would find his or her own identity disintegrated, degraded, or even defiled in the process, rather than integrated, elevated, or ennobled.

The transformation of self that occurs during copulation, then, can be either positive or negative. But the mere possibility that it might be negative exposes the extreme vulnerability of those who copulate. By turning off the defenses that normally preserve the integrity of the identity, sexual arousal temporarily opens[6] the identity to essential change—whether for better or for worse.

Since one's partner appears to be responsible for this self-transformation, one may feel as though the new aspects of one's identity have flowed into it from the partner in the sexual process. It is in this sense that people may be said to "acquire" components from their partner's identity during intercourse, "absorbing" their partner's social and personal attributes. Moreover, since copulation normally comprises two individuals who acquire components from each other's identity, we may speak of sex as involving not merely *identity acquisition* but *identity exchange*.[7]

These fresh components of self injected by one copulant into the other may seem indelible enough to transform the latter permanently. As selves begin to recrystalize after intercourse, components of the partner's identity may appear to resolidify within one's own, becoming so embedded that they cannot be expelled. From this point on, these alien elements in the essence will become part of the self-conception. Consequently, whoever fears that his/her revised self will outlive the sex act that engendered it will chose his/her bedmates with great care.

But this is not the only problem with identity transformation through copulation, for those who feel that sex can alter their own selves will also believe it can alter the selves of others. The new identity an individual develops during intercourse may exist not only in his or her own mind, but in the mind of other members of his or her social group. They too may come to believe that sex has changed a person essentially and permanently. And even if one feels unaltered by a sexual episode oneself, one may still worry about being redefined by others as different in essence and value—especially if one has reason to suspect that others will regard a particular sex partner as having changed one's identity for the worse.[8]

This conception of sex—as an activity in which each partner may transform the other's identity—can help us understand why Jehovanists fear and despise it so much. It is commonly thought today that the Jehovanist distaste for sex is an instance of their disdain for all forms of physical pleasure. But in fact, they do not condemn all other pleasurable activities. There is no evidence, for instance, that the Puritans, those exemplary Jehovanists, did not enjoy their first Thanksgiving dinner. Rather, Jehovanists object to sex because they know it is much more than merely a pleasurable activity. The biblical expert Herold Stern tells us:

> Since the essence of the sexual act is the relationship between two living bodies, in which the male body enters the female body and deposits part of its substance there, Biblical man . . . would deny the viewpoint of modern society which tends to look on the sexual relationship as *essentially* one for the mutual transference of pleasure. [1966, pp. 89–90]

If people were inclined to copulate solely for physical pleasure, the object of their sexual interest would not matter to them as long as it "felt good." But there is only a trivial difference in the amount of physical pleasure obtained by making love to an attractive person, to an animal, or to a soft plastic gadget. Yet most people would by far prefer to copulate with the first than with the last two. In fact, a common "dirty" joke or cartoon depicts the suprise and horror that results whenever a sex object turns out to be not what it first appeared. A man who thought he was having intercourse with a beautiful young woman through a hole in a fence is shocked to discover, when looking over the fence, that he had just fucked a pig.

Of course, this "lower" biological motive for physical gratification might override the "higher" social psychological motive for psychical gratification if the sex objects that can satisfy the latter are unobtainable. Lenny Bruce, whose wildly extravagant exaggerations are often more insightful than the social scientist's more measured inferences, points out how the single-minded pursuit of physical pleasure can produce an utter disregard for a sex object's other qualities:

> You put guys on a desert island and they'll do it to mud. *Mud!* So if you caught your husband with mud, if somehow you could get overseas there,
>   OUTRAGED FEMALE: *EEEEEEEKKK! Don't talk to me!* That's all. . . . Go with your mud, have fun. You want dinner? Get your mud to make dinner for ya. [Cohen 1967, p. 194]

Modern technology is beginning to develop surrogates for the frequently unavailable human partner. If a person cannot relieve all sources of sexual tension with a human being, at least he can relieve its physical sources with "the next best thing":

AUTO SUCK

> Do you spend many uninteresting hours in your car? You can make them sexually exciting with AUTO SUCK. Powerful vacuum suction will travel with you anywhere. AUTO SUCK plugs into your car cigarette lighter. Its soft rubber female orifice will stroke and suck you with erotic vacuum energy. Feel the juices of orgasm actually sucked from your body. Inner lifelike vaginal lips cradle the penis and give hours of driving or parking pleasure.
>   [Common advertisement in sex magazines
>   and newspapers, 1973–1974]

As sexual technology improves, its products will doubtless compete even more with human beings as potential sex partners. But this competition will increase precisely because these advanced technological products will come to look more human, will come to have a more recognizable—or even creatable—identity:

PLAY GIRL

Life size—Life-like in every detail!

Marilyn is the ONLY human-like ACTION DOLL available in America. . . . Let her life-like reproduction female qualities astound you as they have others.

. . . Her breasts are human-like in EVERY detail, both in texture and structure, right down to the finest point. . . . Her open mouth is an achievement in design. The human-like action, tight-flexible cheeks inside her mouth, work on the principle of air suction. . . .

Imagine coming home to your own 21st Century play-girl always ready for action. Dress her up in lingerie, bathing suit, dainty underclothes, tight fitting chic dresses, pant outfits, mini skirts or leather. . . . Think of the fun you'll have dressing Marilyn the way YOU feel a woman should dress. . . .
                    [Common advertisement in sex magazines
                    and newspapers, 1973–74]

Plainly, human beings must possess something sexually arousing that animal species, natural phenomena, and technological products lack. That something is a social self. To be satisfying in a social-psychological sense, then, the sex object with which a person reverses the polarity of his or her identity must possess the appropriate social attributes. As Sartre puts it:

Although the body plays an important role, we must—in order to understand [sex]—refer to being-in-the-world and to being-for-others. I desire a human being, not an insect or a mollusk, and I desire him (or her) as he is and as I am in situations in the world and as he is an Other for me and as I am an Other for him. [1956, p. 384]

Even frequent sex, however pleasurable physically, with persons (or things) who do not possess the appropriate social attributes will not be satisfying in a social-psychological sense.[9]

Although copulation alters everyone's identity to some extent, Jehovanists believe, several social groups need special protection because it changes them more than their counterparts.

✳ Females and Males

Jehovanists do not assume that sex transforms the identities of each gender equally. Females are more affected by male components during intercourse than males are by female components. Hence their "double standard"; for the identities of promiscuous women will become more contaminated than those of promiscuous men.[10] Herold Stern explains why:

Biblical man would maintain . . . that in view of the simple physical nature of the sexual act, he cannot look on it as a mutual relationship. For the male enters the female, the female does not enter the male. [Therefore] principles and laws holding true for one member of the relation will not necessarily hold true for the other member. . . . The double standard is a result of the biological fact that the male's body remains intact no matter how many women he has intercourse with. Physically he possesses them, they do not possess him. [1966, pp. 90, 96]

A husband caught in an extramarital affair can say, "It didn't mean anything to me"—meaning that his identity has not been contaminated by his sex partner as much as his wife believes it has been, and certainly not as much as his wife's identity would have been under similar circumstances.

For Jehovanists, the female identity is more unstable than the male identity because a woman exists in only two states: pure or polluted, madonna or whore, saint or slut—with no intermediate category. G. Rattray Taylor points out one consequence of the binary conception of women during Victorian times:

> Victorians were careful to create a supply of prostitutes by making it impossible for those who once had erred ever to recover their respectability. . . . The result of a [single] misstep was . . . likely to be condemnation to a life of prostitution. [1973, pp. 218, 191]

Thus the common cry of the Victorian maiden who has been seduced by a philanderer: "I've been ruined!"

* The Innocent and the Experienced

Sexual experience is inversely correlated with the extent of transformation of self. The less one's sexual experience, the more a person will be affected by his or her partner's identity components during each act of intercourse, and vice versa. Jehovanists regard children, adolescents, and virgins as "pure" because they have not yet been contaminated with the identity components of others, and "innocent" because they are not even aware that their self is so porous as to be susceptible to this contamination. But they regard profligates, prostitutes, and the promiscuous as "corrupt" because they have already been contaminated with the identity components of others, and "jaded" because their self has so hardened that it is no longer transformed by each new sex act.[11]

Children, Jehovanists feel, are unable to bear the knowledge that structural flaws will appear in their identity at puberty. After all, they themselves were devastated by this awareness as they grew up. Consequently, Jehovanists try to keep the young ignorant of these impending "holes" in their selves by portraying sex in a way that omits its key social-psychological elements: identity reversal, exchange, and transformation. Thus they are likely to tell children about sex solely in terms of the analogous behavior of "birds and bees"—a description that always mystifies these social-psychological processes.

This purity and innocence of the young is fragile, however, because they are so impressionable, so likely to acquire components from their sex partners that may disrupt their identity. Virgins, in particular, are especially vulnerable to corrosive new components. The continuing influence of this Jehovanist view can be found in the following passage from Mary McCarthy's *The Group*:

> Some women, they said, never got over the first man . . . he left a permanent imprint. Why, they even said that a child conceived with the legal husband would have the features of the first lover! . . . It excited her foolish fancy to think that a man who took a girl's virginity had the power to make her his forever. [1964, p. 183]

Even Freud (1963, pp. 70–71, 85) felt that a girl becomes "enthralled" by the man who takes her virginity.

So delicate are the young, Jehovanists believe, that any sexual contamination of them will spread through the life cycle to infect their adult selves. A single homosexual teacher, for example, can thoroughly corrupt them, despite all the heterosexual role models available in their environment.

Of course, not everyone agrees with Jehovanists that sexual intercourse is necessarily the dividing line between innocence and corruption. In the Marquis de Sade's novels *Justine* (1966) and *Juliette* (1968), for instance, Justine retains her innocence even after she has been debauched hundreds of times, whereas her sister Juliette loses hers even before being "deflowered." Terry Southern's *Candy* (Kenton 1965) portrays a modern Justine who sustains her innocence through a series of sexual misadventures; Vladimir Nabokov's *Lolita* (1958) portrays a modern Juliette who is corrupt even before she sleeps with the protagonist.

Despite this dispute over whether sex actually harms juveniles, Jehovanists have enacted strict laws to protect the innocence of the young, against their own will, if necessary. Since the middle of the nineteenth century, Jehovanists have legally restricted juveniles from reading about or seeing—not to mention participating in—any sort of sex.[12] The oft-cited 1868 Hinklin test of obscenity reads:

> whether the tendency of the matter charged as obscenity is to deprave and corrupt those whose minds are open to such immoral influences, and into whose hands a publication of this sort may fall. [*The Report of the Commission on Obscenity and Pornography* 1970, p. 363]

Even now Jehovanists still use the "well-being-of-the-young" argument to suppress sexual knowledge. A Los Angeles city councilman protesting nude beaches stated:

> "When we send our children to the beaches, we have an obligation to see that they are fully protected." . . . [He] maintained that . . . the display of private parts in public is offensive and harmful to young persons. Even though people were "born nude and ignorant," he remarked, they shouldn't stay that way [*sic*]. [*Los Angeles Times*, 19 July 1974, p. 19]

Children are still the most sacred social category of Jehovanist society, for profaning them portends its end:

> Mayor Abraham Beame . . . said, "We have not yet sunk to the level of savage animals, but if we don't draw the line against . . . child pornography, we can kiss goodbye to civilization as we know and cherish it." [*Los Angeles Times*, 1 June 1977, p. 7]

Because the child molester desecrates this sacrosanct entity, Jehovanists have designated him (or her) as the most evil social type in our society. As such, he (or she) has been shunned not only by other criminals but also by other sexual outcasts, like homosexuals and ordinary pornographers. So strong is the stigma against child "molesting" that, in contrast with the actions of other sexual minorities, no militant "out of the closets and into the classrooms" social movement has formed, and there is little chance that one will. Even those who have tried the reasonable approach have provoked vehement—often hysterical—hostility, such as the response of detective Lloyd Martin, who established the Los Angeles Police Department's sexually exploited child unit:

> "Pedophilia is a subculture. We have the Rene Guyon Society, based in Los Angeles, which is working to say sex with children is OK. . . . They claim it is not sick, but a way of life."
>
> Martin, however, regards pedophilia as "the worst crime of all, worse than homicide or armed robbery or burglary. A crime against a child has no equal." [*Los Angeles Times*, 3 May 1981, part V, p. 14]

* Leaders and Followers

In addition to demanding sexual purity from women and children, Jehovanists demand it from those supposed to uphold their world view in theory (clergy), in practice (government officials), and over time (teachers). Any hint of sexual impropriety in members of these professions scandalizes Jehovanists. (A "scandal" occurs when knowledge of a sexual indiscretion spreads rapidly through a community of Jehovanists, allowing them to coordinate their censure.) If even one sexual deviant is allowed to remain in these professions, they fear, it will open a Pandora's box for a multitude of others:

> [Dr. Lewis Stommel, Emeryville school superintendent and principle of Emery High] sounds absolutely grim as he describes what could happen if Steve Dain [a transsexual teacher he has fired] wins [reinstatement]:
> "They'll be coming out of the closets everywhere,

thousands of them— transsexuals, transvestites and every other weirdo—all demanding teaching jobs. Every school in America will have to fight them." [*Los Angeles Times*, 22 November 1976, part II, p. 1]

Why Sex Can Be Physically Repulsive

The nebulousness of personal identity has caused it to be commonly conceived in concrete form as coextensive with the physical body. Modern social psychologists, such as George Herbert Mead (1934, pp. 135–50) and Erving Goffman (1959, pp. 252–353), have complained of the confusion produced by equating immaterial identity with material body, and have insisted on distinguishing them. But too rigid reliance on such a distinction would not allow us to understand the thinking of the classical Jehovanists, who believe that whatever affects the body also affects the identity:

> Since Hebrew man considered the person to be a psychosomatic unit, his emotions were inextricably bound up with the body. . . . When the male physically penetrates the woman, he penetrates to the very center of her soul or emotions. He not only physically possesses her through intercourse, but she feels herself emotionally possessed. Farnham and Lundberg agree with this ancient viewpoint: "The sexual act . . . has the aspect of the violation of a woman's person, of the invasion of her physical self and ego by another person. . . ." [Stern 1966, p. 91]

Since biblical times, the Jehovanists' fear that intercourse may threaten the integrity of the identity has been behind their emotional reaction to its violation of the body through anatomical, physiological, and behavioral channels.[13]

Jehovanists have always been physically repulsed by the parts of the anatomy employed in intercourse. Until recently, they succeeded in restraining the exhibition of the genitals in nearly all public presentations and representations of the human body. They have attempted to edit the

genitals out of existence through clothing (even in swimming), omission (in children's dolls and adult mannequins),
deletion (in air-brushed *Playboy* centerfolds), position (in
nude painting or photography having the model turned
away from the viewer or with crossed legs), idealization (in
statutes),[14] censorship (with an obsuring blotch or
rectangle),[15] or if necessary, through actual castration:

> That good man who, when I was young [in the sixteenth
> century], castrated so many beautiful ancient statues in his
> great city, so that the eye might not be corrupted . . . should
> have called to mind that nothing was gained unless he also
> had horses and asses castrated, and finally all nature. . . .
> [Montaigne 1958b, p. 653]

In the 1960s, art and theater audiences were shocked by
what critics called "frontal nudity"—the sudden thrusting of
the genitals into their visual field. In shape, color, texture,
pilosity, humidity, and orderliness, the genitals differ
markedly from every other visible organ of the body. It
would be almost impossible for an extraterrestrial being (or
even a sheltered child) to imagine or predict the appearance
of the adult genitals from the appearance of the rest of their
body. John Ruskin, whose image of woman was formed
soley from contemplating hairless classical statues, was so
revolted by the sight of his bride's pubic region on their
wedding night that he never slept with her, nor with any
other woman. Those accustomed to conducting social commerce with the civilized, regular, smooth, hairless, dry, neat
features of another's torso will be unprepared for the discovery of the primitive, irregular, varicose, rough, hairy, moist,
unkempt region in the boondocks of that body. The genitals,
a comedian has recently suggested, must be God's idea of a
joke on humanity.

The even texture of most of the human body implies that
whatever it encloses is sharply separated from whatever is
outside. But the uneven texture of the human genitals suggests the opposite. The genitals constitute that region of the
body where its substance shades into its environment in-

stead of being distinct. The Victorians, those extreme modern Jehovanists, were so horrified to discover this aperture in the body/world boundary that they tried to conceal all evidence of its existence:

> Women, *ex definitione* sexless, hardly existed below the waist; or, if they did, they were not bifurcated. When advertisements of underclothing first began to appear in Victorian papers, the bifurcated garments were always shown folded, so that the bifurcation would not be remarked. [Taylor 1973, p. 214]

This view of the genitals explains why Jehovanists can allow young children to appear naked in public but are aghast if adults try to do the same. They regard children as more pure psychologically in part because they are less perforated physically, for prepubescent genitals lack many of the penetrative-receptive characteristics of postpubescent genitals. These permeable features of adult genitals, which suddenly appear at puberty, are difficult to integrate into the image of the body as hermetically sealed that coheres during childhood. Thus the same conception of the relation between identity and anatomy that makes children "pure" makes adults "polluted."

Other physical aspects of sex that disgust Jehovanists are the seminal and vaginal fluids:

> When a man has a seminal discharge, he must wash his whole body with water and he shall be unclean until evening. Any clothing or leather touched by the seminal discharge must be washed and it will be unclean until evening. . . . When a woman has a discharge of blood, and blood flows from her body, this uncleanness of her monthly periods shall last for seven days. Anyone who touches her will be unclean until evening . . . [Leviticus 15:16–17, 19]

Such words impress upon everyone who upholds Old Testament law that the physiological fluids involved with sex are somehow "dirty." (See Douglas 1966, pp. 145–150, for a general discussion of the contaminating properties of bodily fluids.) To Jehovanists, these sexual fluids distill a person's substance, converting him or her into an uncontainable form. They are discharged from the body, thus demonstrating that its walls are too weak to keep vital qualities from draining away. And they are viscid: they stick to whomever they touch and are difficult to remove. Moreover, they can insinuate themselves into another person, even without physical contact by their strong smell alone.[16] For these reasons, Jehovanists have always viewed the sexual fluids as capable of "staining" the substance of one person with the subtance of another ineradicably:

> The attitude of Biblical society was that . . . the woman . . . in a very fundamental physical sense becomes the possession of her husband through the act of intercourse. The possession . . . is intensified by the fact that as a result of the substance deposited in her body, the physiochemical composition of the female body is modified by it. [Van de Velde states:] "The vaginal walls absorb as well as secrete. Thus, chemicals in contact with the vagina may be absorbed and incorporated into the other bodily secretions. They circulate in the blood. . . ." [Stern 1966, p. 90]

Those who feel that their sex partners' essential characteristics can seep into their own through the sexual fluids will insist on showering, or at least washing their hands and genitals, after intercourse. The Old Testament, in fact, made this postcoital cleansing ritual mandatory:

> When a woman has slept with a man, both of them must wash and they will be unclean until evening. [Leviticus 15:18]

Those who have such fear must conceive of the body as a sacred but sievelike entity easily subject to contamination from others through the physiological processsesses of sex.

Finally, Jehovanists are repelled by the physical behavior

required by sexual intercourse. The short, choppy spasms used to hammer home its finale are especially difficult to execute in a disciplined and harmonious manner. Critic Susan Sontag's image is apt when she observes:

> making love surely resembles having an epileptic fit at least as much, if not more, than it does eating a meal or conversing with someone. [1970, p. 57]

The copulators' loss of control over limb and torso, their palsied and spastic bodily gyrations, all indicate their physical vulnerability.

But Jehovanists find another feature of sexual behavior much more abhorrent: the insertion of a part of the body into the body of another person.[17] They have forbidden any depiction of this "ultimate act" whenever possible. Such interpersonal interpenetration demonstrates, to their dismay, that the body—and consequently the self—is not an impenetrable fortress but a pregnable one. Even worse, copulators are not satisfied with treating this insertion as their final accomplishment, but insist on simulating it again and again through a series of partial withdrawals and reinsertions. For the sex act comprises not a single penetration of another's bodily citadel but a continual one, an all-out attack that does not stop with surrender. From the Jehovanist point of view, this reiterative nature of sexual intercourse adds insult to injury.

In short, Jehovanists conceive of the human body as a sack of personal and social qualities whose underside is perforated. It appears to them as a bipolar phenomenon whose top implies separation from other people but whose bottom implies connection with them. Since aspects of identity seem to "leak out" or "trickle in" through the genitals, intercourse always threatens interpersonal pollution.

Why Sex Can Be Socially Taboo

In the Jehovanist world view, the processes of intercourse that affect identity have repercussions for society at large as well as for the body. In order to determine how a private act can have public consequences, we must first examine the Jehovanist conception of society.

The individuals who constitute a society are tied together in many ways: by territory, economics, values, customs, culture, and so on. In the phenomenological tradition of Edmund Husserl (1970), Max Weber (1968), and Alfred Schutz (1962, 1964, 1966), as well as in the symbolic interactionist tradition of George Herbert Mead (1934), the most crucial connection between individuals is their involvement with one another's minds. Each member of society is able to imagine the way he and the world appear from the perspective of all other members of society.

It must be this intersubjective linkage between copulators and everyone else that motivates Jehovanists to transform a seemingly individual—or at most dual—activity into a social taboo, for copulation affects those uninvolved in it in no other way (except indirectly in the event of pregnancy). If Jehovanists can believe that intercourse changes the identity of the individuals who engage in it, they can believe that this sexually induced alteration of identity can spread to every member of their society through the channel of intersubjectivity. For Jehovanists, no couple ever has sex alone. Those who discover that an act of intercourse has occurred are (so to speak) dragged into the bed by the copulating couple, forced[18] to reexperience in fantasy what they think the copulators have experienced in fact. In this way, the alteration of the identity of a single individual can affect the identities of all.[19]

How do the identity transformations of intercourse affect others? The intersubjective connections between members of a society link segments of their individual selves together. As we have seen, however, the identity of a copulating individual is an identity in transition. Others may fear, therefore, that, if someone who anchors their own identity has intercourse, this act will deprive their identity of one of its indispensable moorings. Furthermore, the separate selves of two copulating individuals are temporarily obliterated by merging into a transient new social unit—Chaucer's "beast with two backs." This engendering of a confused and precarious being intersubjectively attached to themselves may also motivate others to fear that intercourse will threaten their own coherence and stability.

Moreover, the new components injected into a person's identity by a partner during sexual intercourse may flow out along these intersubjective channels into everyone else. And if they disintegrate, degrade, or defile the copulator, they may do the same to anyone cognitively connected to him or her. Because of the dangers produced by this ripple effect, Jehovanists attempt to restrict not only their own sex partners but also the sex partners of everyone else in their society.

Thus sex is much more than merely a matter of individual preference for Jehovanists because of their belief that whomever (or whatever) one person screws, all persons screw. Consequently, they do not regard illicit sex as the "victimless crime" liberals currently contend it is. Its "victims" are those whose identities are intersubjectively chained to the copulator's and who therefore fear that *his* or *her* sexual activity will undermine *their* identity, a sickening and terrifying experience.

Unable to restrain sexual activity entirely through calls for celibacy and chastity, Jehovanists have tried to contain its effects through the institution of marriage, which stabilizes the relationship—and thus the identities—of the copulating couple. Marriage provides a psychological prophylactic and a sociological abortion for sex, reducing its risks for the individual while arresting its repercussions for society. From biblical to modern times, Jehovanists have stressed this remedial ability of marriage to diminish the damaging consequences of sex.

Paul:

> It is a good thing for a man not to touch a woman; but since sex is always a danger, let each man have his own wife and each woman her own husband. . . . If they cannot control their sexual urges, they should get married: for it is better to marry than to burn. [Corinthians 7:1, 2, 9]

Martin Luther:

> By the grace of God a good remedy for fornication is marriage.
> . . . In order . . . that it may be easier . . . to avoid unchaste-
> ness, God has commanded marriage so that everyone may
> have his moderate portion and be satisfied with it. [Verene
> 1972, pp. 141, 139]

The Vatican:

> Experience teaches us that [sexual intercourse] must find its
> safeguard in the stability of marriage . . . a conjugal contract
> sanctioned and guaranteed by society. [1976, p. 11]

Jehovanists encourage marriage in part because they
know that restricting sex to a single partner will reduce its
overall frequency.[20] Marriage translates a maximum of
opportunity into a minimum of desire by continually allowing the release of sexual tension before an ample amount of
erotic passion can accumulate (de Rougemont 1966). Thus
marriage seems almost intentionally designed to make sex
boring. By discouraging intercourse in the long run, marriage minimizes the number of times the spouses' identities
are in a transitional state, thereby gradually closing a vulnerable opening in self and society.

Marriage also mitigates the psychological and social perils
that result from conjugal intercourse.[21] First, if copulation
threatens to transform the self only transiently, marriage can
prolong the new character of the self by situating the sexual
act within the material world. By encouraging the acquisition of common possessions, such as house furnishings,
which physically embody the selves of the copulating couple, marriage helps sustain their social relation and consequently their new psychological identities (see Davis 1973,
pp. 171–88).

Perhaps the consummate material embodiment of this
transient psychological merger is children, who represent
the concrete continuation of their parents sexual union
through time. In describing the desire for children, Schopenhauer has written:

[Two lovers] feel the longing for an actual union and fusion
into a single being, in order to go on living as this being; and
this longing receives its fulfillment in the child they produce.
In the child the qualities transmitted by both parents continue
to live, fused and united into one being. [1958, p. 536]

Similarly, Thomas Aquinas has argued teleologically that
the goal of every sexual union is (and should be) children
(Verene 1972, pp. 119–33). Interpreted from a social-psychological perspective, this argument suggests that these
prospective children are necessary to secure retrospectively
the social relation that produces them. Jehovanists try to
restrict sex to procreation, then, because potential children
provide a stable anchor in the future for unstable identities in
the present.

Second, if copulation threatens to disintegrate the self,
marriage can maintain the self's coherence by situating the
sexual act within an intimate relationship (see Davis, 1973).
Marriage eliminates the problem of harmonizing components of the identity that derive from two or more different
sources by ensuring that the "seductive other" and the "significant other" (Sullivan 1953, p. 21) are the same person.
Since marriage restricts sexual activity to those whose selves
are already largely coordinated in other areas, it helps prevent incompatible components from disorganizing their
identity and through them the identities of others.

Unfortunately, it is not always easy to integrate a narrow
sexual relationship into the broader context of an intimate
relationship. Most Western commentators, in fact, have traditionally regarded them as inimical. The Greeks contrasted
earthly love with divine love and the Christians contrasted
eros with *agape* (see Ricoeur 1964, pp. 135–38). More recently,
Kant transposed this conflict from the philosophical to the
ethical level by arguing that sexual relations per se were
immoral because merely a segment of each copulator's
identity was involved, unless such relations occurred within
a marriage involving each copulator's entire identity.[22] Schopenhauer transposed this conflict to the biological level by
arguing that the species' goal of reproduction is opposed to

the individual's welfare, thus explaining why an individual often desires sexually those he or she doesn't even like personally.[23] Freud further transposed this conflict to the psychological level, arguing that it is difficult for many people to unify their sexual desires with their affectionate feelings because of the latter's association with childhood's incest taboo.[24] I suggest we can obtain a deeper understanding of this conflict if we transpose it once more to the historical-sociological level. There an examination could be made of the Victorian social conditions, socialization practices, and ideologies that have widened the gap between parlor personality and bedroom behavior. Because these two parts of each person's self have not been on speaking terms since this period, the four-part conversation that must ensue whenever two persons attempt to relate both sexually and intimately has remained extremely discordant.

Third, if copulation threatens to degrade or defile the self, marriage can maintain its quality by situating the sex act within a social group. By confining sexual activity to a socially certified partner, marriage helps prevent low-status or polluted components from contaminating a person's identity and indirectly everyone else's. Even the legal requirement of a blood test before marriage—ostensibly to insure the marriage partners' physical purity—symbolically insures their psychological purity in order to protect society against the formation of a polluted social subunit.

Finally, if copulation threatens to dissolve the structure of the self, marriage can justify its dissolution by situating the sexual act within a cosmos.[25] In order to legitimize this disorienting transitional state between the old and the new identity, marriage construes it as part of a grander, more permanent pattern—alleviating the terror of Becoming by encompassing it within a more compassionate Being. But those unable to comprehend this tranquilizing power of marriage themselves will continue to be perplexed by its ability to mitigate the fearful aspect of sex for others:

Speaking of her parochial high school education, one student remarked, "I could never figure out how sex could be so nasty and ugly one day, and the next day, because of a ceremony, become beautiful and sacred. [Petras 1973, p. 50]

We can now see why Jehovanists so strongly condemn those who copulate without the psychological and social safeguards of marriage: the premarital fornicators who never wanted them and the extramarital adulterers who no longer want them. Both assault not merely their own identities but also the identities of everyone else in their society.[26] For such psychic carnage, it is not surprising that Jehovanists inflict upon them their ultimate punishment—ostracism from the cosmos:

Be not deceived: neither fornicators . . . nor adulterers . . . shall inherit the kingdom of God. [1 Corinthians 6:10]

Conclusion

Let me clarify a point for the reader who feels that my description of the social-psychological effects of sex goes against common sense. When I assert that a person acquires components of identity from a partner during sexual intercourse, I of course do not mean that these components visibly alter the person. Obviously, a man who copulates with a woman does not thereby become a hermaphrodite. I mean that they disrupt the coherence and clarity of the person's image. Images of people's identities are held in the mind and include, beyond their mere physical appearance, their nonvisual characteristics such as their personality and social status. (Behaviorists who equate the self with the body cannot understand processes involving these mental images.) The desire to protect the mental image of a person's identity, held by both that person and by others, from the threat of sexually induced disintegration is the prime motivation for the Jehovanist restrictions against sex.

This consequence of normal sexual activity can be danger-ous for only one conception of identity. To condemn sex as much as they do, therefore, Jehovanists must believe that ideally each human being has a self that is highly structured, sharply bounded, unique, integrated, pure, and separated from the selves of others completely and permanently.[27] They dread that this delicate identity will be easily punctured during copulation. The alien elements that intercourse can inject into an individual's essence may disrupt its existing structure and produce a new one that is incoherent, debased, or contaminated. Ultimately, this debilitated identity might itself become socially and temporally stabilized.

Jehovanists express their fear of these psychological effects of sex, which undermine their ideal self, through their revulsion at its physical aspects, which undermine their ideal body. To be repelled by the genitals, by semen or smegma or menstrual blood, and by sexual penetration, Jehovanists must believe that the human body—like the human self—is a clearly demarcated vessel, strictly segregated from the world by an impermeable membrane. The physical aspects of sex seem so fearsome precisely because they breach this boundary of the body.[28]

Mary Douglas traced this conception of body and self to the formative period of the Jehovanist world view:

[In the Old Testament] the ideal of holiness was given an external, physical expression in the wholeness of the body seen as a perfect container. . . . To be holy is to be whole, to be one; holiness is unity, integrity, perfection. . . . [1966, pp. 65, 68]

And in the New Testament, Paul points out that pollution can cross these bodily walls during intercourse to contaminate the God within:

Your bodies are members making up the body of Christ; do you think I can take parts of Christ's body and join them to the body of a prostitute? Never! . . . [A] man who goes with a prostitute is one body with her, since *the two become one flesh*. But anyone . . . joined to the Lord is one spirit with him.

> [Therefore] keep away from fornication. . . . To fornicate is to
> sin against your own body . . . , the temple of the Holy
> Spirit. . . . If anybody should destroy the temple of God, God
> will destroy him, because the temple of God is sacred; and
> you are that temple.
>
> [1 Corinthians 6:15–10; 3:17]

In the Jehovanist conception of the cosmos, then, the integration of the body is the physical analog of the integration
of the self. This unity of the individual, in turn, is the
psychological analog of the unity of society, the social analog
of the unity of its monotheistic God. Thus whatever desecrates the body—and nothing does so more than sex—has
ominous consequences for the entire system.[29]

In sum, Jehovanists fear normal sexual activity because it
weakens a major structural component of their cosmos.
They would like to believe that the identities of human
beings are independent, integrated, and invariant. Instead,
intercourse reveals the individual to be not the closed container they imagined but rather an open sieve, liable to
contamination through contact with the unclean. Consequently, cognitively corrosive elements can enter the Jehovanist cosmos at its most vulnerable point—via the self of the
sexually active individual—and spread rapidly throughout
their society via intersubjective channels. Jehovanists have
attempted to stop these repercussions at their root by enforc-
ing sexual abstinence, which seals off the individual exter-
nally from the contamination of others. Failing that, they
have attempted to prevent this epistemological infection of
individuals from becoming the epidemic of society by insti-
tuting the pair partition of marriage, which seals off society
internally from the contamination of its sexually active members.

4.

Perverted Sex:
The Destruction
of the Social

*I*f normal sex alarms Jehovanists, perverted sex terrifies them. Even in the 1970s, they still retained sufficient power in America to punish severely anyone caught performing what they label "sexual perversion":

> A Chula Vista couple has been sentenced to one to 15 years each in state prison on charges of sex perversion. . . . The [married couple] pleaded no contest July 3 to charges of sex perversion involving each other. . . . [*The San Diego Union*, 22 August 1975, p. A-24]

Why should "all heaven break loose" to chastize those who practice these sexual perversions? It should, Jehovanists feel, because perverted sex threatens components of their cosmos that are even more basic than those normal sex threatens. So extreme is the potential for harm that it cannot be contained by ordinary social safeguards. A recent Vatican pronouncement, for instance, ruled out the possibility of accepting homosexuality even within the confines of marriage (1976, p. 11).

From the Jehovanist point of view, prostitutes, homosexuals, transvestites, and other sexual "outlaws" inhabit a "twilight world" in which "ambiguity reigns" (Segal 1970, p. 70). In this chapter, I will try to derive the primary categories of cosmic light that, when juxtaposed to the darkness of specific sexual perversions, produce this indistinct, shimmering, mysterious demimonde on the the margins of Jehovanist society.

Jehovanists specify what they regard as "perverted" in the sexual behaviors they attempt to outlaw and in the sexual literature or art they attempt to censor. I have compiled a list of "sexual perversions" from these sources and from the medical, scientific, and popular catalogs of such non-Jehovanist commentators on Jehovanism as Freud (1972); Ullerstam (1966), Marshall and Suggs (1971), and Margolis (1974). All these sources generally agree on what sexual behaviors are anathematized, although their enumerations vary in extent.

In deriving my account of the Jehovanist cosmos, I have not attempted to examine all the minor sexual perversions mentioned in some of these sources (though I am confident it would be possible to do so). Conversely, whenever the logic of the Jehovanist system seems to demand the existence of a particular sexual perversion that is not named in these sources, I have supplied the missing label, designating my neologism with the letters "nl," and have tried to explain why it has remained anonymous. I will also examine here other nonstandard sexual phenomena such as pornography and prostitution, which Jehovanists at least deplore as corrupted if not despise as perverted.

Jehovanist sexual perversions have been categorized in various ways.[1] Kant[2] classified them according to the normative ends they violated (procreation or marriage); Freud[3] classified them according to whether they violated normative means (the sexual "aim") or normative ends (the sexual "object"). The classification scheme I have developed also entails a binary division, but one based on intersubjective rather than instrumental criteria.

In the last chapter, we saw that Jehovanists condemn normal sex because it opens identity to potentially destructive alterations. In this chapter, we will see that they condemn perverted sex even more stridently because it can actually devastate identity. Some sexual perversions alter identity in a detrimental manner by connecting people through "deviant sexual linkages." Other sexual perversions alter identity in a detrimental direction by connecting people to "deviant sexual objects."

In order to determine the structure of the remaining constituents of the Jehovanist cosmos, we will again work backwards from what threatens them with destruction. Since this framework is manifested only when attacked, we can observe it only indirectly in the dark distorted mirror of the two types of sexual perversions that nullify its existence. The charts on pages 157–59 present a schematization of the Jehovanist world system that is generated by this procedure.

Deviant Sexual Linkage

* Sex through Distant and Contact Sense Receptors

Toward the end of part one, it was noted that a person usually[4] comes to experience sex partners' selves as coalescing around their genitals, their entire identity riding on the sensory stimuli that their genitals emit. But it should be added here that the person can receive these identity inputs from his sex partners through the sensory stimuli taken in not only by his own genitals, but also by such major sense receptors as eyes (voyeurism), ears (auralism), mouth (fellatio or cunnilingus), anus (sodomy), or even by such minor ones as skin (frotteurism) or nose (olfactory eroticism). Jehovanists, of course, require identity to be received only via the genitals for sex to be normal, and stigmatize interpersonal sexual linkages through all other receptor organs as perverted.

Since the eyes and ears receive sensations from a distance, they produce a far wider sexual interval between partners than does genital intercourse. These forms of sexual interaction affect a person's identity only slightly, for the boundary of identity seems to be less porous through the eyes and ears than through the genitals. Therefore, Jehovanists who condemn *voyeurism* and *auralism* more than ordinary intercourse must believe that, if one is going to engage in sex at all, one should do it in a way that makes one's identity susceptible to alteration above some minimal degree.

Consider the following passage from Sartre's short story "Erostratus." Erostratus has just taken a whore to a room where, remaining fully clothed himself, he orders her to undress:

> She dropped her panties . . . [then] tried heavily to kneel between my legs. I got up brusquely.
> "None of that," I told her.
> She looked at me with suprise.
> "Well. What do you want me to do?"
> "Nothing. Just walk. Walk around. I don't want any more from you."
> She began to walk back and forth awkwardly. Nothing annoys women more than walking when they're naked. . . . I was in heaven: there I was, calmly sitting in an armchair, dressed up to my neck, I had even kept my gloves on and this ripe woman had stripped herself naked at my command and was turning back and forth in front of me. [1956, p. 45]

A recent champion of censorship in the Jehovanist tradition, Harry M. Clor, complained that the connection between the sex partners in this passage is insufficient. The voyeur looks at the woman from too great a distance, one at which she is "stripped of all human qualities and reduced to a 'thing'—a sexual organ" (1969, p. 229). Sartre himself, conversely, was trying to demonstrate how voyeurism heightens an individual's feeling of selfhood. By expanding one's distance from others, it increases one's experience of differentiation from them. (For an abstract discussion of the same process, see Sartre's comments on the "look" in *Being and Nothingness* [1956, pp. 252–302].)

Jehovanist condemn all *pornography* in part because it portrays tactile sex through a nontactile medium, whether visual or aural. Except when depicting voyeurism or auralism, the content of pornography always contradicts its form. Jehovanists believe that pornography must distort its consumers psychologically because its content compels consumer and sex object to converge while its form forces them to diverge. Another modern Jehovanist, Walter Berns, argues for censorship on the grounds that this psychological distortion is socially harmful:

> Whereas sexual attraction brings man and woman together seeking a unity . . . the voyeur maintains a distance . . . and because what he looks at he objectifies, he makes an object of that with which it is natural to join; objectifying, he is incapable of uniting and is therefore incapable of love. . . . And a polity without love . . . would be an unnatural monstrosity. [Rist 1975, pp. 49–50]

The sexual interval between partners who employ the contact sense receptor of mouth or anus is much narrower than that between partners who employ the genitals alone. Since a person's identity seems to be even more permeable through mouth or anus than through penis or vagina, he or she will be more affected by *fellatio, cunnilingus*, and *sodomy* than by genital intercourse. (According to Taylor 1973, pp. 123, "the Devil was . . . frequently accused of sodomy." Beyond the obvious fecal symbolism, it was appropriate for the most evil deity to have the most extreme input into the identity of those whom he damned.) By condemning these sexual perversions more than normal sex, Jehovanists must believe that there is some maximal degree above which intercourse should not alter people's identity.

Phillip Roth's novel *My Life as a Man* provides an illustration:

> Earlier, caressing her body, I had been made uneasy by the unexpected texture of her genitals. . . . The vaginal lips appeared withered and discolored in a way that was alarming

> to me. . . . I was tempted to imagine some connection here to
> the childhood victimization by her father. . . .
>   The reader may by now be able to imagine for himself how
> the twenty-four-year-old I was responded to my alarm: in the
> morning, without very much ado, I performed cunnilingus
> upon her. . . . [1975, pp. 71–72]

Roth demonstrates here that the most intense way he can be
affected by an essential characteristic of his sex partner's
identity—victimization—is through oral assimilation of its
apparent embodiment. Jehovanists, of course, would regard
the connection between the sex partners described in this
passage as repulsively excessive.

In the Jehovanist view, then, voyeurism, auralism, fellatio, cunnilingus, and sodomy are all "gradational" perversions. Relative to normal sex, they connect sex partners to an
abnormal degree—voyeurism and auralism separating them
too widely, fellatio/cunnilingus and sodomy fusing them too
closely.

Unlike normal sex, gradational perversions are asymmetrical because each sex partner affects the other's identity
with unequal intensity. The voyeur is changed more than
the voyee, the sodomized more than the sodomizer. One
way to equalize their identity alternations is to perform these
perversions mutually—either simultaneously ("69") or sequentially ("first you, then me"). Another is to switch positions not physically but mentally. By actively stimulating the
other in the desired manner while identifying with the
other, one can receive from the other in imagination the
same sexual stimulation one gives to the other in reality. This
technique allows more precise control over the extent one's
identity is sexually altered, for one can carefully regulate
both the amount of stimulation to the other and the amount
of identification with the other.

Jehovanists seem to condemn these "transpositional" perversions as much as the gradational perversions on which
they are based, but do not always distinguish them with
special nomenclature. Since contact sense receptors reduce
the distinction between the sex partners, no specific terms

are necessary to discriminate the "active" transpositional forms of fellatio, cunnilingus, and sodomy from their "passive" gradational forms. But since distant sense receptors expand the distinction between the sex partners, specific terms are necessary to discriminate their two forms. Thus the gradational perversions of auralism and voyeurism have their transpositional counterparts in *telepathism* and *exhibitionism*. The telepathist expounds on his or her genitals to sex partners, as in obscene telephone calls; the exhibitionist exposes his or her genitals to sex partners, as in this woman's sexual fantasy:

> I'm on one of those stirrup tables that gynecologists have, where they spread your legs and look deep into you. But the table is in the middle of the ring, in Madison Square Garden, and it's mounted on a revolving platform. Thousands of men have paid fifty or a hundred dollars each for tickets, and the ushers are selling binoculars so they can get a better view. . . . [Friday 1974, p. 107]

* Sex through Pain and Provocation

The extent to which intercourse affects a person's identity depends not only on the sensitivity with which sexual stimulation is received but also on the intensity with which it is given. In *masochism*, a person elicits a painfully extreme amount of sensory stimulation from sex partners in order to overwhelm the homeostatic defenses that ordinarily prevent his identity from changing. Physically, masochists punish their bodies by having their flesh beaten, cut, or burnt, their limbs stretched or twisted. Mentally, they mortify their self-conception by inviting insults to batter it or by assuming servile roles to distort it. A collection of erotic fiction by the sex educators Phyllis and Eberhard Kronhausen provides an example of "personal growth" from one form of masochism to the other:

> For the first time since he had been assaulted so brutally, David realized that this was his secret dream! Never had he

dared imagine undergoing physical violence at the hands of a woman! His dreams had always involved only moral humiliation, such as being a woman's servant. But now that the actual pain had stopped, the past five minutes seemed, in retrospect, the most beautiful he had ever known! [1970, p. 216]

If Sigmund Freud was one of the first to explore variations in the organ receptors of sexual stimuli (oral, anal, genital), his English contemporary, Havelock Ellis, was one of the first to examine variations in the signal strength with which they are sent (normal, masochistic).[5] Ellis suggested that a more intense sexual stimulus—pain—might be necessary to arouse those with weaker organic constitutions:

Normally the sexual impulse is sufficiently reinforced by the ordinary active energies of the organism which courtship itself arouses. . . . But in a slightly abnormal organism . . . the sexual impulse is itself usually weaker. . . . An organism in this state become peculiarly apt to seize on the automatic sources of energy generated by emotion. The parched sexual instinct greedily drinks up and absorbs the force it obtains by applying abnormal stimuli to its emotional apparatus. . . . Pain acts as a sexual stimulant because it is the most powerful of all methods for arousing emotion. [1936, *Love and Pain*, pp. 172–76]

Since Jehovanists regard masochism as a perversion, they must believe that there is a maximal level of intensity beyond which people should not allow a sex partner to attempt to alter their identity.

Sadism is the transpositional counterpart of the gradational perversion of masochism because the sadist torments his sex partners while identifying with them. By stimulating their senses to a painful degree, the sadist weakens their defenses against identity alteration. By identifying with them, the sadist experiences a similar weakening of his own defenses. The Marquis de Sade achieved his notoriety in part by pointing out that one's physical impact on a sex partner's body can produce a proportional psychological impact on oneself:

> There is no more lively sensation than that of pain; its impressions are certain and dependable, they never deceive as may those of the pleasure women perpetually feign and almost never experience. . . . One never better irritates one's senses than when the greatest possible impression has been produced in the employed object, by no matter what devices; therefore, he who will . . . procure himself the heaviest possible dose of voluptuousness . . . will . . . impose . . . the strongest possible dose of pain upon the employed object. [1965, p. 606]

A small amount of sexual stimulus, by definition, affects a person very little. Consequently, Jehovanists do not regard an attempt to alter identity with less than a minimal level of intensity as a very serious sexual perversion. Nevertheless, they do disparage activities in which people are sexually provoked only slightly as merely *titillation* or its transpositional counterpart, *coquetry*. People are titillated physically when tickled or vellicated. Although a rare taste, physical titillation is not without some partisans, as the following notice in the personal columns of the pornographic newspaper *Screw* attests:

> ATTENTION! If your thing is tickling, you have many friends who want to meet you. Our new club is for correspondence, but personal contact at your pleasure. Don't feel alone in the world. We would be tickled to meet you. Write Dr. Tickle. [3 January 1972]

More common, of course, is the mental titillation of teasing or flirting. Burlesque strippers, semi-nude dancers, and amateur coquettes wear provocative clothing or act provocatively to tantalize their audience. By prefiguring normal sex, they implicitly promise a more satisfying degree of identity alteration to come, which never actually arrives. Rapists often claim that such provocation from a coquette disequili-

brated their identity, the balance of which they were simply
trying to restore. Titillation and coquetry, in short, annoy
Jehovanists because these quasi-sexual activities destabilize
identity slightly without restabilizing it entirely.

Deviant Sexual Objects

* Sex with Things

Jehovanists have strict rules governing not only how
much identity should be altered sexually but also by what or
who, for they believe that whatever or whoever one copulates with determines the kind of person one will become.
Deviant sexual objects, they feel, produce deviant sexual
subjects. Intercourse with any sex object that belongs to a
class Jehovanists regard as deleterious will be called a "categorical perversion."

The lowest class of sexual objects is made up, of course, of
objects themselves. *Fetishism* is the term for activity in which
a person seeks sexual satisfaction from things rather than
from beings. Not just any thing can be a fetish, however;
only those things associated with, but dissociated from,
beings. Fetishistic sex objects are the subvital slices of vital
wholes, whether inorganic segments (like shoes)[6] or organic
segments (like feet). Jean Genet, who has both participated
in and thought about the seamy side of sex more deeply than
nearly anyone else, observes that the appeal of fetishistic
objects comes from their ability to distill the essence of a
being or class of beings:

> I was excited chiefly by the invisible presence of his inspec-
> tor's badge. That metal object had for me the power of a
> cigarette lighter in the fingers of a workman, of the buckle of
> an army belt, of a switchblade, of a caliper, objects in which
> the quality of males is violently concentrated. [1965, p. 172]

Fetishistic sex objects, then, confuse things and beings by
carrying vital meanings on the symbolic level but not on the

material level. Since Jehovanists regard fetishism as a sexual perversion, they must believe that the boundary between the inorganic realm and the organic realm should be clearly defined.

There is another, more dynamic form of sexual perversion in which people do not merely choose a deviant sex object but manufacture one. Intercourse with any sex object that involves transferring it from a normative category into a counter-normative category will be called a "transformational perversion." Jehovanists dislike transformational perversions even more than categorical perversions: it is one thing to acquire evil identity components passively; it is another to create them actively out of what were once good ones.

Necrophilia is one perversion that involves such a category transformation. Necrophiles enjoy sex with the "dead," i.e., with sex objects in a transitional state between living beings and nonliving things. The recently deceased possess characteristics of both realms, for they are still unified, like beings, but are nonvital, like things. Grave robbers discover sex objects in this transitional state; sex-murderers create them. (For examples, see Vadim's movie *Charlotte* and Oshima's movie *In the Realm of the Senses*.) If people can copulate with the dead as well as with the living, the boundary between these two categories must not be as distinct as Jehovanists would like to believe. Jehovanists regard necrophilia as even more perverted than fetishism not merely because it brings home the inevitability of the living rejoining the nonliving eventually, but because sex is precisely the activity that separated these two categories originally.

A related sexual perversion is *pygmalionism*, the love of statues or mannequins. Here the sex object has the form of a being but the content of a thing. George Bernard Shaw based his play *Pygmalion*, updated as *My Fair Lady*, on sanitized version of the original Greek myth.

Necrophilia and pygmalionism are both instances of what I will call *reiphilia* (nl), a general transformational perversion that involves sex with entities in the process of crossing the boundary between beings and things. It is reiphilia that Montaigne was describing in the following passage:

> Such frenzy is close to that of the boy who went and defiled out of love the beautiful statue of Venus that Praxiteles had made, or that of the frantic Egyptian hot after the carcass of a dead woman he was embalming and shrouding; which gave rise to the law . . . that the bodies of beautiful young women . . . should be kept three days before being put in the hands of the undertakers. [1958, p. 672]

Sex is the only human activity in which the professional has lower status than the amateur. Jehovanists have always condemned *prostitution*,[7] in part because this profession transforms its practitioners into objects. The Kantian version of Jehovanist morality forbids one to treat a fellow human being as an object (1930, pp. 155–66). Karl Marx held that whoever performs a human activity for money is transformed into a thing (1967, pp. 264–300). In exchange for the means (money) of satisfying vital human needs in the future, one person agrees to become a manipulable object for another in the present. Although Marx had productive activity in mind here, he and Engels later generalized this description to reproductive activity as well, for prostitution is the direct exchange of money for sex.[8] Through a similar but more micro-analysis, the German sociologist Georg Simmel portrays prostitutes as giving the most individual and personal part of themselves—their bodies—in exchange for the most general and public remuneration—money (1971, pp. 121–26). Indeed, they usually keep only a small portion of their earnings, the rest going to pimps or madams. Thus prostitutes often become little more than intermediary conduits—mere machines that circulate money to their managers while pumping pleasure to their customers.[9]

Jehovanists criticize *pornography* for a similar reason: it transforms vital beings into subvital abstractions. Pornography can achieve a broad appeal only by abstracting external behaviors and social typifications from sexual interaction.

This abstracting process allows the consumer to "fill in the blanks" of the pornographic sex object with as much individuality and interiority as he wishes. A pornographic novel, for example, might tell its readers only that its heroine is a stewardess or a nurse, and describe only the way she "does it"—not why. Steven Marcus (1967, pp. 283–84), Susan Sontag (1970, pp. 39–40, 51, 54, 58), and Joseph Slade (1971, pp. 39–40) all contrast this abstractness of pornography with the concreteness of "authentic" literature.

Jehovanist critics of pornography have objected specifically to this foreshortened perspective of sexual interaction:

> [Senate candidate Hayakawa] complained that the full meaning of the sex act is missed by pornography. . . .
>
> "There are all sorts of reasons for which men and women go to bed together—but don't forget, in the eye of the camera, they're all doing the same things and that's the terrible thing about pornography. It reduces the sexual act to its mechanics and not to its human relations."
>
> [*Los Angeles Times*, 27 October 1976, part I, p. 28]

Other critics, like George Steiner (1965), believe this aspect of pornography stupefies its audience in the same way that all products of mass culture do. Far from encouraging imagination, pornographic abstraction actually reduces it by replacing private fantasies with its mass-produced shallow images. The portrayal of others as only abstract sex objects also dehumanizes public attitudes, according to Steiner.

* Sex with Beast and Gods

Jehovanists have also prohibited *bestiality* (or zoophilia) since biblical times.[10] In twentieth-century America, many laws remain on the book that forbid carnal knowledge of mammals (especially dogs, horses, and sheep) and even fish and fowl. If modern Jehovanists no longer justify these prohibitions against animal contact primarily on religious grounds, they still assume that their violation indicates some psychological problem.[11] (For examples, see the confessions of "pig-fucking" in Bertolucci's movie *Last Tango in Paris* and of "horse-love" in Schaffer's play *Equus*.) Bestiality disgusts Jehovanists because it undercuts the category of "humanity" at its lower bound. Those who have intercourse with animals acquire bestial identity components, thereby denying the distinction between man (or woman) and beast:

> This nymphomaniac friend of mine remembered that the ape is the animal which most closely resembles man. Her father, as it happened, owned a magnificient orangutan. . . . Urged on by her folly, she bent one of the bars on the cage, and the lewd animal immediately took advantage of the opening. . . . She . . . raised her skirts with determination and stooping over, bravely backed toward the fearsome spear. . . . The first thrusts struck home, the ape had becomes man's equal. [She] was bestialized . . . and monkeyfied. . . . [Kronhausen and Kronhausen 1969, pp. 328–29]

For Jehovanists, this intrusion into humanity from below spreads cognitive confusion and even physical disease. (It was thought to be the source of veneral disease in the eighteenth century, according to MacDonald [1967, p. 431]). Imagined offspring off such unions would be monsters with part human, part animal characteristics, the sort found in horror stories and classical myths, thus blurring the boundary between human and subhuman even further.[12]

But beasts can be made as well as born. If, as Jehovanists believe, an essential difference between human beings and beasts is that the former avoid contact with bodily excretions, then human beings can be transformed into beasts by defiling them with excrement (*saliromania*), specifically urine (*urolagnia*) or feces (*coprolagnia*) (see Ullerstam 1964, pp. 75–80):

> White male seeks dominant mistress to serve as body servant and toilet slave. Crave humiliation, golden showers and oral toilet debasement. Phone "Toilet Mouth" at. . . .
>   [*Fetish Times* #14 (no date), personal columns]

Excrement is especially suitable for defilement because it is the decayed byproduct of living systems, attracting and teeming with lower orders of life. Since its potential for spreading disorder and even death is high, it can contaminate whatever it touches. Saliromania, then, is the transformational counterpart of the categorical perversion of bestiality, for saliromaniacs use excrement to transform humans into subhumans.[13]

At the opposite end of the scale from bestiality is *theogamy*, in which human beings copulate with suprahuman beings, both gods and devils. Many stories involving such sexual indiscretions are related in folk tales, myths, and legends. Although also well-documented in witchcraft trials, theogamy seems to have become a rare "social problem" in recent times.[14] In most cases these mixed marriages did not work out very well. Occasionally, unions with gods produced gods, like Christ, or heroes, like Hercules; more often they produced villains like Clytemnestra, or even dehumanized the human partner, as when Io was turned into a cow. Unions with devils were always detrimental to the human partner and sometimes produced monstrous offspring. Like bestiality, theogamy is a categorical perversion. Unlike bestiality, it has no transformational form. There is no perversion that raises sex partners into suprahumans the same way saliromania lowers them into subhumans—probably because no transubstantiating substance or technique has yet been found that functions as the elevating counterpart to excrement.

* Sex with Too Few and Too Many Others

Autoeroticism differs technically from both onanism and masturbation, although all three terms are used synonymously at present. *Autoeroticism* is a categorical perversion in which one chooses oneself as a sex object,[15] whereas onanism is coitus interruptus practiced for contraception,[16] and masturbation is a transformational Perversion (see below). The autoerotic is excited by the sight of his own body. One's

own body, of course, is too convenient a sex object for
Jehovanists to tolerate, for it allows its lover to tour erotic
reality almost at will.

The prolific English essayist and novelist Colin Wilson
(1966, pp. 38–63) notes the connection between autoeroticism and promiscuity. If Jehovanists regard autoeroticism as
perverted because it involves too little relation to others,
they regard *promiscuity* as perverted because it involves too
much. Don Juan is the archetypal promiscuous pervert:
Casanova, Frank Harris, and Henry Miller are some of his
incarnations. Promiscuity may be simultaneous ("orgies,"
"Saturnalia," "circles," "gang bangs") or sequential ("sleeping around," "sowing wild oats," "nymphomania," "satyri-
asis"). Some forms include both or alternate between them
("swinging," "group sex," see Bartell 1971). Since different
sex partners alter a person's identity in different directions,
promiscuity eventually splinters the self in the Jehovanist
view.

In contrast, the promiscuous themselves often feel that
intercourse with many different partners actually strength-
ens the self, for it helps to integrate the many sides of their
identity that remain unsatisfied by sex with a single
partner.[17] Marco Vassi criticizes the privileged place of two-
sided sex in his essay "Beyond Bisexuality":

> The assumption that *two* allows the most prefect erotic union
> is a misconception rooted in primitive bisexual conscious-
> ness.
>
> When one transcends male-female dualism, eroticism be-
> comes suceptible of a more subtle mathematical understand-
> ing. For each number, there is a different and unique quality
> of consciousness, and no one is intrinsically superior to any of
> the others. [1976b, p. 172]

Vassi goes on to describe how the quality of sexual experience varies with the quantity of sexual partners. Like some
perverse Simmelian, he combines geometry and phenomenology to analyze autoeroticism, troilism, and higher
orders of simultaneous promiscuity (see also his essays,

"The Metasexual Manifesto," and "A Working Model of Promiscuity," 1976b, pp. 178–206).

For Jehovanists, *prostitution* doubly damns its practitioners, not only debiologizing them through objectification but also decomposing them through promiscuity. The prostitute's identity becomes blurred from being continually buffeted by the various social and personal characteristics of many diverse customers. The exchanges of identity with customers are fractional as well as multiple, for "the female [prostitute] contributes her entire self, with all its worth, whereas the male [customer] contributes only part of his personality," according to Georg Simmel (1971, p. 124). Copulating with those who aren't "all there," who are not fully involved in the intercourse, distorts identity still further. From the prostitute's perspective, however, her occupation may not be so debilitating as it seems to Jehovanists. If customers aren't all there, prostitutes aren't always all there either. They often hide behind make-up, extravagant clothes, or affected personalities. Jehovanists like to believe that every prostitute will inevitably end up miserable because of her attempt to take in too many unassimilable identities, but a prostitute who can separate herself psychologically from her professional sexual behavior may well become, like Xaviera Holland, a "happy" hooker (see Hollander 1972).

Masturbation is a transformational sexual activity that alters the objects of both autoeroticism and promiscuity. The masturbator transforms himself into many others in fantasy and transforms many others into himself in actuality. Unlike autoerotics and the promiscuous, who caress their own and other people's bodies for the sake of the bodies themselves, (the masturbator caresses his own body as though it (body and/or caress) were actually another person's.) Jean Genet has helped to elevate the "masturbative imagination" into an art form:

Beneath the sheet, my right hand stops to caress the absent face, and then the whole body, of the outlaw I have chosen for

that evening's delight. . . . I have dreamed myself in many
agreeable lives; my mind, which is eager to please me, has
concocted glorious and charming adventures for me, made
especially to order. The sad thing about it is . . . that the
greater part of these creations are utterly forgotten, though
they constitute the whole of my past spiritual concert. . . .
Pleasure of the solitary, gesture of solitude that makes you
sufficient unto yourself, possessing intimately others who
serve your pleasure without their suspecting it, a pleasure
that gives your most casual gestures . . . that air of supreme
indifference toward everyone. [1964, pp. 55, 121–22, 129]

Note that most people are unaware of the extensive sexual
activity in which their image may be engaging. Although an
accepted occupational hazard for professional pinup models, (the rest of us would probably be shocked to discover
how masturbators are sexually abusing our likenesses) especially since we are often acquainted with them in other
contexts.

Jehovanists have always had difficulty specifying precisely what's wrong with masturbation,[18] especially since the
only biblical reference they cite (see no. 16) condemns it only
within a limited context. The norm the masturbator breaks
by relating to too few others in reality and too many others in
imagination is overly obscure to be persuasive. Unable to
make a convincing case for the ethical deficiencies of masturbation, Jehovanists have been forced to posit its physical
and pyschological dangers.

In his superb historical study of the alleged maladies of
masturbation (1967), Robert MacDonald traced their origins
to an anonymous pamphlet printed in 1707 entitled
"Onania: or, The Heinous Sin of Self-Pollution, And all its
Frightful Consequences, in Both Sexes consider'd, &c." The
frightful physical consequences were these:

Masturbation hinders the growth, is the cause of many a
phymosis and paraphymosis—"I shall not explain these
Terms any further, let it suffice that they are very painful and
troublesome"—stranguries, priaprisms and gonorrheas, thin

and waterish seed, fainting fits and epilepsies, consumptions, loss of erection and premature ejaculation, and infertility. From the wretches that survive, children may be expected so sick and weakly that they are "a Misery to themselves, a Dishonour to the Human Race, and a Scandal to their Parents. . . ." Female masturbators suffer from imbecility, *flour albus* (leucorrhoea), hysteric fits, barrenness and a "total Ineptitude to the Act of Generation itself." [1967, p. 425][19]

By the nineteenth century, Jehovanists had shifted their attack from the physical consequences of masturbation to its psychological effects:

As early as the end of the XVIIIth century some of the more scientific physicians became sceptical about the relation between masturbation and physical disease. . . . The physical consequences of masturbation were generally limited in the responsible textbooks to what was vaguely known as degeneration. The emphasis now shifted to the mental effects. Fielding Blandford in his textbook on insanity typifies this new approach: the brain, he says, undergoes "permanent damage from the constant irritation to which it has been exposed by the habit." [MacDonald 1967, pp. 428, 429]

MacDonald (1967, pp. 430–31) does not attempt to explain why masturbation evolved from being one Jehovanist vice among many during the seventeenth century to become their central sexual sin during the eighteenth and nineteenth centuries. The conjunction of certain intellectual and social trends during this period, however, may have reinforced Jehovanists' customary abhorrence of it. For masturbation, more than any other activity, embodied the tension of the dawning modern age. Enlightenment philosophies stressed human dignity and universal membership in the common category of humanity. But at the same time capitalist economic pressures were undermining human beings as ends in themselves and pitting them against each other. Masturbation symbolized the clash between capitalism's instrumental individualism and the Enlightenment ideal of

common human dignity, for it isolates the individual from
other human beings in reality while they are treated merely
as means for his own gratification in his imagination (see
Marcus 1967, p. 22, for another economic explanation).

* Sex with Ingroups and Outgroups

Confining sexual orientation narrowly to members of
one's own social group may be termed *endophilia* (nl). Jehovanists prohibit selecting a sex partner from only two such
ingroups: one's own family (*incest*) and one's own gender
(*homosexuality* or, specifically for women, *lesbianism*).[20] Incest
and homosexuality are to society as autoeroticism and, in
part, masturbation are to the individual: all are intracategory
activities that Jehovanists associate with insanity, either as
cause or consequence.[21]

Just as the sexual activities of autoerotics and, in part, of
masturbators fail to cross the border between individuals, so
those of the incestuous and the homosexual fail to cross the
border between certain social categories. To attribute a perverted character to both sets of sexual activities, Jehovanists
must believe that in neither set are subject and object distinct
enough for their sexual interchange to take place properly.
(Jehovanists single out homosexuality, above all other sexual perversions, for special condemnation because it involves both a deviant [intragender] sexual object and a deviant [oral or anal] sexual linkage.) Of course, it is precisely
this similarity in family and gender categories that attracts
endophiles to each other. Thus Thomas Mann on incest:

> "You are just like me," said [Sieglinde's brother Siegmund],
> haltingly. . . . "Everything about you is just like me—and
> so—what you have—with Beckerath [Sieglinde's fiancé]—the
> [sexual] experience—is for me too. That makes things even,
> Sieglinde . . . it is a revenge. . . . They forgot themselves in
> caresses, which took the upper hand, passing over into a
> tumult of passion, dying away into a sobbing. . . . [1936, p.
> 319]

And the Marquis de Sade on homosexuality:

"The crime committed with a creature completely like yourself seems greater than that with one who is not" [Greene and
Greene 1974, p. 67]

These two intracategory sexual activities are often related.
Freud (1972, p. 32n) found that incestuous temptations lead
to homosexual temptations during the psychogenetic development of the individual; Taylor (1973, pp. 80, 149–50)
found that incest taboos alternated with homosexual taboos
during the historical evolution of Western society. Whoever
does not cross a sexual boundary between social groups that
it is normative to cross implies that this boundary is too
strong for him. Every instance of incest or homosexuality,
then, raises the specter that the sexual boundaries around
family or gender groupings in our society have become too
impermeable for some individuals to break through them.

It is not fully clear why Jehovanists forbid sexual intercourse within gender and family groupings but not within
other groupings such as size or eye color; though their
homosexual and incest taboos are at least reinforced, if not
primarily caused, by socioeconomic organization. Sexual
pairing within work groups is often prohibited on the
grounds that it would interfere with the group's ability to
coordinate responses to environmental threats. Consequently, homosexuality is less likely to be tolerated whenever economic organization segregates the sexes in the work-
place. (The current decline in gender segregation at work
has paralleled the decline in hostility to homosexuality.)
And whenever environmental threats increase, there is
likely to be greater demand for the gender differentiation
that homosexuality blurs by mingling the biology of one sex
with the behavior of the other. Americans look back on such
perilous periods as the settlement of the West or World War I
and II as times when "men were men and women were
women." Incest undermines social organization in the same
way that homosexuality undermines economic organization. Thomas Aquinas pointed out that it subverts the power
structure of the family and short-circuits the friendship
structure of the community:

Since there is in matrimony a union of diverse persons, those persons who should already regard themselves as one because of having the same origin are properly excluded from matrimony. . . . Besides, it is unfitting for one to be conjugally united with persons to whom one should naturally be subject. . . . Therefore, it would not be fitting to contract matrimony with one's parents. . . . Moreover, . . . friendship is increased among many people when unrelated persons are bound together by matrimony. Therefore, . . . matrimony should be contracted with persons outside one's family. . . . [Verene 1972, pp. 130–31]

The desire to copulate with members of groups to which one does not belong may be termed *exophilia* (nl). Jehovanists disapprove of selecting sex partners from almost all outgroups (other than family and gender) but they regard selecting them from outside certain major social classes as especially perverted. Their antipathy is particularly intense toward those who venture outside their own age group for partners who are either much younger[22] (*pedophilia*) or much older (*gerontophilia*) than themselves, although they are not prohibited in the Bible. The desire to deflower prepubescent girls became widespread during the eighteenth century, apparently as a result of changing child-rearing practices that elevated their status while segregating them from adult society (see de Ropp 1969, pp. 184–85, 210). But this same period also heard Benjamin Franklin's advice: "In your amours, you should prefer old women to young ones; they are so grateful" ("On the Choice of a Mistress"). Despite the general repugnance that is felt toward the old in American today, gerontophilia must be much more common than it is thought to be, considering the surprisingly large number of older women who are sexually attacked. In 1974 there were sixty-nine rape victims over sixty years old in Los Angeles (*Los Angeles Times*, 21 July 1975, part IV, p. 6).

Jehovanists have also forbidden people from selecting partners outside their own racial group (*miscegenation*). In the nineteenth century, racial categories were narrow enough for them to condemn sexual intercourse between members of different European countries as at least a mild form of miscegenation. Today, of course, even sexual liaisons between members of much broader racial categories are not longer prohibited by legal sanctions, except in South Africa. Nevertheless, certain forms of miscegenation still bother many Jehovanist Americans:

> Stanley Kramer's situation-comedy pilot for ABC—. . . one envisioned by the network as in the new bold mode—sank . . . when the schedules were devised this spring. There was just one problem . . . : a bedroom scene in which a black man kisses a white woman on the mouth. Several executives who had been at the screening said that, despite their being prepared for it, they had experienced shock. . . .
>
> Kramer's project was a situation-comedy adaptation of his 1967 movie hit "Guess Who's Coming to Dinner?" . . . The theme of the plot was miscegenation. A well-born white girl marries a brilliant black scientist, and the comedy develops around the reactions of their parents.
>
> "Kramer did it as tastefully as you could ask for," one executive said. "But the physical contact was clearly going to cause hell out in the boondocks."
>
> Asked why "The Jeffersons" on CBS was able to get away with the black-and-white kissing scene last season without causing much of a stir, the executive contended . . . "In 'The Jeffersons,' a white man kissed a black woman and, terrible as it is to say, that's somehow not as objectionable in this society as when the sexes are reversed." [*The New York Times*, 13 June 1975, sec. II, p. 21]

Although Jehovanist opposition to miscegenation per se has weakened, this account suggests their continued belief that, even though the racial group in question is no longer as stigmatized as it once was, the more sensitive female identity is still susceptible to the sexual effect of what stigma remains.

Jehovanists also discourage intercourse that goes beyond the boundaries of class and religion. D. H. Lawrence's *Lady Chatterley's Lover* provides the most famous literary illustration of the hardships encountered by those who take lovers from outside their own socioeconomic class; Phillip Roth's *Portnoy's Complaint* provides a similar illustration for those who take lovers from outside their own religious group.[23] For some reason, Jehovanists refer to the activities that involve these deviant sexual objects only in circumlocutions. Therefore, I will take it upon myself to designate the former as *strataphilia* (nl) and the latter as *sectiphilia* (nl).

To the dismay of Jehovanists, exophiles who transgress forbidden frontiers demonstrates that their society's internal boundries around specific age, racial, socioeconomic, or religious groups have become too permeable to be sustained. Since those who identify strongly with a social category defines their very selves against its opposite, sexual intercourse between ingroup and outgroup members will breach the membrane that keeps evil, chaotic elements out of their system. Jehovanists in biblical times, for instance, claimed that Jews who copulated with non-Jews were punished with venereal disease (Rosebury 1973, pp. 91–92)—a caution concerning intercourse between ingroups and outgroups still heard today.

If a potential sexual partner is not already a member of a tabooed ingroup, he could conceivably be changed into one. Since it is impossible to change others into family members, however, there is no sexual activity that Jehovanists can condemn as the transformational version of incest. (A case could be made, though, that this is precisely what marriage is.)

But Jehovanists do condemn the transformational version of homosexuality: *transvestism*, or its extreme form, *transsexualism*.[24] Transvestites, who change their clothing and behavior to those of the opposite sex, sever the social determinants of gender from its biological determinants. Transsexuals, who change their biological characteristics as well as their social characteristics to those of opposite sex, sever current gender from previous gender. Transvestism disorients Jehovanists by undermining the coherence of their gender classification; transsexualism disorients them by undermining its stability. Note that transvestites or transsexuals, unlike other transformational perverts, change not their sex partners' characteristics but their own, though the oppositional relation produced between subject and object is the same. This indirect method of transforming the sex object gives transvestism and transsexualism, as commonly practiced, the added characteristics of transpositional perversions.

Conversely, a person can change potential sex partners into members of social categories other than his own by inducing them to dress and act as do real outgroup members. The lack of terms for the outgroup transformations condemned by Jehovanists is puzzling. When certain types of clothing are involved, the term "fetish" has been used. But since the clothing coveted almost always belongs to particular age, racial, socioeconomic, or religious groups other than the wearer's own, it is more fruitful to see these practices as transformational perversions, which we can now rename to reflect the specific social category they shift. A man who prefers his wife to dress like a young girl has transformed her life cycle stage through *transageism* (nl). A woman who prefers her white lover to abuse her in black ghetto dialect has transformed his race through *transcegenation* (nl). A man who prefers his mistress to exchange her business clothes for the raiments of royalty has transformed her socioeconomic class through *transstratism* (nl). And a woman who prefers her non-Catholic suitor to dress and act like a priest before she will make love to him has transformed his religion through *transsectism* (nl). In Bernard Malamud's episodic novel *Pictures of Fidelman*, for example, the Jewish art student Fidelman stumbles upon the only way to bed the tempestuous Italian with whom he shares a studio:

> The art student hastened to a costume shop and settled on a cassock and fuzzy black soupbowl biretta, envisaging another Rembrandt: "Portrait of the Artist as Priest." He hurried with his bulky package back to the house. . . . He quickly changed into the priest's vestments. . . . Annamaria, after stealthily re-entering the studio, with heaving bosom and agitated eyes

closely followed his progress. At last, with a cry she threw herself at his feet. . . .

She grabbed his knees. "Help me, Father, for Christ's sake."

Fidelman, after a short tormented time, said in a quavering voice, "I forgive you, my child."

"The penance," she wailed, "first the penance. . . ."

Gripping his knees so hard they shook she burrowed her head into his black-buttoned lap. He felt the surprised beginnings of an erection.

"In that case," Fidelman said, shuddering a little, "better undress."

"Only," Annamaria said, "if you keep your vestments on."

"Not the cassock, too clumsy."

"At least the biretta."

He agreed to that.

Annamaria undressed in a swoop. Her body was extraordinarily lovely, the flesh glowing. In her bed they lightly embraced. She clasped his buttocks, he cupped hers. Pumping slowly he nailed her to her cross. [1975, pp. 67–69]

All these transformational activities associated with sex can also appear in transpositional forms, as when middle-class men prowl gay bars in lower-class guise.

* Sex with the Subjugated and the Subjugators

A yearning for partners vastly different from oneself in status and consequently in power increases the importance of the hierarchical dimension of the sexual relation. Tyrannizing over those far inferior in status and power is called *domination*. Being tyrannized by those far superior in status and power is called *submission*. The more the higher-status sex partner imposes his own rhythms of moving through erotic reality on the lower-status sex partner while ignoring or overriding the latter's rhythms, the more the former demonstrates an ability to affect the latter's identity without being similarly affected in return. Those who dominate others sexually possess the greatest social power there is: the power to control another person's focus of attention. Con-

trol over a person's physical behavior and cognitive orientation implies total control over that person's essential being—
but with consequent responsibility for it, too.

In Western society, of course, men have traditionally
played the dominant role in sex while women have played
the submissive role, although excessive emphasis in the
bedroom on the difference in status and power has been
perceived as perverted. This gender stratification has usually been reinforced by socioeconomic stratification, as when
upper-class men lay lower-class women. But these two social stratification systems can also counterpoint each other,
producing more intricate psychological ramifications. Lina
Wertmuller's movie *Swept Away*, for example, concerns the
emotional complications that ensue when an upper-class
woman has an affair with a lower-class man.

It might seem that domination and submission are merely
forms of strataphilia, since both concern class differentials.
But the nonparity preversions direct attention only to the
relative position of the classes, whereas strataphilia directs
attention to their other characteristics. *Lady Chatterley's Lover*
deals with strataphilia more than with domination or submission because Lawrence focuses on the vitality of the
lower class rather than on any notion of its inferiority.

Domination and submission have also been regarded as
forms of bondage and discipline or of sadism and masochism, but the subtleties of these sexual perversions are
obscured unless all three pairs are carefully distinguished.
Domination and submission are categorical perversions that
involve the choice of sex partners, whereas *bondage* and
discipline are transformational perversions that involve the
conversion of sex partners. The heroine of Pauline Réage's
Story of O (1967) was not born a sexual slave—she was transformed into one. Sex partners of equal status and power are
transformed into sex partners of unequal status and power
through chains and fetters (bondage), physical force (discipline), or verbal threats to use either or both. Bondage keeps
the lower-status sex partner in his new place; discipline
returns him there if he attempts to leave it. Sadism and

masochism emphasize the output intensity of the sex partner's original identity, whereas bondage and discipline
emphasize the creation of a new identity for the sex partner.
S and M stresses fear and physical pain; B and D stresses
frustration and psychological pain (humiliation) and may
even involve physical pleasure.[25] Sadism and masochism, of
course, are often used to enhance the transformational
effects of bondage and discipline. The higher-status sex partner may flagellate the lower-status sex partner sadistically to
ensure that the latter will make a disciplined effort to remain
in role. Bondage and discipline are designed to weaken one
partner's resistance to the sexual alteration of his identity
while strengthening the other's ability to prevail.

The reluctance to allow any sexual modification of the self
can be overcome not only through physical props such as
whips and chains but also through the social supports of
certain occupational and institutional roles. A third transformational perversion in which these roles are used to establish hierarchy will be call *genetism* (nl), after Jean Genet,
author of the play *The Balcony* (1958). In genetism, both sex
partners play-act the complementary social roles of various
types of superiors and subordinates (see Green and Green
1974 for the importance of imagination and ritual in this sort
of sex). Some of Genet's characters in *The Balcony* impersonate authority figures such as "bishop" and "judge," while
prostitutes impersonate their underlings such as "penitent"
and "thief." In general, the higher-status sex partner may
play "master" to the lower-status sex partner's "slave,"
"servant," "page" (eighteenth and nineteenth centuries), or
"serf" (nineteenth-century Russia); "warden" to "pris-
oner"; "teacher" to "student"; or "adult" to "child." Sometimes the superior may cast the subordinate into a subsocial
role, playing "trainer" to "animal" (horse, dog), or even
"living being" to "lifeless object" (footstool, doormat; see
Ullerstam 1964, pp. 85–86). In all these instances, the relative
statuses of complementary social roles are used to reinforce
the relative statuses of complementary sexual roles.

The transformational perversions of bondage, discipline, and genetism differ from the categorical perversions of domination and submission. Putting others into (or back into) high- or low-status social roles may be more enjoyable than merely finding them already there. The superior sex partners may issue impossible or contradictory commands, continually compelling the inferior sex partners to violate their role requirements, in order to justify disciplining them for breaking role, thereby "putting them (back) in their place." Moreover, unlike "domination" and "submission," the terms "bondage," "discipline," and "genetism" do not distinguish whether the sex object is subjugated or subjugating, implying that the practitioners switch between both roles easily and often.

Those into bondage, discipline, and especially genetism often employ other sexual perversions to humiliate or to exalt their partners, for example, commanding them to behave like children (transageism) or encouraging them to act like aristocrats (transstratism). They expand the status difference between sexual partners by superimposing traditional hierarchical relations between social partners—economic, occupational, institutional, familial, or even those involving gender itself.[26] The Kronhausens show how involuntary transvestism can be used to demote a male:

> Male clothing is the symbol of male superiority which is precisely the reason the young man has to be divested of it in order to learn submission. Female attire is thus the symbol of submission and inferior status, and consequently Julian is not only stripped of the male status symbols, but made to wear the mark of the inferior or "second" sex: he must stand in a corner with a petticoat over his head; he is forced to wear a pair of women's drawers as a shirt, his arms stuck ridiculously through the leggings; and so forth. [1969, p. 184]

Considering their conservative respect for authority and rank in other areas of life, Jehovanist opposition to all these hierarchical erotic activities reveals a sexual ethos that is

surprisingly egalitarian (except perhaps where gender stratification is concerned). Since neither domination nor submission nor genetism is specifically forbidden in the Bible,
they must have become known as "sexual perversions" only
recently. Such reconceptualizing seems to have developed
from the opposite responses of different groups to the same
social and cultural changes. Libertines reacted to slipping
social status by intensifying the stratification of their sexual
status, while prudes reacted to growing democratic ideologies by condemning stratification in sex but condoning it in
other social spheres. Thus it was during the eighteenth and
nineteenth centuries that Jehovanists found a new form of
sex to forbid.

The following excerpt from Kenneth Tynan's play *Oh!
Calcutta!* parodies all the hierarchical sexual perversions described in this section, as well as the Jehovanist condemnation of them:

MAN IS DISCOVERED CENTER STAGE IN ARMCHAIR, RELAXED,
LEGS CROSSED. . . . GIRL A ENTERS RIGHT. SHE IS DRESSED LIKE A
VICTORIAN PARLOR MAID. . . . SHE CARRIES A BIRCH ROD. MAN
WATCHES HER AS SHE CROSSES TO THE CHAISE LONGUE AND
KNEELS ON IT, PLACING THE BIRCH ROD NEAR HER FEET. SHE
BENDS FORWARD, RESTING HER HEAD ON HER FOLDED ARMS. SHE
RAISES HER SKIRT AND TUCKS IT ABOVE HER WAIST. . . . GIRL B IS
NOW LOWERED FROM THE FLIES. . . . SHE IS ENCASED IN A NET OF
STOUT ROPE, WHICH DANGLES FIVE FEET ABOVE STAGE LEVEL.
SHE IS WEARING A BIKINI. HER WRISTS AND ANKLES ARE TIED,
HER MOUTH IS GAGGED, AND SHE IS DOUBLED UP. . . .

MAN (easy, slow, conversational tone): Like most civilized
people I believe in democracy. . . . I don't believe that any one
person is essentially more important than any other. Or less.
On the other hand, there are obviously differences between
people. . . .

HE INDICATES GIRL B

Have a good squint at Susan. This girl is where she is as a
direct consequence of physical coercion. Brute force and nim

ble fingers have been at work. The principle of choice—the very heartland of liberty—has been rudely violated. It's an outrage to the human spirit.

HE TURNS TO GIRL A

Now let's take . . . [a] look at Jean. She kneels there—or squats there—in a posture that must be profoundly embarassing. You might even call it humiliating. However, if the spirit moves her, she is at liberty to get up and go. Jean, the submissive household servant in temporary disgrace, is a free agent. . . .

. . . will you please make a sign if you wish to leave the stage?

SHE DOES NOT MOVE. PAUSE

As I was saying, I'm a strict believer in democracy. [199, pp. 105–9]

The Periodical Table of Sexual Perversions

I have grouped the following charts under the title "The Periodic Table of Sexual Perversions" because the elements of (one conception of) our social world organized in this table are as fundamental as the elements of (one conception of) our natural world organized a hundred years ago in Mendeleev's periodic table of chemical elements. Although the arrangement of social elements in this table is analogous to the arrangement of chemical elements, the social elements themselves are more similar to some of the elementary particles of physics (which have not yet been successfully schematized). What are considered sexual perversions in a society are, as it were, antimatter particles that reveal (by contradiction) the fundamental building blocks of the society. Just as the collision between particles of antimatter and matter results in their mutual annihilation in a release of energy, so the collision between sexual perversions and social organization results in their mutual annihilation in an explosion of emotion.

Conclusion

It did not take an excessively procrustean effort in this chapter to show that the Jehovanist loathing for specific sexual perversions is not arbitrary but stems from a unified system, reducible to a small number of underlying dimensions. Jehovanists consider it normative, we have seen, for a person to be only moderately sensitive to the input of identity characteristics from a sex partner who outputs them with only moderate intensity. The person should relate sexually in this moderate way only to another who is vital and human, neither identical nor multiple, different in family and gender but similar in other major social characteristics, and approximately equal in status and power. These qualities of the subject, the sex object, and their relation are the fundamental constituents of the Jehovanist cosmos.

In the last chapter we saw that Jehovanists criticize normal sex for undermining the integrity of the *individual*. In this chapter we have seen that they criticize perverted sex even more for also undermining the integrity of the *social* on both micro and macro levels. Deviant sexual linkages blur the "natural" boundaries of the *relation between individuals*. Fellators are too close to their partners to retain autonomy; voyeurists are too distant to retain connection. Deviant sexual objects, on the other hand, blur the "natural" boundaries of the *structure of society*. The sexual perversions that undermine society's external boundaries—its place in the cosmos—include fetishism (which breaches the biological membrane between the living and the nonliving) and bestiality (which breaches the anthropological membrane between the human and the subhuman). The sexual perversions that undermine society's internal boundaries—those separating subsocial elements—breach various sociological membranes. These include promiscuity (between individual and group), miscegenation (between ingroup and outgroup), and domination (between equals and unequals).[27]

In the last chapter we viewed society as a collection of intersubjectively connected individuals, whose internal

The Periodic Table of Sexual Perversions
(sexual perversions marked "nl" are neologisms defined in the text)

Table 4.1: Deviant Sexual Linkages

Dimension	Subject's input sensitivity				Object's output intensity	
Normative degree	moderate					
Counter-normative degree	immoderate				immoderate	
	insufficient		excessive		insufficient	excessive
Transpositional perversion	exhibitionsim	telepathism			coquetry	sadism
Gradational perversion	voyeurism / visual pornography (form)	auralism / verbal pornography (form)	fellatio and cunnilingus	sodomy	titillation	masochism
Sexual linkage	eyes	ears	mouth	anus	provocation	pain
	distant organs		contact organs			

Table 4.2: Deviant Sexual Objects

Dimension	Biological		Anthropological	
Normative category	vitality		humanity	
Counter-normative category	nonvitality		nonhumanity	
	subvital	—	subhuman	superhuman
Transformational perversion	reiphilia (nl) 1. necrophilia 2. pygmalionism — prostitution (objectification) pornography (content)	—	saliromania 1. urolagnia 2. coprolagnia	—
Categorical perversion	fetishism 1. partial 2. clothing	—	bestiality	theogamy
Sexual object	things	—	beasts	gods

Table 4.2a: Deviant Sexual Objects (cont.)

Dimension	Sociological					
	Quantificational		**Differential**		**Hierarchical**	
Normative category	relationality		transactionality		parity	
Counter-normative category	nonrelationality		nontransactionality		nonparity	
	subrelational	superrelational	reflexive	transgressive	subordination	superordination
Transformational perversion	masturbation		transvestism transsexualism	transageism (nl) transcegenation (nl) transstratism (nl) transsectism (nl)	bondage discipline genetism (nl)	
Categorical perversion	auto-eroticism	promiscuity 1. simultaneous 2. sequential prostitution (disintegration)	endophilia (nl) 1. incest 2. homosexuality (and lesbianism)	exophilia (nl) 1. pedophilia and gerontophilia 2. miscegenation 2. strataphilia (nl) 3. sectiphilia (nl)	domination	submission
Sexual object	oneself	many others	ingroups	outgroups	subjugates	subjugators

psychological organization, Jehovanists believe, normal sex attacks. In this chapter we have viewed society as possessing its own microsocial relations and macrosocial structures, the emergent social organization of which, they believe, perverted sex attacks. If normal sex threatens the integrity of every individual *in* society, perverted sex threatens the integrity *of* society itself as well.[28]

Jehovanists divide their society into different parts, the distinctness of which they attempt to maintain by regulating the interchange of identities between the entities that belong to each part. Since sexual intercourse facilitates this interchange far more than mere association, restricting sex is the main means by which they attempt to control the interpenetration of separate spheres.

Jehovanists, in short, believe that everyone should work continually to maintain the "good" sociocosmic order against the "evil" anarchy, to fence off the natural, moral, and sacred borders and subdivisions of the cosmos from their unnatural, immoral, and polluted counterparts. Jehovanists fear the sexual pervert because he is, they believe, the weak link in their chain of defense against social, and even cosmic, chaos. Every sexual pervert is, they fear, a Samson liable to pull the whole universe down upon their heads.[29]

With this in mind, we can supplement Freud's contention that the "energies available for 'cultural' development are thus in great part won through suppression of the so-called perverse elements of sexual excitation" (1963, p. 27). Repression of sexual perversions affects the content of culture as well as the level of cultural energy. What has been repressed to make our civilization possible is not merely a biological instinct, as Freud thought, but each of the countersociocosmic orders implicit in every sexual perversion. Sexual perverts, then, turn out to be sociologists and cosmologists, engendering societies and worlds alternative to our own.

We have yet to consider what motivates people to persist in practicing sexual perversions, despite the tremendous penalties against doing so. Freud and his followers have already described the biographical origins of these practices, but behind these lies a social source. The social factors that produce sexual perversions must be distinguished from those that produce their repression. The reason some people suddenly want to perform a particular sexual perversion is not necessarily related to the reason other people suddenly want to enforce a law against it, although both may share the same epidemiology. Jehovanists have always opposed sexual perversions, but sometimes they attempt to suppress one of them with special vehemence, revealing local and temporary variations in the aspects of their world view that are vulnerable.

Those who were situated at the stress points of their society while their identity was forming are especially inclined toward deviant sexual activities. The precise nature and location of the stress points that affect the incidence of sexual perversions remain to be specified empirically, but their existence is as certain as the existence of those that affect the incidence of suicide, which were found by the French sociologist Emile Durkheim (1951). We can surmise, however, that the frequency of sexual perversions in a society will vary with the level of social stress and that the most prevalent, or at least most notorious, sexual perversion— e.g., pedophilia among the early Greeks, incest in the Renaissance, sadism in the eighteenth century, homosexuality in the late nineteenth and early twentieth centuries, oral sex today—will vary with the particular social stresses that arise.

In the last chapter we saw that normal sex promotes self-renewal through periodic identity reversal. Now we can see that some forms of perverted sex enhance this self-renewal by reversing and thereby refreshing more aspects (human status, class status, etc.) of identity more emphatically (through pain, orality, etc.). Other forms of perverted sex temper this self-renewal for more sensitive identities by reversing fewer aspects (homosexuality, incest) less emphatically (voyeurism, titillation). Thus those whose identities have been "distorted" (from the Jehovanist point of view) by social stresses may be drawn to perverted sex because of its potential for relieving their psychological tensions more extensively, more powerfully, or more precisely—in any case more effectively—than can normal sex.

Still greater self-renewal can be obtained by combining several deviant sexual objects (like the women who masturbated themselves with human bones, mentioned by Lely 1970, p. 173). Deviant sexual linkages can also intensify the psychological effects of deviant sexual objects. The asymmetrical power of sexual linkages whose output or input is excessive (sadism, sodomy, etc.), for instance, especially reinforces the inequality of sexual objects whose relative statuses are hierarchical (domination, bondage, etc.).[30] The unsurpassed master of reinvigorating individual identity while weakening Jehovanist sociocosmic order is, of course, the Marquis de Sade, who attempted to combine all deviant sexual linkages with all deviant sexual objects systematically in *120 Days of Sodom* (see Barthes 1967, especially pp. 29–30, 157). In another work, one of de Sade's characters cries out: "Behold all that I simultaneously do: scandal, seduction, bad example, incest, adultery, sodomy!" (1966, p. 272)

Sexual perversions can revitalize certain selves so powerfully because the segments of identity that participate in them represent segments of more encompassing entities. The reverberations that result from bringing together these larger social and even cosmic cleavages greatly amplify the psychological effects of individual sexual chords, causing coitus to resound as though the segregated subdivisions of the whole world were engaging in forbidden intercourse through the medium of the copulating couple.

Part Three
The War of
the World Views

Sexuality
and Ideology

*I*n part one we examined the way everyone presumably experiences the transition between everyday and erotic reality. In part two we examined the reasons why some people —those I call Jehovanists—interpret this transition as obscene. Jehovanists, we found, filter their experience of erotic reality through a particular cognitive-normative grid. Consequently, they are distressed to discover that their erotic experience— especially the softening of the self and the transformations that entails— clashes with their ideal conception of personal identity, interpersonal relations, and social organization.

Whatever this Jehovanist cognitive-normative grid is called—world view, paradigm, belief system, ideology, or ethos—those who believe in it usually do so wholeheartedly. Imprinted in childhood, it becomes so fundamental a part of their self-definition that they may even be willing to sacrifice their very lives for it. Taylor cites the historical example "of the virgin Gorgonia, who 'with all her body and members thereof . . . bruised and broken most grievouslie' yet refused the attentions of a doctor because her modesty forbade her to be seen or touched by a man . . . (1973, p. 53)." This world view is central to the lives of true believers in Jehovanism because it provides the markers by which they locate their place in the cosmos. It constitutes the warp and woof of their existence, the sacred threads that tie their entire universe together. Anyone who cuts those cords is accursed.

One reason the Jehovanist belief system has been so persuasive for so long is that it includes a set of several slightly different arguments for denouncing sex. Jehovanism has waxed and waned several times during the course of Western civilization. Every time Jehovanists have returned to power, they have accused sex of violating new aspects of self and social life while continuing to condemn it for its old transgressions. I will briefly review the history of illicit copulation to show the accretion of reasons for condemning sex, an accumulation that has turned sex, for Jehovanists today, into a multi-dimensional miasma.

The earliest indication of what would become the Jehovanist world view occurs in Genesis when Adam and Eve suddenly feel compelled to conceal their genitals after eating from the Tree of Knowledge:

> Then the eyes of both of them were opened and they realized that they were naked. So they sewed fig leaves together to make themselves loinclothes. [Genesis 3:7]

Adam and Eve were the first to sift their sexual experience through Jehovanism's conceptual and moral mesh. In other words, they suddenly realized that their world was now divided into two realms—a "good" everyday realm and an "evil" erotic realm—and that they had to suppress the latter as much as possible by concealing the physical features that generated it. But except for this reference to nudity and the Ten Commandments' condemnation of adultery (Exodus

20:14), the earliest books of the Jewish Bible contain few restrictions on sex.

The first elaborate formulation of Jehovanist sexual proscriptions appears in Leviticus (especially chapters 15, 18, and 20). These sexual proscriptions were originally transcribed after the Jews fled from Egypt around 1240 B.C. but apparently were not followed closely until the Jews returned from their second exile—the Babylonian captivity—around 538 B.C. (Taylor 1973, pp. 244–45). The ancient Jews feared that sex would pollute the body, and, through it, the self and all of society (Stern 1957; 1966).

The early Christian view, propounded by the apostle Paul (A.D. 5?–67), maintained the Jewish belief that the self can be polluted by physical sources but added that fornication with prostitutes could spread pollution even to God himself because "the body is the temple of God" (1 Corinthians 6:15–19; 3:17).

Jehovanism crested again in the fourth and fifth centuries A.D., now in the guise of Hellenistic idealism, after the Roman Empire had crumbled in all but name. The Eastern-oriented Church Fathers condemned carnal desire for dragging the self downward to the earth instead of allowing it to float upward to God. Their sexual proscriptions were part of a more general asceticism, which accused all physical pleasure of diverting attention away from the highly valued spiritual realm toward the lowly valued material realm (Stern 1966, pp. 96–97; Bullough and Bullough 1977, pp. 10–18).

The leading Western-oriented Church Father, Augustine (A.D. 354–430), condemned sex not so much for weakening the spiritual orientation of the self as for weakening its ability to control the body:

It is right, therefore, to be ashamed of this lust. And it is right that the members which it moves or fails to move . . . not in complete conformity to our [will or] decision should be called *pudenda* ('parts of shame'), which they were not called before man's [original] sin. . . . [Then] the flesh did not yet . . . give proof of [Adam and Eve's] disobedience by a disobedience of its own. . . . [1972, p. 578][1]

Both these early Christian attitudes toward sex abated somewhat during the Middle Ages, especially within the general population. But their occasional intense revival within Church circles can be inferred from penitentials that declared fornication to be a worse crime than murder (Taylor 1973, p. 293).

The power of the Jehovanist world view peaked again toward the end of the High Middle Ages. In his recent book (1980), the historian John Boswell argues that the hostility of the Catholic Church toward sex in general and homosexuality in particular was much greater during the last half of the thirteenth century than ever before. The most influential theologian of this period, Thomas Aquinas (1225–74), tried to shift the essence of sex from the activity itself to its possible consequence by equating copulation with procreation:

> It is good for each person to attain his end, whereas it is bad for him to swerve away from his proper end. . . . [Therefore,] each and every part of man, and every one of his acts, should attain the proper end. . . . What is sought in the case of semen . . . [is] to emit it for the purpose of generation, to which purpose the sexual act is directed. [Verene 1972, pp. 120–21]

Consequently, Aquinas condemns all forms of sex that do not bring this creative union of selves to completion:

> Every emission of semen, in such a way that generation cannot follow, is contrary to the good for man. And if this is done deliberately, it must be a sin. [Verene 1972, pp. 121ff]

Such completion cannot be accomplished quickly, for Aquinas holds that the sex act is fulfilled not merely by conception or even birth, but by the child's reaching full adulthood, which requires that its parents be joined in a

long-term monogamous marriage to bring up the child properly (Verene 1972, pp. 121ff). In effect, then, Aquinas believes that each act of intercourse is not fully finished for
nearly twenty years.[2]

The Renaissance was a period of contraction for Jehovanism or, from its perspective, a period of licentiousness. But
by the mid-sixteenth century, the gathering forces of both
Protestantism and Counter-Reformation were restoring
Jehovanism to the influence it had at the end of the Middle
Ages. Beginning with Luther (1483–1546) and especially Cal-
vin (1509–64) in northern Europe, and culminating in the
Puritan seizure of power in England (1640–60), Jehovanists
once again were able to restrict sexual activities. But these
early Protestants differed from their predecessors in trying
to restrict sexual thoughts as well as activities. Even thinking
about sex, they feared, would disrupt the integrity of the
self. If the main effect of Protestantism was to intensify
individuality, the autonomous but isolated self it created
was under great tension. Such a hard but brittle self was
continually in danger of being shattered by the psychic diffusion of the sexual process. Consequently, the task of holding
this sort of self together was a "constant struggle" against
sexual temptations. And these temptations, Martin Luther
warned, were everywhere:

> If no other work were commanded than chasteness, we
> would all have enough to do, so dangerous and raging a vice
> is unchasteness. It is furiously active in all our members: in
> the thinking of our heart, in the seeing of our eyes, in the
> hearing of our ears, in the speaking of our mouth, in the
> acting of our hands, our feet, and our entire body. To keep all
> of these under control calls for labor and exertion. . . .
> [Verene 1972, p. 143]

Meanwhile, the Counter-Reformation was imposing new
restrictions on sex in Catholic countries, though these were
less stringent than those imposed in Protestant countries.
Protestant countries have remained more hostile to sex than

Catholic countries because of the more fragile psychic structure created and maintained by the Protestant ethic, at least
until its recent decline.

After another hundred years or so of relative sexual freedom during the Restoration in England and the Enlightenment on the Continent, Jehovanism began to return toward
the end of the eighteenth century. Its most important
theoretician was the German philosopher Immanuel Kant
(1724–1804). Kant saw sex as undermining the essential distinction between human beings and beasts:

> All men and women do their best to make more alluring not
> their humanity but their sex, and direct their activities and
> lusts entirely toward the latter. Humanity is thereby sac-
> rificed to sex. . . . By making human nature an instrument to
> satisfy their lusts, they dishonor it by lowering it to the level of
> animal nature. Sexuality, therefore, exposes mankind to the
> danger of equality with beast. [1930, p. 164]

Kant, and the later Protestants generally, condemned sex for
motivating human beings to relate to each other as parts and
means rather than as wholes and ends.[3]

Kant's teaching, together with other social and cultural
factors,[4] produced the last great flowering of Jehovanism.
The sexual restrictions of this final surge were stronger in
England than in the rest of Europe throughout the reign of
Queen Victoria (1837–1901), that paragon of prudes. Its influence on Americans, despite their Puritan heritage, was
less than on the English until after the Civil War. The framers
of the First Amendment to the Constitution did not specifically include (or exclude) obscene materials because it never
occurred to them that such materials would ever be censored
(see Richards 1974, pp. 58, 75–76, on the enactment of
obscenity laws long after the Bill of Rights). During the late
1860s, however, the social reformer Anthony Comstock
(1844–1915) joined forces with the YMCA to enact and enforce antisexual legislation at both the state and federal
levels, much of which still remains on the books. By the end

of the century, Americans restricted sex even more stringently than the English, a situation that prevailed until the 1960s (*Report on the Commission on Obscenity and Pornography* 1970, p. 353).

Today, the Jehovanist arsenal of arguments against sex consists of all the allegations mentioned above, which allows them to bring out one or another as the moment demands. Thus Jehovanists can implicitly accuse sex of polluting the self (ancient Jews and early Christians), profaning its orientation (Hellenistic Christians), weakening its control (Augustine), inhibiting its fulfillment (Aquinas), disintegrating its integrity (early Protestants), or constricting its totality (Kant).

Until very recently, nearly all who grew up in Western society had this Jehovanist ethos impressed into them to some degree. Even those who think they have freed themselves from it intellectually might still be shocked emotionally were they to encounter its violation in fact rather than in theory. In everyday reality it is one thing to read about, say, bestiality; in erotic reality it is quite another thing to come face-to-snout with it.

Although Jehovanism proper has produced no original argument against sex since Kant, its critical thrust has continued in other forms. We may label "neo-Jehovanist" those utterances that express the antisexual impulse euphemistically without acknowledging its religious inspiration.

Michel Foucault (1980) contends that talk about sex was not completely curtailed during the centuries before Freud but was carried on in different languages, the Church monopoly over sexual discourse being dispersed to medicine, criminal justice, pedagogy, demography, biology, and psychiatry. But if sex was silenced in its former aspect and retranslated into other tongues, so was the Jehovanist critique of sex. The spreading of rationalism began to force Jehovanists to conceal the religious origins of their antisexual pronouncements. Eventually, a "closet" Jehovanism developed, becoming what Oscar Wilde might have called "the

fear of love that dare not speak its name." Each social institution and intellectual discipline Foucault describes appeared
to condemn sex in its own terms and for its own theoretical
and practical reasons, but the search of these disciplines for a
seemingly rational argument to justify an essentially emotional antipathy toward sex betrayed a Jehovanist influence
at base.

A similar neo-Jehovanism can now be found in those more
extreme members of the women's movement who have radi-
cally expanded the application of Jehovanism's egalitarian
component. Jehovanists have traditionally condemned only
certain sexual perversions (such as bondage, discipline, and
genetism) for being undemocratic; but these radical feminists condemn even normal heterosexual intercourse itself for
being undemocratic ("Women Up from Under!").[5] Although
they would probably prefer to think of their views as van-
guard rather than inspired by the spirit of an old-fashioned
fundamentalist religion, only the heirs to a puritanical ideology like Jehovanism would consider abolishing sex entirely
to end whatever taint of inequality there may be in it.

In chapter 5 we will examine two other lenses through
which sexual experience can be observed, which I will call
the "Gnostic" and the "Naturalist." Seen through these
other optics, sexual experience appears completely different
from the Jehovanist version. Gnostic and Naturalist world
views are not the only alternatives to Jehovanism, but they
are the most common ones in Western civilization. All three
world views, I should add, are "ideal types": although one is
usually dominant within a person, group, or entire society at
any given time, the others are likely to be present as well—
repressed, perhaps, but still competing.[6]

In chapter 6 we will examine the transitions from one
world view to another. Specifically, we will look at the sexual
theorists responsible for shifting paradigms, the theoretical
and practical compromises that each world view's disciples
must make with the adherents of other views, and the confusion of laymen who must muddle through these transitional
states as best they can.

5.

Sexual Ideologies: Moral, Immoral, Amoral

Sex in the Gnostic World View

*I*n sex, as in religion, it is difficult to understand those whose behavior or belief is different from one's own. Both sex and religion seem to require a choice among incompatible strategies for dealing with the fundamental issues of human existence.

Jehovanists regard everyone who refuses to go along with their sexual restrictions as sacrilegious. But only those who believe that they possess a monopoly on morality can entertain such a parochial conception of religion. Sexual activities that violate traditional sexual norms do not attack all religions—only the religion of Jehovanists. Sexual heretics are not necessarily without religion—they may simply worship at a different altar.

In this section we will consider the religious alternative of "Gnosticism," which sanctifies sex and all its associated phenomena as much as Jehovanism condemns them.[1] Pornographic books are its sacred texts, to be reread over and over for hidden implications that may have escaped earlier detection. Pornographic pictures are its sacred icons, to be collected, cared for, and contemplated in private. "Adult" theaters are its public temples.

Although attending an adult theater may seem far removed from attending a church service, their form is similar even if their content is different. In the "restrained" type of adult theater service, the "worshipers" sit in rapt attention, alternately involved with and alienated from the performance on stage or screen while meditating on their actual sex life, their potential sex life, and the gap between them. In the "enthused" or "pentecostal" type of adult theater service, the worshipers exclaim "God!" or "Jesus!" at revelations of the divine—which suddenly appear before them incarnate in erotic persons or organs.

The ancient religious tradition of Gnosticism took root in the Near East several thousand years ago, originally competing with Judaism and Christianity and eventually influencing certain sects within both religions. Although Gnosticism comes in many forms, most Gnostics postulate a cosmos similar to that of the Jehovanists. But they evaluate it negatively rather than positively, making Gnosticism almost the mirror image of Jehovanism.

Gnostic doctrines are difficult to describe. Very roughly, Gnostics believe that the phenomenal cosmos was created not by the supreme God but by another god—the god of the Jehovanists—who is evil, or at least inferior to the supreme God. Beyond this iniquitous or incompetent god who created human existence as we experience it there stands the true God, the discovery of whom is every Gnostic's goal. Behind the apparent physical structure of the universe—the so-called "laws of nature"—lies the true universe; behind the apparent psychological structure of the self in every individual—the so-called "laws of human nature"—lies the true self. Hans Jonas summarizes this complex conception in his classic study, *The Gnostic Religion*:

The theological aspect [of Gnostic doctrine] holds that the divine has no part in the concerns of the physical universe: that the true God, strictly transmundane, is not revealed or even indicated by the world, and is therefore the Unknown, the totally Other, unknowable in terms of any worldly analogies. Correspondingly, the cosmological aspect holds that the world is the creation not of God but of some inferior principle, whose inferiority is a perversion of the divine, and whose main traits are dominion and power. And the anthropological aspect holds that man's inner self is not part of the world, of the demiurge's creation and domain, but is within that world as totally transcendent and as incommensurate to all cosmic modes of being as is its transmundane counterpart, the unknown God without. [1963, pp. 251–52]

The true universe consists of the major portion of the divine substance; the true self consists of a small fragment of it. It is the task of every Gnostic to reunite his own small piece of the divine substance, which is hidden behind his false phenomenal self, with the larger piece of the divine substance, which is hidden behind the false phenomenal universe. Through this means the Gnostic overcomes the alienation or separation of the true God from Him/Herself, restoring the divine wholeness of which each Gnostic is (or has) a part. "Sparks" of the divine have been ensnared in every individual by the false phenomenal structure of the laws of nature and of human nature, and especially by the norms of society which are based on natural law. To free these fragments of the trapped God, therefore, Gnostics must violate social rules. This antinomian thrust of Gnosticism is designed to break up the customary psychic organizations and, if possible, the laws of nature that bind the divine spark (Jonas 1963, pp. 272–74).

If Jehovanists take the boundaries of their cosmos as guides, Gnostics hold them to be prison walls.

It is almost by exaggeration that [Gnostics turn] the divinity of cosmic order . . . into the opposite of divine. Order and law is

the cosmos here too, but rigid and inimical order, tyrannical
and evil law, devoid of meaning and goodness, alien to the
purposes of man and to his inner essence, no object for his
communication and affirmation. . . . Thus, the metaphysical
devaluation of the world extends to the conceptual root of the
cosmos-idea, that is, the concept of order itself. . . . "Cosmos" thus becomes . . . an emphatically negative
concept. . . . [Jonas 1963, p. 250]

Only by causing chaos in this claustrophobic cosmos can
Gnostics achieve their goal of enabling human beings to
shed the secular skins that conceal their sacred selves.

One important branch of Gnosticism tries to achieve this
goal by shattering social rules, psychic organizations, and
even natural laws, through sex. For these Gnostics, the
libertine is the savior of the universe for both human beings
and for the Godhead itself.[2] Sex is an especially appropriate
technique for freeing the entangled divine sparks because
the Gnostic supreme God is essentially sexual—unlike the
Judaic and Christian god, who does not engage in sex, and
unlike the Greek and Roman gods, who are only incidentally
sexual. In the Jewish version of Gnosticism—stemming from
the Cabala—the true God is a purely sexual being, in fact a
bisexual. In *Major Trends in Jewish Mysticism* (1961) Gershom
Scholem traced this Cabalistic development of sexual Gnosticism from its inception in the late Middle Ages, through its
dissemination by such prophets as Isaac Luria, Sabbatai
Zevi, and Jacob Frank, to its eventual contact with the main
tradition of Western thought during the Enlightenment.

The works of several prominent figures in the European
Enlightenment indicate descent from this libertine line of
Gnosticism: the autobiographical *Memoirs* of Giacomo Casa-
nova, the opera *Don Giovanni* of Wolfgang Amadeus Mozart,
the scandalous novel *Dangerous Liaisons* of Choderlos de
Laclos, and, above all, the voluminous pornography of the
Marquis de Sade (1740–1814).

In the Gnostic manner, de Sade attempts to undermine

the legitimacy of the cosmos by accusing the god who created it of being evil or inferior:

> "I believe," this dangerous woman answered, "that if there
> were a God there would be less evil on earth; I believe that
> since evil exists, these disorders are either expressly ordained
> by this God, and there you have a barbarous fellow, or he is
> incapable of preventing them and right away you have a
> feeble God; in either case, an abominable being, a being
> whose lightning I should defy and whose laws contemn."
> [1966, *Justine*, p. 698]

Having disposed of the Jehovanist god—the theological
linchpin of absolutist morality—de Sade can use the argument of anthropological relativism to attack the moral restrictions of Jehovanist society:

> Dolmance—Ah, be in no doubt of it, Eugénie, these words
> *vice* and *virtue* contain for us naught but local ideas. There is
> no deed . . . which is really criminal, none which may be
> really called virtuous. All is relative to our manners and the
> climate we inhabit; what is a crime here is often a virtue
> several hundred leagues hence, and the virtues of another
> hemisphere might well reverse themselves into crimes in our
> own. There is no horror that has not been consecrated some-
> where, no virtue that has not been blasted. When geography
> alone decides whether an action be worthy of praise or blame,
> we cannot attach any great importance to ridiculous and
> frivolous sentiments. . . . [1966, *Philosophy in the Bedroom*, pp.
> 217–18]

Ultimately, de Sade attacks nature itself:

> In everything we do there are nothing but idols offended and
> creatures insulted, but Nature is not among them, and it is
> she I should like to outrage. I should like to upset her plans,
> thwart her progress, arrest the wheeling courses of the stars,
> throw the spheres floating in space into mighty confusion,
> destroy what serves Nature and protect what is harmful to

her; in a word, to insult her in her works—and this I am
unable to do. [1966, quoted in Blanchot, p. 63][3]

De Sade's work can be read as a continual attempt to dig
through the Jehovanist world layer by layer to uncover the
divine sparks beneath its debris:

> Sade explains [that] . . . . "[Virtue] is illusory, a fiction; [vice] is
> authentic, real. . . .." Virtue . . . encloses us in a world of
> appearances; whereas vice's intimate link with the flesh
> guarantees its genuineness. [1967, de Beauvoir, p. 52]

In the psychological dimension, he recommends sexual ex-
cesses and perversions as well as other crimes, not merely
because they allow the expression of violent instincts but
because they allow the piercing of false selves and consequently the revelation of true ones:

> Pleasure's effects, in women, are always uncertain; often
> disappointing; it is, furthermore, very difficult for an old or
> ugly man to produce them. When it does happen that they are
> produced, they are feeble, and the nervous concussions
> fainter; hence, pain must be preferred, for pain's telling
> effects cannot deceive. . . . [1966, *Philosophy in the Bedroom*, p.
> 252]

The need to use these drastic techniques to strip off false
selves appears to be greater in times of much social pretence,
as the eighteenth century and perhaps today.

The influence of de Sade's brand of Gnostic sexuality has
been subterranean but tenacious. All but forgotten for nearly
seventy-five years, it resurfaced toward the end of the
nineteenth century in the French authors Joris Karl Huysmans (*Against Nature*) and Charles Baudelaire (*Flowers of
Evil*), and in the English authors Algernon Swinburne (*The
Whippingham Papers*) and Oscar Wilde (*The Picture of Dorian
Gray*). It became more widely disseminated during the twentieth century, especially in France by Georges Battaile (*Story
of the Eye*), Jean Genet (*Our Lady of the Flowers*), and Pauline

Réage (*Story of O*); and in America by Norman Mailer ("The Time of Her Time"), Lenny Bruce (*How to Talk Dirty and Influence People*), William Burroughs (*Naked Lunch*), John Rechy (*City of Night*), and Marco Vassi (*The Saline Solution*). Today, this Gnostic view of sex has even trickled down into mass culture in the pornographic magazine *Hustler* and in the aggressive bisexuality of such popular musicians as Mick Jagger, Alice Cooper, Tim Curry (of *The Rocky Horror Picture Show*), and recent devotees of "punk rock."

Like Jehovanists, these modern Gnostics see sex as evil, for it can destroy the self, the society, and even the universe. Unlike Jehovanists, they believe it should. Gnostics loathe the Jehovanist cosmos for its inhumanity. They are contemptuous of Jehovanists for accepting the limitations of the human condition. This accusation of inhumanity always disconcerts Jehovanists, who believe their cosmos is humane. But, for Gnostics, what Jehovanists regard as "humane" is only a dead crust that must be removed. Consequently, Gnostics like Marco Vassi have suggested various means of pealing away this outer, falsely human self in order to reveal the inner, truly human self:

> I formulated the notion that this was the essence of revolution: the realization that one has had one's humanity robbed by the civilization one lives in, and the effort to break through the conditioning to some fullness of expression, no matter what form it takes, whether it is fighting at the barricades or wallowing in orgy houses. [1976b, p. 161]

The main Gnostic technique to decorticate the false self from the true is extreme forms of sex. Although Susan Sontag does not mention Gnosticism by name in her essay "The Pornographic Imagination" (1970), it is clearly the religious tradition that lies behind the French pornography she analyzes, for she points out that these works also treat sex as a means to transcend ordinary—"false"—consciousness:

> Such is the understanding of sexuality—as something beyond good and evil, beyond love, beyond sanity; as a

resource . . . for breaking through the limits of consciousness—that informs the French literary canon I've been
discussing. [1970, p. 58]

The more extreme the sex act, the more effectively it
breaks through the psychological, social, and other barriers
that prevent the true self from merging with the true God.
Sontag (1970, p. 68) observes that Pauline Réage's *Story of O*
is an "ascesis"; the extreme sexual activities portrayed in it
are actually a spiritual discipline leading to salvation. We can
read the *Story of O* as a Gnostic attempt to strip away the
inessential outer self layer by layer in order to lay bare the
essential inner self. One by one, the heroine relinquishes the
objects and activities in which her false earthly self is embodied—her clothes (she is stripped), her freedom of movement (she is bound), her vision (she is blindfolded), her
power of speech (she is gagged), etc. Through this degrada-
tion of her false earthly self by sexual humiliations and even
physical torture, she experiences the exaltation of her true
spiritual self. (The more "altruistic" characters in de Sade
provide similar services for others.)

We saw in part two that sexual arousal increases people's
vulnerability by weakening the defenses that protect their
identity. The most effective way for Gnostics to pierce what
they see as the false outer self, then, is through seduction or
rape. Having forced open psychological gates by compelling
sexual arousal, they often employ sexual perversions to
break up the Jehovanist social organization and interaction
patterns that had previously stabilized the "victim's" identity. They forcibly join members of social categories that
Jehovanists try to keep apart—such as women and dogs—
through interaction linkages that involve too intense an impression for Jehovanists to tolerate—as do mouths or whips.
They copulate with persons especially revered by Jehovanists, such as children or virgins,[4] in order to corrode particularly vulnerable ("impressionable") identities. Conversely,
they may copulate with those especially taboo to Jehovanists, such as freaks or prostitutes, in order to erode their

own undesirable identities. Gnostics intend all these extreme ("outrageous") sexual activities to delegitimize the Jehovanist prototype of the person, and thus the entire Jehovanist cosmic scheme.

The main vehicle by means of which Gnostics express their contempt for the Jehovanist order is pornography. Pornography reveals the fundamental organization of the Jehovanist world by portraying its sexual disorganization. Everything prohibited by Jehovanists is permitted—even encouraged—in pornography, particularly the sexual transfer of identity components between social entities whose coital conjunction is forbidden. Susan Sontag observes that these interchanges pervade pornography:

> All action is conceived of as a set of sexual *exchanges*. Thus, the reason why pornography refuses to make fixed distinctions between the sexes or allow any kind of sexual preference or sexual taboo to endure can be explained "structurally." The bisexuality, the disregard for the incest taboo, and other similar features common to pornographic narratives function to multiply the possibilities of exchange. Ideally, it should be possible for everyone to have sexual connection with everyone else. [1969, pp. 66–67][5]

Gnostics, then, employ all forms of sexuality, normal and perverted, to attack the major axes of the Jehovanist cosmos. They thus use sex in precisely the way Jehovanists fear it could be used—as a weapon to batter away at the foundations of the Jehovanist universe at its weakest points.

We can now see that feminists who criticize pornography for being "antiwoman" (see especially Andrea Dworkin [1981]) have too narrow a view of what it is "anti." Female characters are not the only ones sexually abused and humiliated in pornography; male characters are commonly exploited as well. Pornography, at least "serious" pornography, is not specifically antiwoman but more generally antihuman and antisocial, for it attacks a conception of humanity and society that Gnostics find oppressive. Pornography is extremely democratic in that it strips the false façades from everyone, not just from women; it peels away the crust of character formed by society or even by the human condition itself to reveal people's authentic inner core.

The Gnostic goal is *knowledge*; specifically, the knowledge that the Jehovanist organization of the world, of society, and of the self is evil or at best unreal. (Gnostics have always despised Jehovanists not only for creating a stupefying cosmos but also for restricting, through sexual censorship, the very knowledge necessary to see through it.) Modern sexual Gnostics like Colin Wilson and Marco Vassi describe sex, particularly its extreme forms, as a way to achieve this consciousness. For Colin Wilson (1966), sex allows awareness of the "alien-ness" of other human beings by overcoming it, however temporarily. Sexual perversions broaden awareness of the "alien-ness" of more aspects of the human world by multiplying the number of taboo social barriers that can also be overcome. For Marco Vassi, this wisdom is the common goal of those who participate in every kind of sexual debauch:

THE FIST FUCKER
By virtue of having lived in the realm of excess, where others were too fearful to venture, he had attained a depth of awareness that set him apart from the human herd.

THE SHIT EATER
I saw that coprophiliacs . . . were probably the only people who had the courage to face, in total depth, the primitive taboo that binds us all and which, once broken, is revealed as little more than a function of communication and curiosity.

THE DRAG QUEEN
I imagine most of us have at one time or another met a drag queen whose presence was so astonishing that we felt compelled to bow acquiescence to that power. It is extraordinary to look upon a facade which partakes of the depraved and the grotesque and see behind it a profound and fierce intelligence. It is what makes so many of us nervous with such people, for they throw a glaring light on the absurdity of

social identity. . . . And they force us . . . to question whether
we have been too fearful to become ourselves most fully.
[1976b, pp. 93, 155, 142–43]

In short, Gnostics believe that every social activity should
have "redeeming erotic importance," should violate some
regulatory principle of the Jehovanist cosmos in order to
reveal its true nature.

Sex in the Naturalist World View

Both Jehovanists and Gnostics see sex as "dirty," as disorganizing the fundamental categories of human existence.
They differ only in their reaction: the chaos that sex spreads
horrifies the dirt-avoiding Jehovanists but delights the dirt-
embracing Gnostics.

But sex need not be considered dirty. An alternative interpretation that sanitizes sex—popularly called the "new
morality"—has become increasingly prevalent. The intellectual historian Paul Robinson calls it the "modernization of
sex" to emphasize its connection with other intellectual and
cultural shifts that have taken place during roughly the first
half of the twentieth century (1977, pp. 1–2). I will call this
view of sex "Naturalism" to emphasize its connection with a
broader historical tradition that interprets sexual phenomena in terms of nature rather than in terms of the
sacred.[6] In contrast to Jehovanists and Gnostics, Naturalists
regard sex as no big deal, but simply as a part of everyday
life, something without repercussions in higher spheres.
The following mail advertisement for *At Home: The Magazine
of Sexual Fullfillment* illustrates this Naturalist tendency to
regard sex as an ordinary biological process like eating or
drinking:

AT HOME was thought of to treat the sexual outlooks of life
today with the same openness and frankness as any other
appetite. Magazines such as BON APPETIT, GOURMET, ARCHI-
TECTURAL DIGEST, VOGUE and others provide creative ideas in

terms of sensual gratification—food, fashion, home decor and other interests—so why not a publication devoted to sexual awareness in all these areas?

Although this Naturalist view of sex has flourished during the modern period, it is not without antecedents—all of whose proponents, unlike Jehovanists and Gnostics, saw sex as a positive and benign activity. In the primitive matrix out of which Naturalism eventually developed, human sex was part of the great cosmic cycle of birth and rebirth experienced by all living things. It was both a biological and a religious activity, whose processes paralleled and reenforced the great cyclic order of creation (Ricoeur 1964, pp. 133–34; Taylor 1973, pp. 225–26). The later Greek and Roman conception of sex descended directly from this primitive view but deemphasized its religious side, coming to see sex more as a merely biological activity largely[7] detached from the sacred (Taylor 1973, pp. 225, 237–38). Sex in classical civilization led neither to the gods, as it had for the primitives, nor away from them, as it would for the Jehovanists.

After being almost totally eclipsed by Jehovanism during most of the Middle Ages, the Naturalist interpretation of sex reappeared among the "earthy" writers of the late Middle Ages and the Renaissance like Boccaccio (1313–75), Chaucer (1340?–1400), and Rabelais (1494?–1553). Since the Renaissance, the influence of Naturalism has risen or fallen in roughly one-hundred-year cycles: falling in the seventeenth century, rising in the eighteenth, falling in the nineteenth, and rising again in the twentieth. Later Naturalist authors like John Cleland in the eighteenth century (author of *Fanny Hill*), Walt Whitman in the nineteenth, and D. H. Lawrence and Henry Miller in the twentieth were often mistaken for dangerous Gnostics. Naturalism's inherent lack of drama, however, renders it unsuitable for many kinds of art. In the twentieth century, therefore, some writers of fiction, as we saw in the last section, did begin to take a more Gnostic approach to sex; but their place was usurped by writers of "nonfiction," like Havelock Ellis, Sigmund Freud, Alfred

Kinsey, and Masters and Johnson, who treated sex from the Naturalist perspective. In the last few decades social scientists have become the main advocates of the Naturalist world view. Magazine publishers like Hugh Hefner (*Playboy*) and Al Goldstein (*Screw*), along with the health and nudist movements, have popularized these Naturalist interpretations of sex.

These later Naturalists are divided between moderates, who tolerate sex, and radicals, who venerate it. Moderate Naturalists find most forms of sex "not harmful"; radical Naturalists find them actually beneficial, particularly for mental health. The sexually enthusiastic radical Naturalists tend to criticize the sexually sober moderate Naturalists even more than the Jehovanists. As the radical Naturalist Robert de Ropp puts it in his book *Sex Energy*:

> Our "sexual revolution" . . . has certainly freed many people from the phantoms that haunted their grandparents. But it has failed to restore to us the joyous Dionysian attitude toward sexual phenomena that characterized the peoples of the Ancient World. [1969, p. 195]

Modern Naturalism is the heir of several historical trends, which have given its conception of copulation a distinct character. Like many formerly sacred activities, sex has been caught up in the process of *secularization*, which has severed its spiritual ties (Gagnon and Simon 1973, pp. 304–5). Thus the most important principle of modern Naturalist metaphysics is that sex has no metaphysics. Sex has none of the tremendous cosmic meaning for modern Naturalists that it has for Jehovanists and Gnostics. Moreover, unlike primitives and to a lesser extent the ancient Greeks and Romans, modern Naturalists no longer regard sex with even a sense of wonder.[8]

A related historical development—*materialization*—disconnected sex from psychological experience. Beginning with the Cartesian distinction between body and mind (or soul or self), the physical aspects of phenomena increased in importance relative to their psychological aspects (Burtt 1954). As all phenomena became "embodied" in this way, conceptions of sex changed correspondingly. Formerly thought to involve both physical and psychological properties, sex came to be seen more as a physical behavior than as a mental experience. The Enlightenment rationalist Sebastien Chamfort even went so far as to describe it as merely the "contact of two epidermises."[9]

Modern Naturalists equate the entire phenomenon of human sexual intercourse not merely with human behavior, but, more generally and fundamentally, with animal behavior. The last hundred years have seen the rise of natural scientists who believed that biological qualities are "more real" than psychological and social qualities. Their *biologism* has strongly influenced the modern conception of sex, particularly through the founder of American sex research, Alfred Kinsey. Kinsey (who began his career as a zoologist) did not consider human sexual activity to differ essentially from animal sexual activity—a sharp contrast to Jehovanists. Consequently, Kinsey could replace human criteria for evaluating various sexual activities—"normal" and "abnormal"—with criteria derived from animal observations—"natural" and "unnatural" (Trilling 1953, pp. 225–26; Robinson 1977, pp. 55–56). Reducing the entire phenomenon of human sexual intercourse to human sexual behavior obscures the mental component of sex; reducing it still further to animal sexual behavior obliterates it.

As social scientists began to conceive of human beings as basically the same as natural objects, they began to study them more and more with the "objective" procedures of the natural sciences. *Positivism* in natural science was translated into *behaviorism* in social science. Since sexual behavior lends itself to being studied by natural scientific methods far more easily than other sexual dimensions, positivistic sex researchers came to believe that it is the only aspect of sex worth investigating. They minimized the significance of sexual experience by redefining it as "predispositions to act in specific ways" and by relegating its study to surveys of sexual "attitudes." They wrote books with "sexual behavior" or "sexual conduct" or "sexual response" in their titles, emphasizing the external features of the sex act rather than its internal experience. One reason that Jehovanists (including at least one member of the Commission itself) rejected the government's *Report of the Commission on Obscenity and Pornography* (1970) was that almost all the resources drawn on by this commission were Naturalist studies of sexual behavior, which Jehovanists felt investigated only the surface of sex instead of its essence. Naturalist sex researchers do often write as though they have frequently observed sexual intercourse but have never performed it; otherwise they would have been obliged to reorder their research priorities to account for the fact that copulators themselves usually[10] regard their inner sexual experience as much more important than their outer sexual behavior. But perhaps at least the more astute researchers equate copulation with conduct less as a theoretical strategy for understanding sex, than as a political strategy for raising its status in our society, for the chaotic potential of sex lies elsewhere than in its innocuous behavior.

Naturalists employ other rhetorical tactics to counter the Jehovanist conception of sex as evil. For instance, they often try to expose as "myths" Jehovanist beliefs about the harmfulness of various sexual activities, such as the "myths about masturbation" or the "myths about homosexuality." (But they seem unaware that, with the increasing influence of Jungian psychology and Levi-Straussian anthropology, the term "myth" has begun to lose its negative connotation of an "illusion" while gaining the positive connotation of an "abstruse but fundamental truth.")

Naturalists also collect large numbers of biological, anthropological, and historical sexual oddities to try to refute the Jehovanist assumption that few of God's creatures copulate in illicit ways. By expanding awareness of the range of sexual behaviors actually performed by different species and in different societies at different periods, they hope to expand standards for the human sexual behaviors tolerated in Western civilization today.

But Naturalists go further than simply denying that forbidden forms of sexuality are rare in other times and places; they also assert that such forms are common even in our society. As Lionel Trilling observed (1953, p. 216), Kinsey's studies of male sexual behavior demonstrated the prevalence in American society of what many men had previously believed to be their own private vices, such as masturbation or homosexuality. Recent studies of female masturbation, such as *The Hite Report* (Hite 1976), have had the same effect on women. Sexual surveys are thus far from being the neutral reports they appear, for they do not merely describe current opinions and actions but actually influence future ones.[11] (This consequence may tempt researchers to omit or alter findings that contradict their ideology.) In a democratic society, any activity performed by numerous people may be legitimized ipso facto. Therefore, social researchers may increase the number of people who engage in a previously forbidden activity just by demonstrating that many are already doing it.

Since Western societies are hierarchical as well as democratic, Naturalists can weaken Jehovanist sexual proscriptions still further by showing that the transgressors are not only numerous but have high status as well. Havelock Ellis pointed out that many homosexuals have led distinguished careers and that many masturbators have been the pillars of their community (1936, vol. 1: *Sexual Inversion, Auto-Eroticism*). *Playboy* magazine transformed America's midcentury cultural conception of sex from that of a lower-class activity spawned by idleness to that of a leisure activity enjoyed by the elite (Gerson and Lund 1971).

By claiming that copulation is only a physical behavior, Naturalists attack implicitly the Jehovanist assumption that identity is fundamentally involved in intercourse. Sometimes, in fact, they explicitly accuse those who fear that sex will affect the psyche of being "sick."[12] Nonetheless, even behaviorists must have some conception of the self that sex is supposed to have no effect on.

To make their views on sex consistent, Naturalists must ground them in a self whose internal structure is amorphous or "fluid" (see Kilpatrick 1975, esp. pp. 41–79). They must see the self as a loose open system, without integrity, continually modifying itself to mirror its environment. Unlike the "rigid" self that resists change, presupposed by both Jehovanists and Gnostics, the Naturalist self adapts easily. On the other hand, sexual input does not stick to the Naturalist self, as it does to the more adhesive Jehovanist and Gnostic self. Identity components of sex partners flow out of this Naturalist self as easily as they flow in, leaving little trace after their departure. Metaphors for the Jehovanist and Gnostic self are rock and flypaper; metaphors for the Naturalist self are rubber and teflon.

The combination of rigidity and receptivity makes the Jehovanist self very precarious, very susceptible to sexual pollution. (The Gnostic self is less susceptible; when Gnostics want to pollute themselves or others sexually, they have to work at it.) In contrast, the rubbery teflon self of the Naturalists cannot be contaminated by copulation, for that self has no persisting and adhesive psychic structure for sex to subvert.

This conception of identity conditions the entire Naturalist view of sex. They are not bothered by nudity, for instance, because they find that the genitals fit into the rest of the body as comfortably as the parts of the identity are integrated into the whole. Jehovanists and Gnostics, by contrast, find the genitals a stark flaw in the otherwise perfect form of the body, just as sexual desire is incompatable with the otherwise inelastic organization of the self. Nor do Naturalists find nudist camps and beaches inevitably erotic places, unlike Jehovanists and Gnostics. The Naturalists who frequent San Diego's Blacks Beach, for example, are aroused by its thousands of totally nude bathers far less than the Gnostics who flock to New York's Times Square area are aroused by its relatively few fully clothed prostitutes. The small number of Gnostics who wander around Blacks Beach with blatant erections appall its Naturalist crowd, who believe the eroticizing power of nudity is, and ought to be, low. (On Blacks Beach, see Douglas and Rasmussen 1977).

Moreover, since Naturalists do not believe in subjective connections between individuals, they do not fear the diffusion of sexual contamination through intersubjective linkages. In a case involving university recognition of a homosexual rights organization, Supreme Court Justice William Rehnquist observed that the (Jehovanist) university saw homosexuality as a potential spreader of infection whereas the (Naturalist) Gay Union did not:

> He noted that to the Gay Union, denying recognition was just as offensive as approving a college Democratic club but disapproving a college Republican club. The university's viewpoint, he said, "is more akin to whether those suffering from measles have a constitutional right, in violation of quarantine regulations, to associate together and with others who do not presently have measles. . . ." [*Los Angeles Times*, 22 February 1978, part 1, p. 12]

If copulation does not contaminate others psychologically, there is no need to contain it sociologically. Therefore, Naturalists can advocate nonmarital sex—that is, sex uninsulated from society by marriage. More radical Naturalists approve of sex outside any intimate relation at all, even love relations.

Naturalists fear perverted sex as little as normal sex. They are unconcerned about the different ways people copulate, or the different partners with whom they copulate, because any identity component encountered during intercourse can depart from the open system of the self as easily as it entered. Since foreign components do not become permanent parts of the identity, Naturalists, unlike Jehovanists, do not feel it necessary to distinguish privileged sexual modes and partners from proscribed ones. So where Jehovanists posit sharp distinctions between differences in kind, Naturalists can posit smooth continuity between differences in degree (see, for instance, Kinsey 1948, pp. 199–201). And what Jehovanists call "sexual perversions" to distinguish them from normal sex, Naturalists can call "sexual variations" to equate them with normal sex.

Nearly all sexual receptors are equal for Naturalists.[13] Unlike Jehovanists, who see oral and anal sex as qualitatively different from genital sex, Freud was the first modern Naturalist to regard all three of them as on the same dimension, as merely occurring during different stages of childhood psychosexual development—although he still believed that genital sex is superior to the others because it is more "mature" (1972, pp. 66–106). Post-Freudians, like Norman O. Brown (1959, pp. 27ff), completed the democratization of these sexual modes by attacking the vestiges of hierarchy that remain in Freud as the "tyranny" of genital dominance.

Naturalists also regard nearly all sexual objects as equal.[14] They have attempted to demonstrate that it does not matter whether one copulates with things or beasts, oneself or many others, ingroups or outgroups. Fetishism or bestiality, masturbation or promiscuity, incest[15] or miscegenation are in no way inferior to "normal" sex with a single, human, extra-familial partner of the same race. Paul Robinson describes how one Naturalist knocked down the taxonomical distinctions that Jehovanists have erected between different kinds of sex:

> The notion of outlet thus allowed Kinsey to bring off a remarkable feat of sexual leveling, and although he was elsewhere to reveal a lingering loyalty to the regime of marital heterosexuality, the fundamental categories of his analysis clearly worked to undermine the traditional sexual order.
> Kinsey called the sum of the orgasms obtained from all sources "total sexual outlet." This concept, too, may have been inspired by a desire to put heterosexual intercourse in its place. It strongly implied that all orgasms were equal, regardless of how one came by them, and that there were accordingly no grounds for placing heterosexual intercourse in a privileged position. [1977, in 58–59]

Sex, as we have seen, is an extremely powerful solvent, capable of dissolving the sturdiest partitions between fundamental categories of existence. Its caustic qualities are neutralized by only one kind of cosmos—one without any solid boundaries for sex to subvert. Only if psychological and physical forms are already indistinct will sex not blur their borders; only if distances of interaction are already variable will sex not shift their grooves; only if locations along the biological, anthropological, and sociological dimensions are already indeterminant will sex not dislocate their places. Such then must be the Naturalist image of the person, of society, and of their relation: an amorphous ball of wax bobbing to and fro on a boundless sea of flux.

The rise of this Naturalist world view in modern society has paralleled the decline of Jehovanist sexual distinctions—penis and vagina versus the rest of the anatomy, genital sex versus nongenital sex, human versus animal, male versus female, heterosexual versus homosexual, madonna versus whore, sex in marriage versus sex outside of marriage. The decline of these former sexual distinctions refutes the idea that *differentiation* is the essential characteristic of modern society, as Herbert Spenser, Emile Durkheim, and Talcott Parsons have argued.[16] These sociologists can make such a claim only by assuming that the economic segment of society stands for the whole. But even though economic differentiation may be increasing, sexual differentiation is unquestionably decreasing. Alexis de Tocqueville, Ortega y Gasset, and Dwight MacDonald have argued that the essential characteristic of modern society is dedifferentiation or *similarization*. These mass-society and mass-culture theorists are closer to the mark if we equate all of society with its sexual segment. The most that can be said about modern society as a whole, without these synecdoches, is that some differentiations—particularly sexual ones—are collapsing while other differentiations—particularly economic ones—are emerging.

Increasing sexual differentiation seems to have the unintended consequence of intensifying sexual desire. The more carnal categories one can transgress, the more erotic tension one will experience. Thus Jehovanists, who multiplied the copulatory modes and objects that are forbidden, came to see eroticism as self-reinforcing. Since the slightest smidgen of smut greatly magnifies their erotic excitement, they are forced to suppress sexual stimulation as much as possible. But the more they try, the stronger it grows. Abstinence, many Jehovanists find, makes the heart grow fonder.

Conversely, decreasing sexual differentiation seems to have the unintended consequence of diminishing sexual desire. Fewer taboos to violate leads to less erotic tension. Thus Naturalists, who forbid far fewer sexual modes and objects, have come to see eroticism as self-limiting. The more sexual stimulation one receives beyond a certain point, the less erotic excitement one will experience. This saturation model of sex prompts Naturalists to predict that those free to receive as much sexual stimulation as they wish will soon find their erotic response blunted by boredom. Consequently, if Jehovanists are trying to reduce sexuality, Naturalists believe they are going about it the wrong way. In response to a Supreme Court decision allowing censorship of pornography, Cris Chase suggested:

> Force every movie house in America to show nothing but dirty movies; at the end of six months, audiences would be sneaking down to their bootleggers to catch "Little Women." [*The New York Times*, 5 August 1973, section II, p. 1]

Having reduced copulation to behavior and having permitted it in any way with anyone or even anything, Naturalists are often surprised to discover that they have succeeded in weakening sexual motivation itself. Those who no longer feel that their sexual behavior transgresses major taboos may find that their sexual desire is no longer reinforced by psychological, social, or cosmic overtones. Already some have even begun to wonder, "If sex isn't dirty anymore, why bother to do it?"

We might expect Naturalists to rejoice over this lessening of sexual desire. After all, they have always tried to minimize its social effects in order to counter Jehovanists, who characterize it as a monstrous threat. With the major exception of Freud, Naturalists have tried to show that Jehovanists have exaggerated concern about the social destructiveness of sex. Sexual desire, Naturalists believe, is too weak a force to be dangerously antisocial, less of a raging menace than a paper tiger (see, for instance, Gagnon and Simon 1967).

But on the personal level, Naturalists see an active sex life as essential for mental health. As one of their body's natural functions, sexual desire must be expressed for human beings to fulfill their potential. Consequently, insufficient sexual motivation is as much of an affliction for Naturalists as excessive sexual motivation is for Jehovanists. If restraining sexual arousal has been problematic for Jehovanists, inciting it has become problematic for Naturalists.[17] Thus Naturalists have managed to replace the old "sin" of giving into sexual desire with the new "sickness" of not having enough sexual desire to give into—a dubious improvement.

Conclusion

Unlike Jehovanists, both Gnostics and Naturalists like sex. But Gnostics admire it because it is evil, because it undermines a morality they believe to be false, whereas Naturalists accept it because it is harmless, there being no fixed morality for sex to subvert. Susan Sontag perceptively points out that (Gnostic) pornographers continue to see sex as a destructive force, in opposition to the (Naturalist) position prevailing today:

> The complex of views held by most educated members of the community [assumes] . . . that human sexual appetite is, if untampered with, a naturally pleasant function; and that "the obscene" is [merely] a convention. . . . It's just these assumptions that are challenged by the French tradition represented by Sade, Lautreamont, Bataille, and the authors of the *Story of O* and *The Image*. Their work suggests that "the obscene" is a

primal notion of human consciousness, something much more profound than the backwash of a sick society's aversion to the body. Human sexuality . . . belongs . . . among the extreme rather than the ordinary experiences of humanity. Tamed as it may be, sexuality remains one of the demonic forces in human consciousness—pushing us at intervals close to taboo and dangerous desires, which range from the impulse to commit sudden arbitrary violence upon another person to the voluptuous yearning for the extinction of one's consciousness, for death itself. [1970, pp. 56–57]

Gnostics feel even greater contempt for Naturalists than for Jehovanists. Jehovanists, who restrict the sexual knowledge that Gnostics seek for salvation, at least believe it is important enough to restrict. But Naturalists allow this sexual knowledge to be freely disseminated because they believe it is trivial. Since no true cosmos exists for them behind the physical cosmos, and since no true self exists for them behind the phenomenal self, they do not see how any information can help people transcend their situation spiritually. Gnostics often complain that Naturalists are cheapening their sacred, hard-won, carnal knowledge by making sex and its perversions seem too wholesome. Marco Vassi, for instance, objects to recent attempts to remove the stigma from homosexuality:

There is no reason why homosexual encounters must dispense with all elements of perversity. I am not at all certain that the gay militants, in their historically necessary role of changing homosexuals' consciousness, have not insinuated an idealized wholesomeness into the homophile mystique. For myself, I still have a sweet tooth for certain kinds of depravity. [1976b, p. 146]

The difference between Jehovanist, Gnostic, and Naturalist world views is most apparent in the ways each treats the relation between sex and violence. Both activities threaten the self through the body. (Etymologically, "fuck" is related to "feud.") Punching and strangling, like sex, embody the self by transforming the body into an object. Knifing and shooting, again like sex, rupture the self by breaking the body's boundary. Sex and violence, however, occur at different psychological intervals. As we have seen, people attempt to merge mentally with their sex partners, but they attempt to distance themselves mentally from their violence partners even as they clash together physically.

Jehovanists are better able to tolerate violence than sex because violence does less damage to their highly integrated (some would say "uptight") conception of the self. By widening the psychic interval between individuals, centrifugal violence sharpens individual selves. But by narrowing the psychic interval between individuals, centripetal sex defuses individual selves. Since self-integrity is more basic to their view of the world than even bodily existence, Jehovanists fear the ability of sex to disintegrate the self far more than the ability of violence to destroy the body. Thus they are far more likely to censor sex (and associated phenomena such as nudity) than violence, for what is one human life—or even a few million—when a world view is at stake?

Officials at some TV stations affliated with NBC want the network to cut two brief scenes containing frontal nudity from its upcoming 9½ hour limited series, "Holocaust," which deals with the Nazi extermination of Jews during World War II.

Representatives of the NBC affiliates . . . were told by programming Chief Paul Klein that the two scenes last only about two seconds each and were in no way salacious. One involves an authentic photograph of Jewish women forced to disrobe before being killed and the other is a piece of dramatic action in which elderly women are being marched to their death. Klein said the point is to show how the women were humiliated before they were murdered.

Several members of the affiliates' delegation urged the network not to use the footage. One said the material would offend many viewers, particularly in the Midwest. . . . [*Los Angeles Times*, 8 March 1978, part iv, p. 20]

In contrast, Naturalists are continually condemning violence (and associated phenomena such as weapons) while condoning sex. For example, the columnist Mike Royko:

> One of the interesting things I've noticed about the first wave of censorship since the Supreme Court decision is that it has come in several of the states where gun controls of any kind get the citizens most outraged.
>
> How did Americans develop such a great affection for .45 caliber pistols and such a great fear of genitalia?
>
> On the Fourth of July, a recent immigrant from Yugoslavia sat in his suburban apartment shooting a pistol out his window, not knowing where the bullets might go. . . .
>
> One of the bullets struck a young boy, who said a few words to his father, then fell dead.
>
> The immigrant had bought the gun at a suburban gun shop. . . .
>
> Had his interest been pornography and had he spent the day reading dirty books, that little boy would be alive.
>
> But most of the fig-leaf people would consider an "Adult Book Store" more dangerous than a place that sells pistols to any goof who walks into the place. . . . [*Chicago Daily News*, 10 July 1973, p. 3]

Naturalists dislike violence not only because it damages the body, which they value more than do the Jehovanists, but also because it attacks their loosely integrated (some would say "hang-loose") conception of self. Naturalists are averse to the way violence forces the self to tighten up whereas they extol the way sex allows it to relax.

Today, our society schizophrenically regards sex and violence as alternatives for cultural depiction, especially in films and television. As romance and action pictures gave way to sex and violence pictures, Jehovanists and Naturalists began to differ over which activity should be censored.[18] The activity actually expurgated indicated the dominance of Jehovanists or Naturalists over a particular medium at a particular time.

Ten years ago, a network censor forced a writer to change a scene in which a man beat up a woman off screen. The censor insisted that the man abuse the woman in front of the cameras. Otherwise, the audience, hearing the woman scream, might think she was being raped. Today—with consumer groups monitoring and protesting television violence—it is the rape that appears in front of the cameras and the violence that must disappear into the next room. [Harmetz 1978, p. 10]

One development that has recently strained the traditional opposition of Naturalists to sexual censorship is the appearance of "snuff movies." Here, it is alleged, actors and actresses are actually murdered for the erotic edification of their audience:

Many are drawing the line at *Snuff*, a wretched soft-core movie in which a woman is eviscerated and sawed to pieces by a sadistic gang leader apparently modeled on Charles Manson. (Though the advertising implies the woman was actually murdered, it is a hoax.) "If anything should be censored," says Psychologist Wardell Pomeroy, co-author with Alfred Kinsey of *Sexual Behavior in the Human Female*, "*Snuff* would head the list." The movie was banned in Baltimore, Wilmington, Del., and Orange County, Calif. In New York City, protestors picketed the theater showing *Snuff*. Such fledgling porn fighters as Critic Susan Sontag, Historian Martin Duberman and Author Grace Paley demanded censorship and prosecution. [*Time*, 5 April 1976, p. 62]

Snuff movies are made by and for Gnostics, being part of their quest for authenticity—for presumably no human expressions are less phony, less distorted by concern for social convention, than those of the dying. All Gnostic cultural productions attempt to violate Jehovanist self structure and social organization. Since these patterns are so entrenched, however, they can be affected only by the most extreme acts committed at the most vulnerable moment. Reason enough, Gnostics feel, to portray the perpetration of violence upon the sexually aroused.

Gnostics operate in the free space that Naturalists have cleared by limiting sexual censorship, much to the embarrassment of Naturalists who feel that Gnostics give sex a bad name.[19] To the consternation of both Jehovanists and Naturalists, then, Gnostics like *both* sex *and* violence—actively encouraging any activity that combines the extreme vulnerability of sex with the extreme aggression of violence, such as sadomasochism or rape.[20]

As idealists, Jehovanists react more violently to any attack on their conception of the cosmos than on their society. Political freedom, which may result in social anarchy, is bad; but sexual freedom, which may result in cosmic chaos, is far worse. In fact, Jehovanists fear political freedom precisely because it may lead to sexual freedom. An interview with California State Senator John Briggs, proponent of an anti-homosexual ballot proposition, demonstrates how much Jehovanists admire totalitarian societies—even Communist ones—that have banned sexual perversions:

> Interviewer: What has led to the ultimate destruction of civilization?
>
> Briggs   : What has? Oh, homosexuality [and] a permissive attitude.
>
> Interviewer: You say that the free world is where this problem is, and in the Communist world they don't have this. . . .
>
> Briggs   : Yes, because the government there believes that it is not healthy for the nation. But in this country, these people are protected by the Supreme Court. . . .
>
> Interviewer: Does[n't] that make the Communist countries less free, because they ban homosexuality? . . .
>
> Briggs   : Less free? No, but it makes them stronger.
> [*Los Angeles Times* 6 October 1978, pp. 26–27]

As materialists, Naturalists respond more vehemently to any attack on their society than on their nebulous conception of the cosmos. It is bad enough for sexual repression to result in cosmic (or moral) absolutism; it is far worse for political

repression to result in social authoritarianism. In fact, Naturalists fear sexual repression precisely because it may lead to
political repression, as a Chicago attorney, Patrick Tuite,
argues:

> The great danger in censorship of pornography is that history
> has shown it does not stop there. Instead, in the name of
> "good government" or "national security" or any of the other
> euphemisms used today, censorship will reach into areas
> such as criticism of government or exposure of corruption.
> [*Chicago Tribune*, 1 July 1973, section 2, p. 3]

Thus the "spreading contamination" model underlies the
outlook of Naturalists as much as of Jehovanists, only the
former fear the spread of censorship whereas the latter fear
the spread of what is censored. Jehovanists and Naturalists,
then, view sex and politics, freedom and repression, in irre-
concilable ways. Having constructed the world out of different building blocks, they worry about its collapsing in opposite directions.

6.

Sex at the Interstices of Ideologies

In the "real world," of course, ideological perspectives are not compartmentalized so neatly as the above discussion implies. The "ideal types" of Jehovanism, Gnosticism, and Naturalism are merely divisions in an analytic scheme designed to differentiate cognitive tendencies that are jumbled together in actuality. But the existential confusion of these ideal types itself has consequences for their agents, their arguments, their applications, and their adherents. In this chapter we will examine how the hodgepodge of reality affects the purity of ideology.

Transitional Theorists

There has been much dispute about the major sexual theorists of the last hundred years concerning just how "modern" their sexual theories actually are. Sometimes they sound contemporary, at other times more traditional. We can determine their degree and kind of modernity more precisely by comparing their views on particular aspects of sex with the tenets of the ideologies we have been considering.

The major nineteenth- and twentieth-century sexual theorists in the social sciences have not been pure Naturalists; their doctrines are more accurately characterized as transitional between Jehovanism and Naturalism. The earliest, Richard von Krafft-Ebing (1840–1902), was nearer to the pure Jehovanist pole. Although he was the first social researcher to investigate sex scientifically (or at least systematically) in the Naturalist manner, his major work, *Psychopathia Sexualis* (1965), originally published in 1886, Jehovanistically stressed the close connection of sex with crime and degeneracy. Most of the other sex researchers have been nearer to the pure Naturalist pole, their sexual theories retaining only traces of Jehovanism. Some are also transitional between moderate and radical Naturalism.

The sexual theories of Sigmund Freud (1856–1939) contain elements of both the Jehovanist and the moderate Naturalist positions. Unlike the radical Naturalists, he certainly did not see sex as a unalloyed joy. Unlike even the moderate Naturalists, his view of copulation was not fully secularized; for toward the end of his life he attempted to establish its link with a cosmic force called Eros, which he believed to be in eternal conflict with another cosmic force called Thanatos. (see Freud 1962)

Freud is similar to other Naturalists in grounding sex in biology, but he differs from them in equating it with biology's dynamic aspect. His conception of biology, derived from the vitalistic *Naturphilosophie* of the German poet Johann von Goethe (1749–1832), led him to view sex as an inner force (instinct) striving to actualize itself outwardly. This conception of biology, and consequently of sex, distinguishes Freud from most other Naturalists, particularly Kinsey (see below). Kinsey's conception of biology, derived from the taxonomic system of plant forms and functions of the Swedish botanist Carolus Linnaeus (1707–78),[1] led him to view sex as a more static outer behavior. Kinsey's behavioristic Naturalism, which harmonizes better with modern scientific positivism, has come to prevail over Freud's vitalistic Naturalism, whose "scientific" status has been under continual attack.[2]

Freud's belief that normal sex does not necesssarily damage cosmos or psyche may make him a Naturalist, but his belief that it threatens society remains Jehovanist. Since sexual desire is insatiable, Freud thought, it would greedily consume the human energy required by society unless continually repressed. Freud hoped, however, that sexual repressions could be reduced somewhat from the almost intolerable levels of the first decade of this century (1963, pp. 20–40). A pure Naturalist, on the other hand, would see no need for society to repress sex at all. Since sexual desire is easily satiable, they believe, it does not compete with society for the scarce resource of human energy.

Freud also remains Jehovanist in attributing bad psychological and social effects to perverted sex. True, he did not consider sexual perversions the epitome of evil, as Jehovanists do, and he was sympathetic to those who felt compelled to engage in them. For example, he wrote to a mother who had discovered her son's homosexuality:

> Homosexuality is assuredly no advantage but it is nothing to be ashamed of, no vice, no degradation, it cannot be classified as an illness; we consider it to be a variation of sexual function produced by a certain arrest of the sexual development. . . .
> [Quoted in Hechinger 1978, pp. 30, 32]

But he did not accept sexual perversions with as much enthusiasm or even as much tolerance as later Naturalists did. Again following the concepts of *Naturphilosophie*, he believed that the sex instinct expressed itself in different ways at various stages of human development. Adults who practice abnormal forms of sex thereby indicate that they have not progressed through the normal course of sexual development but have fixated at a childhood stage—a conception we might term "psychosexual lag" (Freud 1972). In effect, Freud continued to justify the Jehovanist effort to suppress sexual perversions by continuing to attribute them to an inferior source, merely replacing the Jehovanist motivation of freely willed moral corruption with the deterministic motivation of childhood problems.[3]

Finally, unlike Jehovanists and even many Naturalists, Freud did not stress the need to secure sex within an intimate relationship. Intimate relations, in fact, actually interfere with sexual desire by reactivating buried incest taboos (Freud 1963, pp. 58–59). Marriage is merely a plot on the part of society to restrict the sex lives of its members (Freud 1963, pp. 20–40).

Freud's English contemporary, Havelock Ellis (1859–1939), was also a transitional figure, though his position fell between a tepid and a fervid Naturalism. Ellis did, however, retain the Jehovanist doctrine that sex should occur only within an intimate relationship. But unlike most Jehovanists, he denied that this close personal relationship must be socially legitimized by marriage, or even that it must be monogamous. He did not go so far as to endorse prostitution, however, for prostitution provides variety merely in the number of sexual partners, not in the number of *intimate* partners, whom he felt to be more beneficial (1936, vol. 2: *Sex in Relation to Society*; see also Robinson 1977, pp. 29–32). Ellis's Naturalism was moderate in its denial that normal sex had bad social consequences but radical in its claim that sex could have good psychological, and even physical, consequences (1936, vol. 2: *The Mechanism of Detumescence*; esp. pp. 169–70). His views on perverted sex also fell between moderate and radical Naturalism. As a moderate Naturalist, Ellis doubted that much psychological or social harm could come from masturbation, homosexuality, or even sadomasochism (1936, vol. 1: *Auto-Eroticism, Sexual Inversion, Love and Pain*). But as a radical Naturalist, he affirmed a positive psychological and social effect for other sexual perversions, believing that they exercise, and consequently develop, the human imagination (1936, vol. 2: *Erotic Symbolism*; see also Robinson 1977, pp. 26–27).

Alfred Kinsey (1894–1956), who retained less of Jehovanism than almost any other major modern sexual theorist, was much closer to the ideal type of Naturalist than Freud or Ellis. In fact, his Naturalism was of the most radical sort, for he was favorably disposed to almost all forms of sex. Kinsey did not find normal sex nearly so dangerous for self or society as did Freud:

> For Freud sex was hedged about with danger, even with the possibility of psychic catastrophe. Kinsey, on the other hand, took an entirely matter-of-fact view of human sexual experience. It might, he allowed, be the source of considerable grief, but it utterly lacked the demonic potential attributed it by Freud [Robinson 1977, p. 45]

Kinsey, who was very enthusiastic about premarital sex and moderately enthusiastic about extramarital sex, did not find it nearly so necessary to embed copulation within an intimate relationship as did Ellis (1948, chaps. 17–19; 1953, chaps. 8–10). (Robinson 1977, pp. 77–78, however, points out that Kinsey still evaluated non–marital and other forms of sex with regard to their contribution to the quality of sex within marriage.) Nor did Kinsey find perverted sex a threat to self or society (Trilling 1953, pp. 232–33). He denied the Jehovanist assumption that sexual contamination necessarily spreads from behavior to being. For instance, by focusing on homosexual activities rather than on homosexual persons (1948, pp. 616–617), Kinsey implied that homosexual behavior has little effect on the psyche of those who engage in it.[4] He also found no social harm, and some benefit, in masturbation and homosexuality, as rehearsals for later heterosexual activities (1948, chaps. 14, 21; 1935, chaps. 5, 11). Almost alone among Naturalist social scientists, he did not disparage even child molesters (1948, pp. 238; 1953, pp. 116–22). (Robinson 1977, p. 116, however, notes that Kinsey could maintain his acceptance of sexual perversions only by glossing over the more extravagant ones—voyeurism and exhibitionism, sadism and masochism, transvestism—

which Kinsey claimed were too insignificant statistically to consider.)

Sexual ideology may now be entering a new phase, which I will call "postmodern." The writings of some recent sexual theorists imply that our society might move away from modernist Naturalism toward Gnosticism. In *One Dimensional Man* (1964), pp. 72ff), Herbert Marcuse attacks sexual Naturalism as an example of "repressive desublimation," contending that individuals should be antagonistic to the present social order and that permissive sexual ideologies deprive them of some of the motivation and energy necessary for criticizing and overthrowing it. In "The Pornographic Imagination" (1967, pp. 70–73), Susan Sontag observes that pornography reveals how to "transcend the personal." Far from being harmless, as most Naturalists believe, pornography is a repository of "dangerous knowledge"—dangerous because what can cause "self-transcendence" for a few extreme visionaries could cause "self-destruction" for most ordinary people. Although not sexual Gnostics themselves, both Marcuse and Sontag have, in effect, rearticulated the Gnostic perspective on sex, which sees it as a means of transcending society and self. But it is unlikely that this trend will consolidate and develop for Gnosticism has always been too stark and sinister to attract more than a few devoted disciples.

Augmented Arguments

Although Jehovanists have no doubt that sex undermines some fundamental axiom of their world, the cosmic collapse it threatens does not seem to bother those who do not share the same metaphysics. These non-Jehovanists remain unconvinced by anti-sex arguments based on the authority of the Bible and other religious tracts that implicitly contain the Jehovanist world scheme. To persuade the indifferent, Jehovanists have been forced to resort to the rhetorical technique of apodixis: the assertion that the forms of sex they condemn also attack aspects of human existence even a non-Jehovanist would value. Consequently, Jehovanists have developed a *theory of concomitant evil* to convince those who do not find illicit sex despicable in itself that they should at least find deplorable the biological, psychological, and social evils that necessarily accompany it.

The most tangible of the unheavenly hosts in sex's entourage, according to Jehovanists, is venereal disease. In *Microbes and Morals* (1973) Theodore Rosebury observes that the first explicit attempt to connect copulation with venereal disease occurred after the end of the Middle Ages (when Jehovanists' absolute domination over Western society abruptly declined). During the Renaissance, the most feared form of bodily contamination from others shifted from leprosy to venereal disease; during the Reformation, the cause most often attributed to venereal disease shifted from religious impropriety to sexual impropriety. Rosebury suggests that (Jehovanist) reactionaries pointed to venereal disease as evidence of divine wrath after humanists had dared to assert that the human potential was unlimited:

> The efflorescence of VD appeared just as the forces of the Renaissance were attempting to liberate the human spirit and to abolish notions of divine vengeance. . . . The conflict raged between such humanistic impulses, which affirmed a pride in the nature of man . . . , and those which sought to restrain his natural impluses. . . . The attempt to free the human spirit fought against original sin. . . . Humanism lost the struggle. [1973, p. 152]

In *Civilization and Disease* (1962, pp. 75–79) Henry Sigerist adds that the link between sexual transgressions and venereal disease was reasserted (by Jehovanists) during Victorian times:

> In religious circles the view that venereal diseases were an appropriate punishment for sin was wide-spread. In 1826, Pope Leo XII banned the use of the condom because it defied the intentions of divine Providence, namely, to punish sinners by striking them in the member with which they had

sinned. And even in the beginning of our century there were church people who were deeply disturbed by Erlich's discovery of salvarsan [a treatment for syphilis]. [1962, p. 78]

Even today, Jehovanists are still trying to associate illicit sex with venereal disease:

> Homosexual cops would not only "destroy both the morale and efficiency of the [Los Angeles] Police Department" . . . they would literally infect the force with disease.
>   "The liaisons that homosexuals spontaneously engage in in public theaters and back alleys and that sort of thing," the chief [Edward M. Davis] explained, "and the high percentage of germs and so forth pose a real health threat to the people who work with them." [New York Post, 29 October 1975, p. 36]

To discourage sex further, Jehovanists have tried to maintain the medical hazards of its other physical side-effect— pregnancy. They have prohibited the distribution of contraceptive drugs and devices, or played up their perils. From AWAKE! (22 January 1973), the newsletter of the Jehovah's Witnesses:

> College students in Canada are being given a powerful "morning-after" birth control pill "by the bucket," according to the Canadian Medical Association. . . . Such pill taking is evidence of the deepening moral breakdown on campuses today. However, medical authorities say a drug utilized in the pill . . . has been linked with cancer.

And at this writing Jehovanists are still trying to reinstitute the medical dangers of illegal abortions by restricting access to legal ones. The intense fervor of those who support this movement can stem only from a determination to protect their cosmos from the sexual assaults I have described. Their slogan—the "right to life"—is merely a front for the right actually desired, the "right to deter intercourse."

Jehovanists have also attempted to associate sex with psychological problems, for even a non-Jehovanist would agree that mental health is good and that whatever harms it

is bad. They have claimed that premarital sex ("sexual freedom," "the new morality") leads to "insecurity and hurt"
and "dashed expectations," as well as "emotional problems" including "depression," "neurotic behavior," and
"feelings of inadequacy," not to mention "loss of appetite"
and "headaches."[5]

> The leading character in NBC's James at 15 series will lose his
> virginity in an upcoming episode centered around his 16th
> birthday. A dispute over how James should react has caused
> story consultant Dan Wakefield to quit the show.
>   Wakefield . . . said he resigned this week after NBC's
> broacast standards department ordered revisions in his script
> to indicate that James suffers remorse after his first sexual
> experience. . . .
>   "We wanted them to show a feeling of guilt or remorse or
> retribution—something to show that it isn't all that proper for
> youngsters to jump in bed and have sexual intercourse simply
> because they have access to contraceptives," said Jerome
> Stanley, head of the network's broadcast standards depart-
> ment on the West Coast. [Los Angeles Times 13 January 1978,
> part IV; p. 24]

But Jehovanists have directed their psychological attack
less against normal sex than against its perverted forms.
Although they no longer claim that masturbation leads to
insanity, they now claim that pornography leads to "un-
healthy sexual fantasies" and "neurosis."[6] Prostitution, they
claim, makes one "full of self-hatred" and "masochistic self-
abuse"; forces one to use sex "as a form of punishment" and
"self-abasement"; and causes one to become "undersexed,"
"frigid,"and often "lesbian." Jehovanists also accuse the
johns who visit prostitutes of being "afraid of intimacy" and
even "latent homosexuals."[7] Jehovanists assert that swinging leads to "sexual problems" such as "impotency and
"infertility" as well as "fatigue" and "strain."[8] And they
insist that homosexuality leads to "psychic disturbances,
personality deformities, socially and personally harmful behavior patterns," as well as "certain paraphilias and other
aberrations."[9]

Jehovanists now draw on social science research if the results support their own positions. More and more today, in fact, they have come to phrase their religiously inspired diatribes against sex in terms of the seemingly neutral language of social science, becoming Savonarolas in scientists' clothing. As we have just seen, they are found among the ranks of amateur and even professional psychologists, reacting with "ritual insult behavior" to those whose sexual activities disconcert them.

Jehovanist social psychologists often accuse teenagers who engage in premarital sex of giving in to "peer pressure." This accusation assumes not only that no adolescent who concluded that the benefits of sexual activity outweigh its detriments could be rational, but also that their own opinion of adolescent sex is completely uninfluenced by the "peer pressure" of their own colleagues.

Jehovanist sociologists, for their part, look for correlations (however spurious) between sex and social problems. In the past, the main social problems Jehovanists have associated with sex (especially its perverted forms) are religious heresy (e.g., that the incestuous are witches) and political heresy (e.g., that homosexuals are communists) (Taylor 1973, pp. 34, 99n, 129–31, 297). Today, the main social problem they associate with sex (especially its public forms) is crime:

[New York Mayor Abraham Beame stated:] "Some people think of the fight against pornography as being an attack against the First Amendment. It's not. It's basically a fight against crime. It's been shown that violent crimes in a sex-oriented area are 75% or more higher than in other parts of the city." [*San Diego Evening Tribune* 31 May 1977, p. 3]

Ever since Krafft-Ebing (1965) collected accounts of sexually motivated murders in the late nineteenth century, Jehovanists have been connecting "crime in the streets" with "crime between the sheets." They now believe this association between sex and crime is so apparent that they need not even prove it. Warren Burger, Chief Justice of the Supreme Court, writing for the majority in the Paris Theater Case, stated:

> Although there is no conclusive proof of a connection be-
> tween antisocial behavior and obscene material, the legisla-
> ture of Georgia could quite reasonably determine that such a
> connection does exist. [*New York Times* 22 June 1973, p. 42]

Thus Jehovanists commonly associate prostitution with violent offenses,[10] and pornography with the mob or Mafia.[11] It
seems appropriate for those who fear that these forms of sex
will disorganize their cosmos to feel that "organized crime"
must lurk behind such activity.[12]

Jehovanists also argue that sexual corruption can spread
from individuals to their territories. Pornography and prostitution in particular, they claim, weaken the economy of the
neighborhoods, and even the cities, that tolerate them. They
have attributed the mid-1970s financial collapse of New York
City to the widespread illicit sexual activities that occurred
there during that period.

> In the wake of an investigation by ABC News, Howard K.
> Smith summed up: "An assembly of sex business is a guaran-
> tee of decay."
>
>   And decay, aside from moral corruption, can be measured
> in terms of economics. In Time Square, for instance, which is
> undeniably a cesspool, a "Clockwork Orange" of depravity,
> the amount of money the area paid to the city in sales taxes
> went down in the last two years by 43 percent. . . . [*The San
> Diego Union* 26 April 1977, section C, p. 7]

It was no coincidence that at precisely the same time New
York City was about to go bankrupt, the previously permissive *New York Times* launched a "clean-up" campaign against
sexually oriented businesses in Time Square. If Jehovanists
cannot convince non-Jehovanists that illicit sexual activities
are immoral per se, they can try to convince them that these
activities are at least costly to the public purse, and ultimately to the non-Jehovanists' own.

Perhaps the one thing that even non-Jehovanists would
agree is worth preserving above anything else is the stability
of society. Consequently, Jehovanists have tried to argue
that sexual license will lead to social collapse:

SACRAMENTO—A bill legalizing all sex acts between consenting adults in private was signed last night by Gov. Brown. . . .

Opponents, several quoting Bible passages, warned the bill would increase promiscuity and contribute to the downfall of society. [*The San Diego Union* 13 May 1975]

The decline and fall of the Roman Empire is the favorite example cited by those who wish to point out the catastrophic consequences of sexual freedom. But closer examination of this example challenges their contention, for it is equally plausible to assert the contrary: that the sexual liberty of the early Roman Empire was responsible for its rise to greatness whereas the sexual repression of the late Roman Empire was responsible for its decline and fall.

For their part, Naturalists do not merely deny the Jehovanist accusations against sex; they also attempt to make sex more appealing to the non-Naturalist by developing a *theory of concomitant good*. Thus they argue that nearly all sexual performances and paraphernalia are beneficial for mental health, whereas abstinence from sex leads to mental illness. For instance, Patrick M. McGrady, Jr., author of *The Love Doctors*, finds pornography to possess this psychotherapeutic virtue:

> Obscenity, pornography, erotic material—same thing—tend to stimulate sexual fantasies which are mystically removed from reality in the same way that dreams are, but as protective of sanity and general health in their way as dreams are in theirs. [*The New York Times* 5 July 1973, p. 29]

Naturalists also argue that enhancement of the individual's sex life will improve the health of society as a whole by actually reducing crime and violence. For instance, Naturalist sex researchers have found that sex criminals were exposed to pornography *less* than noncriminals (*Report of the Commission on Obscenity and Pornography*, 1970, pp. 276–78). Of course, neither Jehovanists nor Naturalists have had much success with these augmented arguments in convincing dedicated members of the opposition, though they might sway those who belong to neither side.[13]

Intermediate Countermeasures

Ideally, neither Jehovanists nor Naturalists should have much problem dealing with sex. If Jehovanists were to dominate a society completely, they would simply suppress sex entirely (except perhaps in marriage). If Naturalists were to dominate a society completely, they would simply permit any sexual activity (except perhaps nonparity perversions). But since neither Jehovanists nor Naturalists have total control over our society, neither can enforce their ideology absolutely. Each must compromise their beliefs by developing a "fallback position," one that takes into account the limits of their power while sacrificing as few of their principles as possible.

When their domination over society has slipped to the extent that they lose unquestioned control over the beliefs and actions of some of its citizens, Jehovanists have sometimes restored continence by falling back on the method of last resort: *extraction*. Apparently taking their cue from the biblical saying, "If thine eye offend thee, pluck it out," they have castrated themselves and, when possible, others. If the "hangman is the ultimate guardian of [political] society," as the French reactionary Joseph de Maistre observed, the castrator is the ultimate guardian of (everyday) reality. Jehovanists have demanded castration especially for incorrigible sexual deviants—particularly rapists, homosexuals, and child molesters—as the "final solution" to the pervert problem.

When their domination has weakened still further and this extreme countermeasure is no longer feasible, Jehovanists may retreat to the milder sexual deterrent of *distraction*. During Victorian times, for instance, Jehovanists instituted compulsory sports for school children and adolescents, hoping that physical exhaustion would keep their minds off copulation and its cosmological perils (Taylor 1973, p. 221). Similarly, as more and more women join the military, one reason behind its fatiguing daily schedule seems to be the prevention of sex:

> Socially and sexually, the relations in coed training are low-key—partly because . . . after a day beginning at 5 a.m. and ending with lights out at 9 p.m., there isn't much time for socializing. . . .
> Jacqueline Landry said, "We're so tired when we get back to the barracks at night all we want to do is take a shower and go to bed." [*Los Angeles Times*]

Jehovanists try to control the external sources of sexual arousal even more than its internal sources. When they cannot prevent pornography from being printed, they attempt to prevent it from being distributed through censorship. In our society, Jehovanists were long able to stop the sensual slide into erotic reality at the chin, as it were, for the only important tactile contact they permitted between potential sex partners in visual media (theater, movies, television) or printed media (books, magazines) was kissing. By editing erotic reality out of the mass media in this way, they managed to maintain the illusion that everyday reality was a seamless weave.[14]

Since they are unable to annihilate sex, Jehovanists fall back on the technique of *containment*. Having failed to stamp out prostitution, for instance, they have informally confined it to "red light districts":

> From the time of Louis IX (Saint Louis), in the thirteenth century, who saw the failure of an attempt to prohibit prostitution, efforts were made to tolerate and regulate the practice. Since that time [according to E. Lancereaux], "special neighborhoods have been allotted to prostitutes. Avignon, Toulouse, and many other towns had, like Paris, Venice, and London, their prostitution districts and special laws in reference to prostitutes." [Rosebury 1973, p. 228]

After the Supreme Court legalized pornography in the late 1960s, pornographic material began to tear random holes in the fabric of everyday reality for many people. Consequently, Jehovanists tried to confine pornography temporally to the "adult" phase of the life cycle and spatially to "adult" magazines, bookstores, theaters, and movie houses. By the mid-1970s, they tried to restrict it further to specific sections of the city:

> The city that once made "banned in Boston" a household phrase is zoning a district that will be the exclusive domain of pornography shops, sex films and girlie shows.
>
> The two-block-long area in downtown Boston will be zoned as an "adult entertainment district" by a planning agency that hopes to keep the pornography businesses from spreading to other parts of the city. . . .
>
> The new district will be in a place known as the Combat Zone, dominated by X-rated theaters, strip tease bars and adult bookstores. [*The New York Times*, 9 June 1974].

During this period Jehovanists also tried to contain the pollution spread by pornographic movies by confining advertisements of the films to specific pages of the newspapers they controlled, such as the *Los Angeles Times*.[15]

Because the sex industry was banned from the rest of society and culture, it became almost the exclusive concern of the pockets where it was permitted. As a result, these areas festered. By the late 1970s, many of the neighborhoods that contained adult bookstores, movies, massage parlors, and prostitution deteriorated economically and became crime-ridden. Jehovanists blamed the corrupting power of sex; but since they could not reimpose their extreme countermeasures, they became more receptive to the Naturalist method of combating its evil effects.

Naturalists, too, have had to moderate their principles to put them into practice. Although in theory Naturalists are unwilling to conceded that copulation has any evil consequences, in practice they are willing to mitigate those that others find in it through *dilution*—a technique based on the assumption that a little dirt can be overwhelmed by a lot of purity.[16] If public manifestations of sex are scattered around a city, for instance, they will not reach a dangerous concentration in any particular neighborhood. A zoning law modeled on this Naturalist method, which originated in Detroit but was later adopted by other cities, prohibits any new sex business from locating near an old one:

> Sex-oriented outlets such as bookshops and massage parlors may have to be scattered about Los Angeles County in the future rather than clustered together.
>
> That shift in emphasis was a major recommendation in a study released Thursday by the country Regional Planning Commission.
>
> The study, a response to complaints over the proliferation and centralization of so-called sex emphasis stores and arcades, recommends at least 1,000 feet of space be required between all adult entertainment businesses [:] . . . adult arcades, adult bookstores, adult theaters, massage parlors and model studios. [*Los Angeles Times,* 17 March 1978, part II, p. 4]

Naturalists also neutralize the dangerous, cognitively disorienting properties of sex by *filtration,* particularly by sifting them through the media of art, science, or medicine. These filters[17] obscure all but a few aspects of sexual experience and activity, making sex as safe as looking at the sun through smoked glass. And since our society considers art, science, and medicine to be among the noblest and purest of human endeavors, they can easily bleach out whatever sexual stain trickles through.

The United States began in the 1930s to switch from the Jehovanist countermeasure of suppressing sex-related activities entirely to the Naturalist countermeasure of filtering them partially. In a 1933 obscenity trial, Judge Woolsey decided that James Joyce's *Ulysses* was not obscene because the author did not intend the book's "dirty parts" to be sexually arousing; instead he intended to portray human consciousness in a new literary mode. When the decision was appealed, Judge Augustus Hand proclaimed the doctrine of "dominant effect": a work can be obscene only when "taken as a whole." In other words, a little dirt can be diluted by a lot of context. In a 1936 case Judge Learned Hand stressed that the good effects of the context could counterbalance the bad effects of the embedded sexual descriptions:

> The [new] standard [of obscenity] must be the likelihood that the work will so much arouse the salacity of the reader to whom it is sent as to outweigh any literary, scientific or other merits it may have in that reader's hands. [Quoted in Clor 1969, p. 22]

In the *Fanny Hill* (Roth) case of 1957, the Supreme Court reaffirmed that obscenity is not protected by constitutional guarantees of free speech, but ruled that sexual representations are not obscene (and are therefore protected) if, taken as a whole, the dominant theme of the work does not appeal to prurient interests, and if the work has even the "slightest redeeming social importance." Throughout the 1960s the courts extended permissible (socially redeeming) filters for portrayals of sex from high to low cultural contexts, from Henry Miller's *Tropic of Cancer* to the likes of *Whip Woman in Chains*.

These legal decisions have permitted Naturalists to temper an audience's experience of nudity and sexual activities by embedding such phenomena in literary and artistic contexts that deeroticize them. Nudes in photography, painting, sculpture, and art films—even live nudes in art modeling classes (Jesser and Donavan 1969)—usually pose artfully enough to prevent their observers from being drawn very far into erotic reality.

But it is not easy to filter intercourse through art. Sex scenes are difficult to integrate into books and movies because sex, like singing, has a rhythm and tempo different from that of ordinary social interaction:

[Gerald] Damiano's major innovation, of course, is the porno plot. But except for "The Devil in Miss Jones," his "plots" are nothing of the sort—they are merely framing material for the hard-core action. True, the framing material provides the *appearance* of a plot (and gives audiences a rationale for coming into the theatre), but every time Damiano moves into another round of hard-core sex, his dramatic structure crumbles. Without plot, believable characters are impossible; and without believable characters, all you've got are impossible inexpressive cocks and cunts. [*The Village Voice*, 2 February 1976, p. 119]

Consequently, two separate species of art have evolved. "Serious" literature and movies portray everyday reality almost exclusively, truncating or omitting nearly all segments of erotic reality, even those necessitated by the plot. "Pornographic" literature and movies portray erotic reality almost exclusively, with few of the ordinary activities of everyday life. If the former are almost all recitative, the latter are almost all aria. Few works of art have managed to bridge the gap between these two genres by combining everyday and erotic reality in realistic proportions with aesthetic transitions.

Gnostics have used these new legal rulings to evade Jehovanist persecution by camouflaging their products behind the Naturalist art filter. They have called their voyeurism parlors "photo studios," their pornographic periodicals "art magazines," and their dirty bookstores "adult museums."[18] At times they have even dared to mock the very way Naturalists legitimize art as an ameliorating context for sexual portrayals. In the pornographic film *The Private Afternoons of Pamela Mann*, a walk-on character gives an incomprehensible opinion survey and, when questioned why, replies that she is there simply to give the film "socially redeeming value."

Jehovanists have always doubted that art was a sufficiently strong antidote for the poisonous effects of sex. "And, as a matter of history," the art historian Kenneth Clark points out (1956, p. 470), "the Victorian moralists who alleged that painting the nude usually ended in fornication were not far from the mark." Recently, Jehovanists have begun to recognize the Gnostic presence that may lurk beneath the Naturalist veneer. In the Miller case in 1973, the new Jehovanist majority on the Supreme Court began a counteroffensive against using art to filter sex. They brought the gradual liberalization of artistic standards for portraying sex to an abrupt halt, substituted the phrase "lacking serious" redeeming value for "utterly without" it, and shifted the criteria for legitimation from the Naturalist "cultural context of their production" to the Jehovanist "community context of their consumption."

Scientific research has become another safe contextual filter for sex since Kinsey's studies of sexual behavior (1948 and 1953). In the words of Lionel Trilling," Professor Kinsey and his coadjutors drag forth into the light all the hidden actualities of sex so that they may lose their dark power and become domesticated among us" (1953, p. 222). But Kinsey's interview method allowed him to tame only sexual *accounts*, although these were accounts of actual sexual activities in natural settings. More recently, Masters and Johnson (1966) extended the claim that science could safely contain sexual dangers. Their experimental method allowed them to tame actual sexual *activities*, although only in a laboratory setting. Critics, however, have pointed out that observing sexual activities in a laboratory might change their nature enough to distort the results (Farber 1978, pp. 34–35; Robinson 1977, pp. 138–40). What is needed is scientific observation of sexual activities "in vivo" rather than "in vitro"—though of course a field researcher would find it difficult to obtain access to such natural settings, not to mention the question of obtaining permission to manipulate them secretly for unobstrusive experiments.

These artistic and scientific filters reduce the power of sex to threaten the observer's organization of his world. Harry Clor describes how the filtered sexual representations of art and science attenuate this risk, in contrast to the naked[19] stare of pornography:

When genuine literature treats of things intimately personal or of things ignoble, the feelings which it arouses are not the same as those which would be aroused by the direct experience of these same things in ordinary life. . . . The objects can be presented in such a way that the audience will contemplate them with a degree of detachment. Works can be designed so that the grosser physical aspects of the phenomena treated will be viewed from a certain distance. . . .

Obscene literature may be defined as that literature which presents, graphically and in detail, a degrading picture of human life and invites the reader or viewer, not to contemplate that picture, but to wallow in it. . . .

The writings of Freud about sado-masochism are not obscene, but an obscene novel could be written on the basis of them. The obscene novel would *portray* the physical phenomena of sado-masochism, and it would do so in vivid detail. It would not maintain aesthetic or intellectual distance between its readers and these details. Its readers would not be invited to reflect upon the nature of degrading human experiences, but, simply, to have such experiences. [Clor 1969, pp. 233–34]

If pornographic representations of a sexual activity encourage audiences to "wallow" in it subjectively, artistic or scientific representations encourage them to contemplate it objectively, with little subjective response.

When scientific studies of sex were first permitted, around the end of the nineteenth century, Jehovanists in authority limited public access to them. They were unconvinced that the scientific filter was powerful enough to prevent ordinary people from being pulled into erotic reality. Until as late as the middle of the twentieth century, publishers, libraries, and bookstores in England and America attempted to restrict the circulation and sale of works that made sexual descriptions "too accessible" to the public:

The 1913 English edition of [Freud's] *The Interpretation of Dreams* contains a message reading: "Publishers Note. The sale of this book is limited to members of the Medical, Scholastic, Legal and Clerical professions." [Ruitenbeek 1974, p. 38]

Scientific studies of sex that did go into general circulation were usually neglected by reviewers;[20] some were even prosecuted legally (Taylor 1973, pp. 291–92) or destroyed (Ruitenbeek 1974, p. 37). Even today, those in the scientific professions must sometimes claim that their unique system of relevances should give them special privilege to obtain the sexual materials denied to others:

> A doctor who specializes in treatment of sexual problems asked a federal court judge here Tuesday to be allowed to receive through the mails pornographic material that he claims is "useful and necessary" to his medical activities.
> Dr. Eugene Shoenfeld . . . is arguing that even if the items are obscene, because of his capacity as a doctor he should have right to receive them—even if the average citizen may not. [*Los Angeles Times*, 12 March 1975, part 1, p. 29]

Scientists themselves have shielded laymen from the dangerous implications of their sexual studies by presenting them in a language that retarded their readers' sensual slide. Krafft-Ebing wrote in his preface to one edition of *Psychopathia Sexualis*:

> In order that unqualified persons should not become readers, the author saw himself compelled to choose a title understood only by the learned, and also, where possible, to express himself in *terminis technicis*. It seemed necessary to give certain particularly revolting portions in Latin. [Quoted in Ruitenbeek 1974, p. 36]

This book, too, neutralizes the cognitively explosive qualities of sex by sandwiching its pornographic passages between thick slices of "scientific" discussion. Most educators would probably find this book too threatening to assign in college courses if its extreme examples were not clothed in technical jargon or imprisoned in a theoretical framework. Nevertheless some readers and conservative critics might not view this book through the scientific filter, regarding it as pornography pure and simple.

There is a point, however, beyond which Jehovanists refuse to compromise their principles. They still deny that the
scientific filter can mitigate sexual dangers for research subjects, even if it can for researchers and their readers:

> A Harvard dean has banned participation by undergraduates
> in an experiment that would have wired their genitals to
> electronic devices to measure whether sexual arousal declines
> as fear increases.
>
> Dean of Students Archie C. Epps said he had acted because
> the experiment was "inappropriate" and could have harmful
> effects on students. [*The New York Times*, 30 November 1975,
> p. 52]

(And at this writing the Supreme Court has just suspended
the art filter for a similar reason: they have banned child
pornography less for its effect on its audience than to "protect" the children themselves from "sexual exploitation.")

The medical filter is also supposed to shield both physicians and their patients from the hazards of erotic reality, but
Jehovanists have been slow to accept its effectiveness:

> Dr. Willoughby, of Derby, tells how, in 1658, he had to creep
> into the chamber of a lying-in woman on his hands and knees,
> in order to examine her unperceived. In France, Clement was
> employed secretly to attend the mistresses of Louis XIV in
> their confinements; . . . he was conducted blindfold, while
> . . . the face of the lady was enveloped in a network of lace.
> . . . In the early nineteenth century, . . . it [was] usual for the
> room to be darkened . . . during an examination. Many old
> pictures show the [doctor] groping in the dark, beneath the
> bed-clothes, to perform operations on women in childbirth.
> [Ellis 1936, vol. 1: *The Evolution of Modesty*, pp. 29–30]

Such sexual modesty before even the shaded eyes of medicine is not confined to the distant past:

> Dear Abby:
>   I was disappointed in your reply to the girl who resented
> having a male physician give her a breast and pelvic examina-

tion. She said she wanted to remain chaste for her husband. You said an examination of that kind would in no way violate her chastity.

I disagree with you. I am no prude, but I place a high value on the privacy of my body, and I do not care to share it with anyone other than the man I marry. A male physician is no different from any other man, and I wonder how many husbands would allow their wives to go to a male gynecologist if they knew how intimately their wives would be touched and examined. . . .

P.J.

Dear P.J.:

It is indeed your right to select a female physician if you wish, but a male gynecologist has about as much erotic feeling while examing female patients as an electrician has when he's looking for a loose connection. [*San Diego Union*, 28 September 1973, p. D-4]

Although some Jehovanists would still rather die than be seen naked by a physician, many are now willing, albeit grudgingly, to give a slightly higher priority to combating illness than eroticism. American network television made a rare exception to its taboo against nearly all visual depictions of the body's erogenous zones when it recently showed naked female breasts to demonstrate a self-administered cancer examination.

The ability of the medical filter to neutralize eroticism can be seen most strikingly in the gynecological examination. Since its participants and activities are similar to those associated with intercourse, the gynecological exam is a point of overlap between everyday and erotic reality where slippage between these two realms can easily occur.[21] Joan Emerson (1970), James Henslin and Mae Biggs (1971), and others have enumerated the elements of the medical filter that prevent both gynecologist and patient from sliding into erotic reality. These factors include the examiner's medical props, costumes, jargon, euphemisms, restrained paralinguistics, briskly efficient and nonchalant manner, avoidance of eye contact, other gaze control, and humor to undercut

any residual sexual tension. They also include the ex-
aminee's undressing out of sight (usually behind a screen)
and continued partial covering (usually with a sheet) to
segregate her vagina from its bodily context, in other words
to sever the physical area of technical concern below from
the social area above that speaks.

Naturalists currently use an offshoot of the medical
filter—the health filter—to screen the erotic effects of nudity
that occur outside a purely medical context, thus providing a
justification for nude beaches, nudist camps, male-female
saunas, and massage parlors.

In the past few years, radical Naturalists have increased
the power of the medical filter dramatically. No longer is it
merely supposed to prevent copulation from occurring.
Now it is supposed to diminish the negative consequences
of copulation itself. Patients can now pay "sex surrogates" to
help them overcome their sexual problems through practice
in a medical context—though this sounds suspiciously like
prostitution to skeptical Jehovanists.

Gnostics sometimes manipulate the medical filter in the
same way as other Naturalist filters—nefariously, to seduce
the innocent. In his book *Candy*, Maxwell Kenton (Terry
Southern) provides an amusingly far-fetched fictional
account of one Gnostic who does so:

> "Well, of course, you should really have a periodic check-
> up," [Dr. Johns] said. . . .
> "Gosh, guess I'd better make an appointment," said
> Candy.
> "Hmmm. The difficulty is, you see, I'm off on two months'
> holiday starting tomorrow," said Dr. Johns. . . . "We can give
> you an examination," he said, "just over there. . . ."
> Candy was amazed. "Here? In the *Riviera* [a Greenwich
> Village cafe]? Good Grief, I don't. . . ."
> "Oh yes," said Dr. Johns. "Just here . . . this will do nicely."
> He had led the girl to the door of the men's toilet, and quickly
> inside. . . .
> "Now I just want to test these clitorial reflexes," he said,

"often enough, that's where trouble strikes first." And he began to gently massage her sweet pink clit. . . . [Kenton 1965, pp. 133–35]

To prove the inefficacy of the medical filter for reducing eroticism, Jehovanists are quick to point out every "scandalous" instance of doctors, especially psychiatrists, copulating with their patients ("We told you so!").

Ambivalent Emotions

The transitional period between one sexual ideology and another is a bewildering time for ordinary people. While theorists can take refuge in conceptual ambiguity, laymen often must endure emotional ambivalence. Sexual shame occurs frequently, for instance, during transitions between Jehovanism and Naturalism (as between pristine childhood and prurient adolescence). Whatever one's sexual inclination during this period, it can always be attacked by the arrière-garde (or sexually retarded) for "going too far" and by the avant-garde (or sexually precocious) for "not going far enough."

Ordinary people may respond to being caught between world views by feeling guilty. Feelings of guilt occur when the influence of a world view has weakened enough for one to acknowledge desire for the forbidden, but not enough to change the negative evaluation that attaches to such behaviors. Until recently, for instance, many people in our society felt guilty for wanting to engage in sexual acts condemned by the dominant but declining Jehovanist world view. But that is not all. Guilt is also felt by those who discover that what was approved by their previous world view is condemned by their new one. Many people now feel guilty about *not* participating in sexual activities that were formerly criticized by Jehovanists, for the increasingly influential Naturalists criticize abstention from such activities with equal vehemence. Religious revivals try to shift the coordinates by which people judge their sexual desires or behaviors toward the Jehovanist pole; psychotherapies try to shift these coordinates toward the Naturalist pole.

If the intrusion into consciousness of Jehovanist interpretations of one's sexual desires or behaviors can produce guilt, the intrusion into consciousness of Naturalist interpretations of them can produce mirth. Mirth, like guilt, is a psychological response to sex on the part of those caught in the battlefield between Jehovanist and Naturalist ideologies. Laughter saves the integration of the self from the disintegration of the world. People laugh when they suddenly recognize that something does not fit into the larger pattern of their cosmos while simultaneously removing the self from this contradiction to a safe distance. The inconsistency in the cosmos remains, but does not concern them essentially (Davis 1979). People who laugh at sex, then, recognize its threat to cosmic consistency, but contain it through self-distancing. Whoever can see the humor in sex need no longer fear its consequences.

Neither of the ideal types I have been describing—pure Jehovanists and pure Naturalists—find fucking very funny. (Not finding sex a laughing matter, they would be "unamused"—if not horrified or annoyed—by much of this book.) Pure Jehovanists are well aware that sex is inconsistent with their cosmos, but the Jehovanist self is bound up with this rigid cosmic structure too closely to be safely distanced, through laughter, from the resulting chaos. Pure Naturalists do not find sex inconsistent with their more loosely organized cosmos; consequently the threat of chaos is insufficient to force them to seek safety in the distancing power of laughter. Only those located between pure Jehovanism and pure Naturalism, only those who can and must distance themselves from the chaos that coitus creates in their cosmos, are able to appreciate sexual humor.

This interstitial sexual humor—the kind of sexual humor Freud examined most frequently in *Jokes and Their Relation to the Unconscious* (1960)—is defensive. It is used by those who try to reconcile Jehovanism and Naturalism in order to shelter the self whenever copulation threatens to rupture the cosmos. Gnostics also find sex amusing, but in a different way. Gnostic sexual humor is aggressive, intended to free the true self by cleaving the false cosmic categories that bind it. Thus Gnostic laughter is always sardonic, never anxious.

Sex is humorized when it has been dehumanized. Susan Sontag (1970, pp. 53–55) points out that pornography is closely related to comedy. The human characters in pornography are often described as though they were fucking *machines*: they are characterized only outwardly and behaviorally, they exhibit meager emotional responses to their extreme circumstances, and they exhaust all their sexual potentials by permuting organs and objects systematically. Henri Bergson (1956) defined comedy as the transformation of the organic into the mechanical, the human into the nonhuman. This definition applies equally to much pornography. Since erotic behavior seems mechanical when it lacks erotic experience to make it human, many pornographic works, as well as other behavioristic descriptions of sex, sound funny, despite the serious intention of their authors.

Like the mechanization of sex, its comercialization in Western society produces metaphors that are incongruent with its human element. Some people humorously refer to various sexual perversions in terms of upper class-Madison Avenue corporate abbreviations ("S and M," "B and D," "AC-DC," "69") or lower-class service industry shop talk ("blow jobs," "hand jobs"). Ghetto blacks even refer to normal sex as "taking care of business." Business metaphors for sex provoke laughter because they describe the human activities of erotic reality, which is supposed to be a refuge from the workaday world, in the most instrumental terms of everyday reality. Although such instrumentality has no place in erotic reality itself, it is required by the often difficult task of transporting both parties there from everyday reality. Thus humor can be used to relieve the tension created by the discrepancy between the unearthly ends of seduction and its mundane means. Both the incongruity and instrumentality of sex were nicely captured in the 1957 movie *The Fuzzy Pink*

Nightgown when Jane Russel attempted to ward off a would-be seducer by exclaiming, "None of that 'funny business'!"

The sudden drowning-out of a word's ordinary denotations by its sexual connotations produces the incongruity behind the humor in sexual wordplay. Shakespeare's works, for example, are far more bawdy than is generally believed (Partridge 1969):

> Hamlet : Lady, shall I lie in your lap?
> Ophelia: No, my lord.
> Hamlet : I mean, my head upon your lap?
> Ophelia: Aye, my lord.
> Hamlet : Do you think I meant country matters?
> Ophelia: I think nothing, my lord.
> Hamlet : That's a fair thought to lie between maids' legs.
> Ophelia: What is, my lord?
> Hamlet : Nothing.
> *Hamlet*, 3.2.119–28

(Psychoanalysis, too, tries to elicit the sexual meanings hidden behind the ordinary meanings of objects and activities, making it sometimes seem like one vast dirty joke.) The same kind of incongruity produces nonverbal sexual humor. The flashers and streakers of the mid-1970s evoked smiles and laughter because their brief semaphores of sexuality suddenly outshone the ordinary meaning of public occasions.

Humor and eroticism have surprisingly similar psychological rhythms. In both, tension slowly increases before suddenly decreasing. But laughter releases this tension much sooner than orgasm, making humor a powerful anaphrodisiac. By shortcircuiting sexual arousal before a person can slide very far into erotic reality, humor constrains its anarchic potential more effectively than do other Naturalist filters.[22] Consequently, those who fear eroticism might be wiser to demand that sexual activities be depicted only in humorous contexts rather than only in serious—artistic or scientific—ones.

Humor and horniness are in fact often found together. Lovers who cannot contain themselves giggle continually to relieve their tension. Since too much erotic tension prevents people from acting in the world, laughter lowers its level enough for them to be able to perform physically the sexual activities they are otherwise too overmotivated to actually carry out.

In the old burlesque houses, baggy-trousered, dirty-punning, leering, slapstick comedians worked to puncture the audience's expanding balloon of erotic reality, which had been pumped up by the sensual strippers who preceded them. Burlesque alternated arousal and amusement; recent hard-core pornographic films have tried to synchronize them, but with less success. The controlled sequencing of arousal and amusement in burlesque succeeded in creating both great tension and great releases, whereas their simultaneity in inane porn films fails to produce either much tension or much release.

Even if an erotic situation is not intentionally funny, audience reaction sometimes makes it so. Audiences who whistle, wisecrack, and catcall during the showing of serious stag movies (which used to be a common occurrence at fraternities and fraternal organizations) demonstrate how laughter can be used to defuse erotic tension before it can accumulate a charge that might shatter a self or a world. The recent decline of audience laughter at pornographic movies, noted by Slade (1971, p. 38), implies that modern audiences are able to sustain erotic tension longer without breaking up.

Since the tension released by humor results from the conjunction of things normally seen as disjunct (Bergson 1956), people who combine incompatible sexual categories in themselves often become butts of ridicule. Homosexuals and transvestites, by defying one of our society's most important differentiations, have inspired humor as well as horror. Some have created their own peculiar brand of wit, which plays on the conjunction of their incongruous categories. A professional male or female impersonator shows

an audience that gender role behavior is largely dramaturgical, but often makes light of his/her own contradications in
order to spare the audience the full shock of recognizing the
extent that they themselves are also merely male or female
impersonators. Through double-entendres in patter and
songs, the impersonator wittily deflates the audience's
growing horror at the discovery that sexual distinctions may
actually be arbitrary.

In contrast to comedy, tragedy evokes the sudden awareness that contradictions in the cosmos do concern the individual in an essentially way (Davis 1979). Overinvolvement
in the cosmic contradictions of copulation produces too
much tension to sustain sexual arousal—as Jehovanists have
often discovered. Underinvolvement in them produces too
little tension to sustain it—as Naturalists have often discovered. Fear puts an end to sexual desire just as surely as
laughter does. Thus tragedy and comedy, horror and
humor, are the upper and lower bounds of erotic experience.

Conclusion

I have tried to show in this part that Jehovanists, Gnostics,
and Naturalists treat sex differently because each group
evaluates it in terms of a different conception of the cosmos,
of society, and of self. Consequently, those who attempt to
refute, say, the Jehovanist interpretation of sex through "scientific" research will seldom disuade a single believer, no
matter how impeccable their logic or irrefutable their facts.
For the world views that underlie sexual interpretations are
not held rationally, but rather are the very conditions of
rationality. They determine which arguments about a topic
seem reasonable and persuasive. Most scientific studies of
sex simply do not seem reasonable and persuasive to Jehovanists because they disregard what Jehovanists regard as
its most important aspects. Thus Naturalist sexologists "talk
past" Jehovanists (and of course Jehovanists do the same to
them).

Belief in the Jehovanist interpretation of sex has almost certainly declined in recent years, but not because it has been proven false. Rather, Jehovanist sexual beliefs are less influential because their fundamental conception of the cosmos has been undermined by a change in the social conditions that support it. New social conditions create a new kind of self, leading to a new interpretation of sex that better accords with this new kind of self than do traditional interpretations of sex. New social conditions in Western, and particularly American, society have undermined the structured self, which grounded traditional Jehovanist (and Gnostic) beliefs about sex, and have given rise to a fluid self that is more harmonious with the new sexual beliefs of Naturalism. Therefore, it is not completely the case—as the jeremiads of Jehovanists have maintained—that the Naturalist sexual ideology is the sole *cause* of a weakening social fabric; instead, the persuasiveness of the Naturalist sexual ideology is more an *effect* of a changing social structure that has already been eroded in other areas.

Although it is difficult to draw more general conclusions about the relation between social, psychological, and ideological cycles in Western civilization, I will tentatively suggest that the three sexual interpretations we have been considering become popular during different phases of social change.[23]

The influence of the Jehovanist world view seems to increase *after* social crises. Whenever society enters a new historical phase, Jehovanists usually become the leading voice in the reformation of the social order by attempting to restore what they regard as its "moral purity." Thus Jehovanist sexual restrictions were enforced with renewed zeal after the expulsion of the Jews from Egypt (the writing of Leviticus), after the Babylonian captivity (post-Exile prohibitions), after the destruction of classical civilization (early medieval Christianity), after embryonic urbanism and nationalism began to disrupt medieval social organization (Thomas Aquinas), after the Renaissance (the Counter-

Reformation and Puritanism), after the advent of industrialism, especially in England (Victorianism), after the Civil War in America (the Comstock laws), after the worst of the Great Depression (the Hayes Movie Production Code), and recently after Vietnam and Watergate (the Burger Supreme Court pornography convictions).[24]

The Gnostic world view seems to become more loudly voiced *before* social crises, becoming more pervasive during the late phase of the previous social order. Whenever traditonal moral categories begin to lose their legitimacy, Gnostics attempt to accelerate their decline by criticizing them as the source of human suffering. Thus Gnostic justifications for extreme sexual license to violate these conventional norms were formulated toward the end of the pre-Roman Mediterranean societies (early Gnostic writings), toward the end of the Middle Ages (Albigensian heresy in Catholicism and Cabalism in Judaism), toward the end of the eighteenth-century monarchies (debauched aristocrats and adventurers such as de Sade, Casanova, and the legendary Don Juan), toward the end of the period when bourgeois dominance of society was unquestioned (aesthetes and decadents such as Baudelaire, Huysmans, Wilde, and Gide), and recently in America toward the end of the Eisenhower era (the early work of then "beat generation" or "Southern decadent" writers such as William Burroughs, Norman Mailer, Tennessee Williams, and Truman Capote). Jehovanists and Gnostics are sometimes contemporaries, but the former are midwives to the birth of a new social order while the latter are morticians for the death of an old one.

Unlike Jehovanists, who are continually seeking to create or reestablish a social order, and Gnostics, who are continually seeking to destroy one, Naturalists have little desire to do either. They are influential during those periods when society is taken so much for granted that many people possess neither the Jehovanist fervor to purify it through sexual restrictions nor the Gnostic passion to pollute it through sexual license. During this relatively tranquil interlude, Naturalists try to reduce society's structural differentiation, despite considerable opposition from the disciples of the Jehovanists who legitimized its original establishment. Naturalists employ their sexual ideology to weaken the traditional social borders between individuals and between groups. By attempting in this way to further liquefy the self, they hope to argue more convincingly that anyone can sexually trespass without risk these previously forbidden boundaries.

The Naturalist interpretation of the history of sex has become increasingly accepted. This history is characterized either by a gradual progress toward sexual freedom from the ancient repressions of the Judeo-Christian tradition or by a return to a "normal" amount of sexual freedom after the relatively recent repressions of the aberrant Victorian period. Some Naturalists attribute this shift toward "sexual sanity" to the rightness of their cause. More sophisticated Naturalists attribute it to the recent qualitative change in social and psychological conditions that has rendered obsolete the dialectic between Jehovanism and Gnosticism. The processual model implicit in Naturalism, they believe, corresponds to the essential character of modern society and selves more accurately than the structural and antistructural models implicit in Jehovanism and Gnosticism. In any case, most Naturalists assert that our society has left its previous sexual restrictions far behind, forever.

But all self-styled "avant-garde" social movements feel that history ends with them. They cannot believe that they too will ever be surpassed by the rush of historical events. We saw, however, that previous movements similar to modern Naturalism occurred not during the terminal stage of social change but merely during a transitional phase of a social cycle. It seems likely, then, that modern Naturalism is occurring at exactly the same turning point today, even if the pendulum at the top of its swing momentarily believes itself to be at rest at last.

Consequently, my reading of the history of sex comes to a different conclusion. I see this history as a series of alternations between periods of sexual liberty and periods of sexual limitation. In the past, the gradual sexual liberalization of society under Naturalist tutelage often set loose so many antinomian Gnostics as to help precipitate the very social crisis that eventually restored hypernomian Jehovanists to power, thus reinitiating the entire process. If this cynical cyclical view of sexual history proves correct, our current period of sexual freedom will only be temporary—and those devoted to the Naturalist ideal had better enjoy it while they can.

POSTSCRIPT: The 1980s have so far seen the resurgence of Jehovanism predicted by my oscillator model of sexual change. The Moral Majority and other avowedly Jehovanist groups have recently increased their membership, their financial basis, and their influence with media. Even the formerly radical women's movement has grown increasingly ambivalent about the sexual freedoms of the 1960s and 1970s, preferring now to picket existing pornography instead of developing its own. The recent epidemics of "acquired immuno-deficiency syndrome" among homosexuals and genital herpes among the sexually promiscuous can easily be interpreted as divine punishment for sexual transgression. Most important, the government and especially the Supreme Court—the economic and legal gatekeepers of new social forms—have become increasingly restrictive, attempting to undo the sexual innovations of the last quarter-century. Although it is perilous to predict the precise point where the pendulum of social movements begins to turn, at this writing the reaction toward sexual conservativism seems to be gaining momentum.

During the past few decades, Freud's contribution to our understanding of our society has been summed up in the phrase, "the return of the repressed"; for the foreseeable future, however, it might become more accurate to characterize our society with a phrase implicit in Freud's darker side: "the return of the repressors."

Conclusion

I do not feel I have fully answered the questions that motivated me to begin my quest (Why do people want to engage in sex? Why do others want to prevent them?). Like other sex researchers, I too have devoted more attention to the how of sex than to the why; although unlike most of the others, I have tried to depict the mental rather than the behavioral aspects of sex. Nevertheless, I do feel that this endeavor has brought me—and, I hope, the reader as well—at least a few steps closer toward understanding sex, for I am convinced that the essential features of a phenomenon must be described in detail before the phenomenon can be explained in depth.

But even the reader who has tried conscientiously to follow the foregoing discussion of sex might have lost the path somewhere along the way, diverted by its necessarily seductive examples. To bring the disoriented back on track let me retrace the argument more abstractly but more rigorously.

In part one, I tried to describe sex phenomenologically, which I believe is a necessary preliminary to explaining it theoretically. Most previous attempts to construct a science of sex, like those of Kinsey and his followers, have tried to base this science on sexual behavior. But the phenomenological perspective allows us to grasp sex from the inside, so to speak, whereas the behavioral perspective permits us to see only its surface. From Kinsey's interview method (which reveals people's screened memory of their sexual behavior) through Masters and Johnson's observational method (which reveals people's actual sexual behavior) to the method of phenomenological reflection on oneself and empathetic understanding—*verstehen*—of others (which reveals people's ongoing experience of their sexual behavior), we move ever closer toward the essential core of sex.

My goal has been to recapture the subject of sex for the social sciences by reemphasizing its uniquely human aspects. Behaviorism, in contrast, locates the study of human sexuality among the biological sciences by focusing on those aspects it shares with the sexuality of other species. Perhaps the main deficiency of an approach that reduces this human phenomenon to animal behavior is that it cannot account for the long history of sexual fears and repressions (except for some sociobiological speculations about their breeding benefits). The phenomenological approach I have been using here, however, can account for sexual anxiety and taboos. It conceives of the person not as a solid object but as an assemblage of various attributes, bundled together only tenuously in the experience of both oneself and others. Intercourse can be perilous, then, because it entails an exchange of the sex partners' attributes, thereby actually reconstituting each sex partner psychologically and socially (with varying degrees of magnitude and permanence).

A phenomenological analysis of sexual experience also points up the inadequacy of seeing sex as an instinct, as Freud and his followers have done. They have examined sex as output and expression whereas we have examined it as input and impression, which permits us to discern entirely different features of the phenomenon.[1] Since only a man, like Freud,[2] would think of sex as something that "goes outward," this shift from outgoing instinct to incoming experience is, in effect, a conversion from a male model of sex to a female model. Thus phenomenology can bring about a Copernican revolution in sex theory from an androcentric to a gynocentric view of sexuality.

Freud's views on sex have set the terms for its discussion during the twentieth century. Even today, words such as "instinct," libido, "cathexis," "aggression," "expression," "repression," and "sublimation" still bear much of the burden of communication in most treatments of sex. Although it has borne much fruit for many years, I believe Freud's approach to sex has finally exhausted its potential. Consequently, I have tried to develop in these pages a new conceptualization and terminology with which to carry on this discussion. I have tried to articulate the characteristics of sexual experience by spreading them out along spatial, temporal, social, and physical dimensions. Sex is not a simple unified phenomenon, but rather a complex and varied one. Failure to see that the term "sex" means different things to different people exacerbates many controversies about it.

This new approach allows us to distinguish the experience of "erotic reality" from the experience of everyday reality, and to describe the way people move from one to the other. It also provides an explanation for why sex can be condemned. The one-time Freudian sociologist Phillip Slater (1963) observed that activities, particularly courtship and marriage, which withdraw individual's "libidinal cathexis" from the collectivity often entail many social rituals and other collective intrusions that remind them of their larger ties. Translating this social-psychoanalytic observation into our social-phenomenological framework, we could say that activities—like sex—that withdraw individual consciousness from socially shared everyday reality can elicit condemnation unless they are hedged with social rituals.[3]

Sex has a greater potential for eliciting condemnation than other forms of cognitive withdrawal, however, because it draws consciousness into a world far more antithetical to the ordinary world, one in which many of the basic components of the ordinary world are actually inverted. The body, for example, is conceived as a closed container of everyday reality, but in erotic reality it is transformed into an open receptacle. Consequently, activities that seem repulsive in everday reality, such as fellatio or cunnilingus, might become attractive in erotic reality. Sex, in short, is not so much a worldly as an other-worldly desire, drawing consciousness away from both the mundane world of everyday life and its traditional spiritual rival.

Though the world seen through the lustful eye is as clear and sharp as the world seen through the unaroused eye, human existence loses its focus when these two visions are superimposed. Those whose glance must shift continually between erotic reality and everyday reality require some interpretive work to smooth out the incongruity. Much confusion has resulted from a failure to distinguish erotic experience itself from its various interpretations.

Popular interpretations of sex cannot be understood by themselves, but only in relation to the ideologies behind them. These ideologies consist of coherent bodies of basic beliefs, in contrast to their seemingly haphazard applications. The principles of these ideologies—their fundamental conceptions of self and society—may be arbitrary, but, once established, the interpretations of specific aspects of sexuality to which they give rise follow logically.

One implication of this observation is that no sexual activity is obscene in itself, but only in relation to a particular ideology. Therefore, the central question in the controversy over sexuality today should be shifted from "What sexual activities are obscene?" to "Relative to what are some sexual activities obscene?"

If the phenomenological analysis of part one revealed that sexual experience has the potential to become obscene because erotic reality differs so much from everyday reality, the ideological analysis of part two revealed that sexual experience can actually be obscene only when erotic reality disrupts a particular interpretive grid, one that reifies every-day reality into rigid and brittle elements and relations. Thus do the vagaries of human experience have ideological consequence.[4]

The feeling that the sexually aroused self is mutable, more than any other feature of erotic reality mentioned in part one, is the principle threat to this particular interpretive system, as I tried to show in part two. For a mutable self may be subjected to "identity exchange," the reciprocal cognitive transfer of some of each partner's defining characteristics to the other during sexual intercourse. Identity exchange is central to both erotic experience and smut structure, provid-ing the link between the sexy and the dirty. It is the "double helix" of sexuality, involved in both sexual attraction and repulsion. Sex partners are attracted to each other because identity exchange allows each to reproduce himself in the other and the other in himself. Those I have called Jehovan-ists condemn sexual attraction because this same identity exchange undermines their conception of the physical, psychological, and social entities of everyday reality. Their responses range from discomfort to agony whenever the genital generators of their erotic experience are squeezed by the fist of their sexual ideology.

In part two I mapped out the aspects of the Jehovanist world view that are violated by the sexual exchange of identity components in erotic reality. We saw that this ex-change normally disrupts the Jehovanists' closed, integrated view of the body and the self—though they usually tolerate such physical and psychological disruptions if socially con-tained within the institution of marriage. But under no cir-cumstances do Jehovanists tolerate "perverted" modes of exchange, which disrupt their view of appropriate distances and intensities for social interactions, nor the exchange of "perverted" components, which disrupt their view of appropriate separations and distinctions between social categories.

This discontinuity between everyday reality and erotic reality deeply disturbs Jehovanists by making them painfully aware that the world is not all of a piece. They have tried to restore its wholeness by constricting erotic reality as much as possible—compartmentalizing the times and places it may occur (e.g., at night in bed), obscuring its activities (e.g., by turning out the lights), and repressing the very words that describe it.[5]

In part three I examined other responses to this disjunction between realities, which bothers Gnostics as much as Jehovanists but for the opposite reason. For Gnostics, it is ordinary life that corrupts the true nature of the self. Consequently, they have tried to make the world whole by expanding erotic reality rather than everyday reality. They have used every means at hand—such as masturbation, pornography,[6] seduction, and rape—to arouse themselves and others sexually as often and as long as possible.

That preeminent sexual Gnostic, the Marquis de Sade, offered perhaps the most ingenius suggestion about the way to maximize the experience of erotic reality:

> We have the right to decree laws that compel woman to yield to the flames of him who would have her. . . . The law . . . will oblige them to prostitute themselves as often and in any manner we wish. . . .
>
> A man who would like to enjoy whatever woman or girl will henceforth be able . . . to have her summoned at once to duty at one of the houses; and there . . . she will be surrendered to him, to satisfy . . . all the fancies in which he will be pleased to indulge with her, however strange or irregular they may be. . . .
>
> If we admit . . . that all women ought to be subjugated to our desires, we may certainly allow them ample satisfaction of theirs . . . and under the special clause prescribing their surrender to all who desire them, there must be subjoined another guaranteeing them a similar freedom to enjoy all they deem worthy to satisfy them. [1966, pp. 319–21]

(De Sade's surprisingly nonsexist codicil should cause feminists to revise their mistaken view of him as the archetype of male chauvinists.) Rather than discourage the formation of erotic reality, as Jehovanist-dominated Western society has done, the Gnostic de Sade would encourage its formation by designating the desirer, not the desired, as the one who makes the final decision whether to copulate or not. If the one desired refuses, he or she could be legally prosecuted. Thus de Sade would replace the Jehovanist laws that explicitly forbid copulation without permission ("rape") with new Gnostic laws that strip the sexually attractive of their veto power.[7]

Gnostic sexuality raises the question of civil liberties in our society, for it has been continually harassed by Jehovanists both in and out of government. So far, civil libertarians have contended that Gnostic sexual expressions are protected under the constitutional guarantee of freedom of speech.[8] But since I have argued that Gnosticism is as much a religion as Jehovanism, attacks on its sacred texts (pornography), rituals (perversions), and priesthood (prostitutes) actually constitute religious persecution. Gnostic practices would thus be more appropriately defended under the constitutional guarantee of freedom of religion. Pornography, perversion, and prostitution celebrate a particular conception of the world, including social organization, pattern of interaction, self, and body. Behind all the specific disputes over obscenity, then, lies the more fundamental constitutional question: Should the right to be heard—previously extended to Marxism, which advocates overthrowing merely our society—be further extended to sexual Gnosticism, which advocates overthrowing our entire cosmos as well?

Gnostics like sex because it threatens the established order, which they believe is evil; Naturalists like sex because it is nonthreatening, even beneficial, to the established order, which they believe is benign. Jehovanists often accuse Naturalists of being antinomian Gnostics, an imputation which Naturalists try hard to deny.

Naturalists render sex harmless by reducing it to body and behavior as well as by regarding psychological entities and social relations as flexible. For Naturalists, the copulators' essential characteristics are not transferred during copulation; and even if they were, there are no rigid and brittle entities or relations in the Naturalist universe for such an identity exchange to shatter.

Freud was the most important transitional theorist between the older and newer responses to the two realms we have examined. Instead of trying, like the Jehovanists and Gnostics, to fuse erotic and everyday realities into a monolithic consciousness by constricting one or the other, Freud tried to unify human experience by demonstrating that its two parts were not entirely unconnected. He pointed out the many small but significant ways that sex can influence ordinary behavior, such as causing compulsive repetitions or slips of tongue and pen. Freud's famous theory of sexual repression—developed specifically to counter the Jehovanist refusal to consider sex a part of human experience—states in one formulation: "What is repressed in sexual life will reappear [in distorted form] in daily life."[9]

Like Jehovanists and Gnostics, Naturalists deny that erotic and everyday reality are as disjunct as they seem to many people. Since sex disrupts the Naturalist interpretive scheme much less than the Jehovanist or Gnostic, most Naturalists feel free simply to disregard the differences between these two forms of experience. Recently, however, some Naturalists have felt compelled to paper over the ontological crack that, they have decided, does after all exist between erotic and everyday realities, and have employed two opposing means to cover it up. Jehovanist-influenced or "straight" Naturalists regard erotic reality as a province of everyday reality, and apply to sex the same Protestant-Puritan ethic their forefathers applied to work. Through the ascetic "technization of sex," they treat copulation as a task to be accomplished, like other tasks of the workaday world, and emphasize appropriate techniques. Gnostic-influenced or "counterculture" Naturalists regard everyday reality as a province of erotic reality, applying to work the same voluptuary ethic that certain religious mystics have applied to sex. Through the hedonistic "erotization of everyday life," they treat ordinary activities as though they were part of a mating ritual, and stress a style of sensuality. If for one kind of Naturalist sex is "making it," the other kind might declare (with the Beatles) that "all you need [in everyday life] is love." Both still remain Naturalists, however, in denying that erotic reality is seriously destructive of everyday reality.

Naturalists propagate their world view through "sex education" and psychotherapy. Sex education provides an introductory course in the Naturalist ideology as an alternative to the Jehovanist ideology; psychotherapy provides a remedial course in Naturalism for those who have flunked Jehovanism. Although Naturalists believe that their sex-education courses teach children about sex in an unbiased way, they actually proselytize Naturalist metaphysics by depicting a cosmos in which sex is merely a neutral, natural, harmless activity like any other. Jehovanist opponents of sex education, skeptical of Naturalist claims to "objectivity," see the contest in the schools today as not between sex education and no sex education but between one kind of sex education and another. The Jehovanist goal for sex education has always been to teach children that sex is something from which the eyes and mind must be averted or else catastrophic consequences will ensue. Their fairly effective teaching technique has been to conspicuously avoid the topic altogether.

Pornography is the Gnostic form of sex education.[10] Pornography upsets Naturalists almost as much as Jehovanists, for its extreme forms portray sex not as an innocuous human activity but as something that can, will, and should get out of control—destroying the whole world as we know it.

Who is right? Having lured his readers all this way with the tacit promise of ultimately revealing the truth about sex, surely the author will inform them at last whose interpretation of sexual experience is correct.

Unfortunately, I cannot do so. There is no easy way to decide who is right because, like scientific paradigms, each interpretive sexual scheme determines the very facts by which it justifies itself. The best I can do is to separate what I have found to be the enduring kernels of these schemes from their ephemeral husks, and to synthesize their partial truths into still another view of sex—one that I hope will be a little less provincial than the others.

To this more cosmopolitan view of sex Jehovanism would contribute its implicit notion of identity exchange, the cognitive transfer of social characteristics between the partners during sexual intercourse.

Gnosticism would contribute its critical stance, which sees as relative the category system that Jehovanists believe to be absolute. Gnostics use sex as a fulcrum to overturn everything Jehovanists take for granted, from the arrangement of society to what it means to be human. Only through this universal destruction, they feel, can a better world be born.

And Naturalism would contribute its ability to disarm sex, reducing the otherwise explosive repercussions of the clash between identity exchange and social organization. By softening our conception of both the self and society, Naturalism minimizes the personal threat of sex, allowing us to contemplate it with some detachment.

In short, (unlike the Naturalists) we should conceive of sex as more than mere behavior, as also a unique experience whose most important feature is the feeling that essential characteristics of each copulator's self have been transferred to the other; and (unlike the Jehovanists) we should conceive of sex as not necessarily obscene, because the category system disrupted by its identity exchange component is arbitrary and alterable, whatever historical and structural factors have sustained it so far.

Although other views of sex are possible, Jehovanism, Gnosticism, and Naturalism have been the only major ones in the West, for they logically exhaust one dimension in which sex occurs: time. Their long and fruitless controversy over sex has occurred in part because each ideology locates the essence of the sex act at different points along its temporal progression. Gnostics, particularly de Sade and Sartre, equate sex as a whole with a characteristic of its preorgasmic beginning: *power*. Manifesting relative status during foreplay motivates potential copulators to initiate and accelerate their slide into erotic reality. Naturalists, particularly Freud and Kinsey, equate sex as a whole with a feature of its orgasmic middle: *pleasure*. Reducing physical tension terminates each copulator's further need for the other, at least temporarily. Jehovanists, particularly Augustine and Aquinas, equate sex as a whole with a consequence of its postorgasmic end: *procreation*. This teleological goal ensures a long-term connection between copulators whose short-term attraction may periodically wane. Jehovanists, Gnostics, and Naturalists focus on only one temporal segment of sex; by combining these viewpoints, however, we can survey the entire act from beginning to end.

Jehovanists, Gnostics, and Naturalists all share the desire to overcome the split between erotic and everyday realities, either by repressing or by ignoring the discrepencies between the two. They want the world to seem whole, even at the price of blinding themselves to the ways in which it is not. But better, I believe, to be aware of the important differences between everyday and erotic realities, to be aware that we experience the world as plural; and neither to distort nor simplify our experience to make it seem singular.

The lack of fit between the experiential realities generated by sexual arousal and the daily round of life is one of the most sublime perplexities of human existence. It is an enigma encountered by all societies, though how much trepidation it evokes depends on the degree of differentiation and rigidity in each society's conception of everyday reality. Certain conceptions of everyday reality can reduce this split, but none can close it completely. Sex everywhere has something indeterminate about it, something extraordinary—for sex involves more than biology; it involves cosmology as well.

Sex is dirty to the extent that erotic reality threatens to undermine the cosmic categories that organize the rest of social life. This is the source of the fears that surround sex, but also the source of its fascination. If sex did not disintegrate the cosmos to some extent, human beings would want to copulate only as much as do animals, which are much less preoccupied with sex. Those who desire to wash the dirt from sex, to scrub it down to a pure and simple behavior whose only point is physical pleasure, should realize that they are polishing away the very impurities that make it worth doing, that allow sex to rise above mere biological process into existential act.

For sex is one of the few activities through which humanity can become conscious of the incompatibility of cosmic principles. Sex is the wedge that forces apart the components of the cosmos long enough for human inspection. By violating what people believe to be the "natural" order of the cosmos, sex can persuade them that reordering it in other, better ways is always possible.

Still further rewards await the "sexually declassé," those who can cast themselves off sexually from all social moorings.[11] These "erotinauts" who set sail from the harbor of established sexual preferences and phobias (avoiding both the old Scylla of the alleged vices of sex and the new Charybdis of its alleged virtues) to navigate the unknown and perhaps perilous seas beyond will be more than recompensed for their efforts by an incomparable ability to chart the shores of social organization from new perspectives.

I hope by now the reader can see why, for this scientific virtue if for no other, a "dirty" mind is a continual delight.

Notes

Introduction

1. Anna Freud clarified her father's work by listing the techniques, thus revealed, by which the ego defends itself against thwarted sexual (and other) instincts: regression, repression, reaction formation, isolation undoing, projection, introjection, turning against the self, reversal, and sublimation (A. Freud 1946, p. 44).

2. Until recently, most social scientists treated sex in terms of this expression-repression model. For instance, Kingsley Davis (1961) and Ned Polsky (1969) showed that our society does not totally repress prostitution and pornography because these two alternative outlets for sexual expression, seemingly so opposed to the institution of marriage, actually support it. Recently John Gagnon and William Simon (1973) have urged social scientists to abandon this expression-repression model for investigating sex.

3. This phrase is commonly used by pimps to refer to the process of transforming neophytes into experienced prostitutes.

4. The precise distinction between a psychoanalytic and a phenomenological approach to sex has been controversial. One side regards Freudian psychoanalysis as essentially a materialistic and mechanical doctrine that centers sex in the organism, in contrast to phenomenology, which centers sex in consciousness (see, for instance, Wilson 1966, pp. 131, 220). The other side argues that Freudian psychoanalysis is not a purely materialistic or mechanical or objectivistic or scientific doctrine but actually contains many phenomenological elements, such as the

attribution of meaning to all human actions (including sex) and the diffusing of sexuality throughout the whole of human existence (see, Merleau-Ponty 1962, esp. pp. 158–59). Paul Ricoeur (1970, esp. pp. 375–418) has subtly and extensively compared psychoanalysis with phenomenology. Although both probe beneath the immediate contents of consciousness to discover their genesis, he concludes, psychoanalytic inquiry is more arduous; unlike phenomenological inquiry it encounters "resistance" to its investigations and therefore must "work" to overcome them. My own view is that it is true that psychoanalytic *therapy* closely parallels phenomenological investigation, but psychoanalytic *theory* is far more materialistic and consequently serves well as a foil for the mentalistic approach I wish to explicate here.

5. Ideally, of course, research is both significant and systematic. But since this ideal is seldom achieved, I believe actual research should give priority to significance, especially at the early stage of investigation. Given enough time and money, significant research can always be made more systematic; but no amount of effort or funding can bring out significance in systematic research if it isn't there to begin with.

6. Several centuries after the fact, his Christian counterpart Augustine related the incident with disgust and disbelief, and declared that it better not happen again:

> The Cynics. . . hold that since the sexual act is lawful between husband and wife, one should not be ashamed to engage in it in public and to have marital intercourse in any street or square. . . . Diogenes once made an exhibition of himself by putting this theory into practice. . . . However, the Cynics did not continue this practice, and modesty . . . prevailed over error—the mistaken idea that men should make it their ambition to resemble dogs. Hence I am inclined to think that even Diogenes himself, and the others about whom this story is told, merely went through the motions of lying together before the eyes of men who had no means of knowing what was really going on under the philosopher's cloak. . . . If any [Cynic philosopher] were to venture to [act like Diogenes again] they would be overwhelmed, if not with a hail of stones, at any rate with a shower of spittle from the disgusted public. [1972, pp. 581–82]

Even today most liberals still favor removing restrictions only from private sexual acts.

7. Moreover, ordinary people don't know any more about sex than anyone else: they tend simply to repeat the platitudes of their time. On the other hand, the important authors, poets, and dramatists of an age can provide more insight into sex because they are more sensitive to and perceptive about its nuances. In fact, their fame or critical acclaim attests to their having articulated what ordinary people have experienced only incoherently.

8. As everyone who has read or seen them knows, most pornographic books and movies are badly constructed, repetitious, and boring. But it is precisely these features of pornography that allow it to be investigated. Without them, pornography would always succeed in seducing its audience into an erotic realm incompatible with theorizing. A person cannot copulate and cogitate simultaneously, for the former requires the merger of subject and object whereas the latter requires their separation. Keeping one foot in *logos* while the other sinks

deeper and deeper into *eros* is a difficult straddle to sustain. Fortunately for the sex researcher, the low quality of most pornography continually undermines the fictive erotic reality that it is ostensibly trying to create—inadvertently producing the same *Verfremdungseffekt* (estrangement effect) that Bertold Brecht's plays produce deliberately. Although this exasperates those who want to lose themselves in voluptuous visions, it is exactly what is needed by those who want to retain their scientific detachment.

9. Specifically, I regard this book as being in the tradition of Georg Simmel and Erving Goffman. Simmel looked for the highest in the lowest, finding a metaphysical principle in a pot handle; Goffman looks for the lowest in the highest, finding a concentration camp in a mental hospital.

It is this same dialectic between highest and lowest, and not the one between mere opposites, that accounts for the explanatory power and continuing appeal of the Freudian and the Marxist social science traditions. Freud connected the highest cultural achievements with the lowest, most despised biological urge. Marx connected the highest hope for a utopian social organization with the lowest, most despised social class.

Erotic Reality and Everyday Reality

1. A dispute over the nature and location of reality is one in which I prefer not to get involved. It would take me too far from my goal of describing the concrete human experience of two particular worlds, whatever their status ontologically. Indeed, I believe we can better resolve the abstract controversies over what reality is and whether it is "out there" or "in our heads" after we examine more concrete experiences of reality's various manifestations rather than before.

2. Some maintain that this split is psychological. The existential psychiatrist Adrian van Kaam, for instance, believes the sexual world that adolescents suddenly encounter clashes with their childhood organization of life; some may even need psychotherapy to reintegrate the two (Ruitenbeek 1970; p. 129). Others maintain that this split is sociological. The behavioral scientists John Gagnon and William Simon believe our society's current ideology has separated our sex life from the rest of our life, but changing our cultural conception of sex may overcome this division (1973, p. 285). Still others maintain that this split is metaphysical. Augustine believes it is inherent in the current human condition; however, it did not exist before the Fall and will be overcome again after the Resurrection (1972; p. 578).

3. Madame Xaviera Hollander, who stage-managed many elaborate sexual fantasies in her house of prostitution, comments:

> The freak world of make-believe is so delicate and sensitive that the essential mood can be shattered by the least lapse in reality. Therefore, the fantasy you spin, the clothes you wear, and the atmosphere you create are absolutely important. [1972, p. 220].

4. The "My Scene" column of the pornographic newspaper *Screw* provides another illustration of the attempt to retain the best of both realms. In this extreme example of "auto" eroticism, a driver tries to determine how much sexual stimulation he can take without smashing up his car:

> Before I knew it, her head was in my lap and her mouth around my cock. . . .
>
> The more she sucked, the crazier it got. If I had been thinking, I might have gotten scared. . . . Every couple of blocks, at least, I'd suddenly realize I was coming far too close to parked cars, and I would quickly jerk the Ford back toward the center line. . . .
>
> Just then I started to come. . . . When I finally got my eyes open, I realized we were skidding. . . . When the car stopped, it was on the wrong side of the road, and the engine had stalled.
>
> [*Screw* #356, 29 December 1975, p. 19]

Chapter One

1. Schutz elaborates his conception of "relevance system" in his essay "The Stranger":

> In so far as [the actor] is interested in knowledge of his social world, he organizes this knowledge not in terms of a scientific system but in terms of relevance to his actions. . . . He singles out those of its elements which may serve as means or ends for his "use and enjoyment," for furthering his purposes, and for overcoming obstacles. . . . The world seems to him at any given moment as stratified in different layers of relevance, each of them requiring a different degree of knowledge. To illustrate these strata of relevance we may—borrowing the term from cartography—speak of "isohypses" or "hypsographical contour lines of relevance," trying to suggest by this metaphor that we could show the distribution of the interests of an individual at a given moment . . . by connecting elements of equal relevance to his acts, just as the cartographer connects points of equal height by contour lines in order to reproduce adequately the shape of a mountain. The graphical representation of these "contour lines of relevance" would not show them as a single closed field but rather as numerous areas scattered over the map, each of different size and shape. [1964, pp. 92–93]

2. The Doppler effect in physics (named after its discoverer, Christian Doppler) states that wave frequency changes when the source and the observer are moving toward or away from each other. For instance, a train whistle drops in pitch after the train passes. The Doppler effect is most commonly used in astrophysics, where scientists have found that a star's light waves shift to the red end of the spectrum if it is moving away from Earth. This "red shift" is one of the principle proofs that the universe is expanding. A person's perception, it is argued here, exhibits a similar shift whenever he wants to move closer to another sexually.

3. In "Fun and Games" (1961, pp. 15–81), Erving Goffman maintains that all human encounters are composed of these elements.

4. To see the great erotic power of horizontal interaction, consider the quaint eighteenth- and nineteenth- century custom of "bundling," defined by Grose in his *Dictionary of the Vulgar Tongue*:

> A man and a woman lying on the same bed with their clothes on; an expedient practised in America on a scarcity of beds where, on such occasions, husbands and parents frequently permitted travellers to *bundle* with their wives and daughters. [Quoted in Atkins 1972, p. 104]

The many admonitory and amusing commentaries on this practice imply that the suppression of the formal rules for vertical interaction enhances erotic reality even more than clothes inhibit it:

> Some really do, as I suppose,
> Upon design keep on some clothes,
> And yet in truth I'm not afraid
> For to describe a bundling maid;
> She'll sometimes say when she lies down,
> She can't be cumbered with a gown,
> And that the weather is so warm,
> To take it off can be no harm. . . .
>
> But she is modest, also chaste,
> While only bare from neck to waist,
> And he of boasted freedom sings,
> Of all above her apron strings.
> And when such freedoms feebly bared,
> I leave for others to relate,
> How long she'll keep her virgin state,
> [Quoted in Atkins 1972, pp. 106–7).

5. In "A Propos Lady Chatterly's Lover" (1968, pp. 340–42), Lawrence recalls an early twentieth-century pope who insisted that women cover their bare flesh, especially their arms, in church. Short skirts and pants are still prohibited in the Vatican.

6. Zetterberg bases erotic rank on "emotional overcomeness" rather than on sexual attractiveness (1966, p. 141), although both sets of rankings would be highly correlated. Still, the notion of erotic rank was an important breakthrough in stratification theory, for it legitimized supplimenting the many studies of macroeconomic rankings with new investigations of microinteraction rankings. Unfortunately, Zetterberg himself did not refine erotic rank into an ordinal scale and overstressed its secretiveness, even to the point of calling his article "The Secret Ranking." Apparently, it had been kept a secret only from sociologists.

7. The *Los Angeles Times* (18 May 1979, part IV, pp. 1ff) reports that the historical passivity of the repulsive—at least the physically repulsive—may be changing. Recently, several organizations such as the "Committee Against Physical Prejudice" and "Uglies Unlimited" have been formed to raise their class consciousness and to protect their class interests.

8. The attractive/repulsive split (which crosscuts the sexes) may be an even more fundamental feature of microstratification in our society than the male/female

split, for the life chances of the attractive and the repulsive may differ far more than those of men and women.

9. The repulsive, however, may become even more repellent in erotic reality than in everyday reality, for in daily life one can at least focus on their nonsexual features. *Psychology Today* (September 1979, p. 92) reports a psychological experiment that involved rating the attractiveness of the opposite sex by subjects, some of whom had been sexually aroused by pornography. The researchers, Gerdi Weidner, Joseph Istvan, and William Griffit, found that "sexual arousal does indeed make attractive men and women seem better looking, but it also makes unattractive ones seem worse." Still to be determined is why the erotic status of those repulsive in everyday life is sometimes raised, sometimes lowered, by viewing them through the optics of sexual arousal.

10. In *Ragtime* E. L. Doctorow suggests that limitations on the population of potential local lovables may also raise the erotic status of the repulsive, at least temporarily. In these passages "Father" has gone with Admiral Peary on an expedition to the North Pole:

> The Esquimo families lived all over the ship, camping on the decks and in the holds. They were not discreet in their intercourse. They cohabited without even undressing, through vents in their furs, and they went at it with grunts and shouts of fierce joy. One day Father came upon a couple and was shocked to see the wife thrusting her hips upwards to the thrusts of her husband. An uncanny animal song came from her throat. . . . This filthy toothless Esquimo woman with the flat brow and the eyes pressed upwards by her cheekbones, singing her song and pushing back. . . .

Later:

> Waiting for Peary to return to the *Roosevelt* he had heard the wind howl at night and had clasped with love and gratitude the foul body, like a stinking fish, of an Esquimo woman. He had put his body into the stinking fish. . . .

Back home:

> Now in New Rochelle [Father] smelled on himself the oil of fish liver, fish on his breath, fish in his nostrils. He scrubbed himself red. [1975, pp. 84, 125]

11. Whether sexual arousal actually does increase the salience of physical characteristics relative to social and psychological ones—and whether it should—has aggravated antagonism between the sexes, between age groups, and between generations. One side sees this ideological battle as a contest between "natural" and "sublimated" conceptions of sex whereas the other side sees it as a contest between "adolescent" and "mature" sexual views.

12. Sartre observes how sexual desire separates the body from its milieu:

> Now at first the Other's body is not flesh for me. . . . We can not perceive the Other's body . . . in the form of an isolated object. . . . The Other's body is originally a body in a situation. . . . Ordinarily it is hidden by cosmetics, clothing, etc.; in particular it is hidden by *movements*. Nothing is less "in the flesh" than a dancer even though she is nude. Desire is an attempt to strip the body of its movements as of its clothing and to make it exist as pure flesh; it is an attempt to *incarnate* the Others' body. [1956, p. 389; italics his]

13. Behaviorists have described how sexual arousal alters a person's body physically: penises erect, nipples stiffen, vaginas lubricate, etc. But phenomenological psychiatrists, like Adrian van Kaam, have suggested we should pay at least equal attention to how sexual arousal alters it perceptually:

> This erotic perception makes us aware how we may sexually enjoy our body and that of the other. . . . We experience our (and the other sex's) body, therefore, not merely as a complex object depicted in a book of physiology. . . . Our perception as erotic reveals the body to us as sexual and outlines for us its sexual articulations and appeals. [Quoted in Ruitenbeek 1970; p. 132]

14. Recent research on pheromones has shown that smell is the prime sexual attractant for many insects, reptiles, and mammals. But the sight of certain curves and kinesics is a much more powerful sexual attractant than smell for most human beings, demonstrating how misleading it may be to extrapolate up the evolutionary ladder.

15. Of course, each culture, historical period, and person finds a different set of curves sexually arousing. Some like thin, some like fat, some very fat:

> King Mutesa I of the Baganda used to feed his wives on cream. They became so fat that they could not stand but had to roll round the floor. [Atkins 1970, p. 201]

But the fact that the particular curves that induce erotic reality vary widely does not deny the possibility that some sexually arousing forms—or some of their transformations—are universal. The science that searches for them could be called "erotometry."

16. It is astonishing how drastically the presence or absence of a few milliliters of bone, flesh, fat, pus, or scar tissue on a person's face can alter the entire course of his or her life—giving new meaning to Freud's remark that "anatomy is destiny." Few other physical factors so small have social consequences so great.

17. The mass distribution of pornographic films, however, may eventually give audiences a taste for larger genitals. Since this is the first time in history when millions of people are seeing realistic intercourse between huge penises and vaginas, one wonders whether they will ever again be satisfied with normal-sized organs.

18. Labeling theorists believe that our society has regarded the aged as unsexy only because of arbitrary prejudice. (Of course, few labeling theorists attempt to prove their theory by copulating with the aged themselves.) It would be a good test of the limits of labeling theory, however, to discover whether the inability of the geriatric to arouse the rest of us sexually is biologically inherent in them or merely cultural conditioning in ourselves. It will probably be found that both these factors determine our sexual response to the aged. The progress of aging actually turns off many erotic generators while activating some new ones, but every society decides in its own way whether to focus on those fading or those intensifying.

19. One way aging decreases sexuality is by making adults look like sexless infants. Both infants and the aged at times share bald heads, round figures, weak, erratic kinesics, and other physical traits. Another way aging decreases sexuality is by increasing the resemblance between older men and older women. Like

the undeveloped gender differentiation between the very young, the reduced gender differentiation between the very old minimizes their sexuality for most people. (The very fat and the very thin exhibit the same desexualization for the same reason.)

20. Of course, these are not the only factors that stimulate mental arousal. I have left unexplored, for instance, the entire dimension of language as a generator of erotic reality. It would be worth discovering the statements that articulate, and thereby reinforce, the sender's high erotic transmission power ("You're beautiful!") or the receiver's high sensitivity to his partner's sexual signals ("I think I'm in love with you.").

21. Al Goldstein, editor of the pornographic newspaper *Screw*, has also developed a scale to measure the erotic power of pornographic movies, which he calls the "peter meter." Many people regard any attempt to measure erotic reality, however, as impossible, immoral, or at best comical. No one inside erotic reality can quantify it, they claim (because numbers do not exist in this realm) and no one outside erotic reality should quantify it, they claim (because numbers that measure only observable behavior debase human experience). Those who wish to quantify the phenomenology of sex, then, can neutralize these qualms about quantification only by inventing a technique for placing themselves and their instruments inside and outside erotic reality simultaneously.

Chapter Two

1. In this chapter I intend to analyze the sex act phenomenologically in the same developmental way that Van de Velde analyzes it physiologically in part three of his book *Ideal Marriage* (1965, originally published in 1926). Although marred by errors of fact, weaknesses of theory, and intrusions of personal taste, his book still remains the classic in its field. It is an awesomely comprehensive attempt to distinguish each of the biological and behavioral elements of sex and to connect them all both statically and dynamically.

2. This is no mere metaphor. From the perspective of the sociology of knowledge, natural scientists *first* encountered accelerating attraction in social experience and *then* projected it onto the natural world. In reading it back into the social world, therefore, I am merely reintrojecting what was previously projected out of it, returning a borrowed metaphor to its original rightful ground.

3. Tantric Buddhists, who believe that increasing involvement in erotic reality is a symptom of cognitive involvement in all earthly activities, try to gain enough control over their experience to stop this phenomenological slide. Most Buddhists reject such worldly involvement as the prime source of human suffering. Tantric Buddhists try to perform physical sex detached from the mental descent it usually entails, both as symbol and practice for their goal of engaging in all human activities without being caught up in them cognitively.

4. Despite the unscientific nature of this collection, it is a valuable resource for sex research. Nowhere else, to my knowledge, do such articulate people expound on such a topic. Even its obvious exaggerations at least reveal the norm.

5. During a person's first few attempts or after a lengthy abstinence, sexual performance is likely to be stilted. Practicing its procedures with an imaginary partner is not the same as performing them with a real partner, whose actual

requirements and rhythms are different. Since the world does not respond as facilely in reality as it does in fantasy, whoever predicates his or her sexual actions on partners' ideal responses will be disconcerted by their actual responses—possibly enough to collapse the whole copulatory interaction. Sex is an activity where practice (at least imaginary practice) doesn't necessarily make perfect. On practicing in general, see Goffman 1974, pp. 59–65.

6. For instance:

> Yesterday, [the Michigan Court of Appeals] upheld the legality of a Liquor Control Commission rule banning nude dancing in bars. . . .
>
> It said the commission may outlaw nude dancing—obscene or not—in licensed establishments when the combination of dancing and drinking "increases to an unacceptable level the likelihood of illegal and/or disorderly conduct."
>
> [*San Diego Union*, 22 August 1979, p. A17]

7. Deriving his conception of sex from Sartre, the American philosopher Thomas Negal theorizes:

> All stages of sexual perception are varieties of identification of a person with his body. What is perceived is one's own or another's *subjection* to or *immersion* in his body, a phenomenon which has been recognized with loathing by St. Paul and St. Augustine. . . . [1969, pp. 12–13]

The religious connotations of Sartre's term "incarnation" are appropriate, for self-embodiment theory in modern sociology (Mead, Goffman) is similar to soul-embodiment theory in early Christianity, whose discussion of this topic is in many ways more extensive and profound.

8. Thomas Negal escapes Sartre's one-sided sexism by viewing the self-embodiment process as operating through reciprocal perception:

> Sexual desire leads to spontaneous interactions with other persons, whose bodies are asserting their sovereignty in the same way, producing involuntary reactions and spontaneous impulses in *them*. These reactions are perceived, and the perception of them is perceived, and that perception is in turn perceived; at each step the domination of the person by his body is reinforced, and the sexual partner becomes more possessible by physical contact, penetration, and envelopment.
>
> Desire is therefore not merely the perception of a preexisting embodiment of the other, but ideally a contribution to his further embodiment which in turn enhances the original subject's sense of himself. This explains why it is important that the partner be aroused . . . by the awareness of one's desire. [1969, p. 13]

He devotes the rest of his article to showing how sexual perversions result from various breakdowns in the reciprocity of this mutual perception.

9. Perhaps the most extreme way to inform someone about the later stages of the sex act is through pornography, which prefigures the activities through which a self will become embodied. Critics of mass culture like George Steiner detest pornography precisely because it preprograms sexual experience in this way, homogenizing society's heterogeneity:

> Sexual relations are, or should be, one of the citadels of privacy, the night place where we must be allowed to gather the splintered, harried elements of our consciousness to some kind of inviolate order and repose. It is in sexual experience that a human being alone, and two human beings in that attempt at total communication which is also communion, can discover the unique bent of their identity. There we may find for ourselves, through imperfect striving and repeated failure, the words, the gestures, the mental images which set the blood to racing. In that dark and wonder ever renewed both the fumblings and the light must be our own.
>
> The new pornographers subvert this last, vital privacy; they do our imagining for us. They take away the words that were of the night and shout them over the rooftops, making them hollow. The images of our lovemaking, the stammerings we resort to in intimacy, come prepackaged. . . . [1965, p. 18]

In any event, it usually takes a clever tongue to persuade acquaintances to expose themselves to pornography, for portraying the later stages of a sexual relation may prove too much for the early stages of an intimate relation ("Well! I never! How dare you suggest such a thing!").

10.
> The [British] Advisory Group on the Law of Rape was formed following a highly publicized case involving a Royal Air Force sergeant who invited three younger Air Force men to his home to have sexual intercourse with his wife.
>
> The sergeant warned them that his wife might struggle a bit, but told them not to worry. In the melee that followed the woman was raped by the three men in turn, and then by her husband. When she was finally released, she grabbed her coat and headed for the hospital and the police.
>
> The three men were eventually convicted of rape, and her husband of aiding and abetting.
>
> The men appealed their case to the Law Lords, Britain's highest court of appeal, where the court ruled that if a man honestly believed a woman consented to sexual intercourse, he should not be convicted.
>
> The convictions were not overturned, however, on the grounds that the jury was not convinced that the men believed that the woman was consenting.
>
> [*The New York Times*, 13 December 1975, p. 22]

11. The recent controversy over whether rapists may claim that they were "led on" by the woman's "sexy clothing" reveals the difference in perspective between arouser and aroused. Those who dress provocatively want their audience to appreciate their looks while remaining firmly anchored in everyday reality. At most they intend to draw others only up to the portico of erotic reality. But should their outfit push one of its viewers too far down the sensual slide for him to stop his momentum, they are startled to encounter a monstrous urge for total sexual satisfaction that can no longer be denied.

12. Goffman (1974, p. 255) states that the absence of this transitional divestment process in art classes and gynecological exams "presumably functions to stabilize the application of a natural framework under difficult circumstances," that is, under circumstances that facilitate the application of a sociosexual

framework instead. From my perspective, Goffman is saying that the erotic reality generated by total nudity is not strong enough to overcome the everyday reality generated by other aspects of art classes and gynecological exams without the additional erotic increment generated by the transitional divestment process. In short, total nudity without undressing is not sexually arousing enough to pull art students or gynecologists from everyday into erotic reality, given other situational constraints.

13. The relation between erotodynamics and thermodynamics is complex. Heat requires less clothing, which exposes more of the body's erotic generators, but exhausts the energy necessary to appreciate them fully. Thus male-female saunas and nude beaches are not as erotic as we might expect, even though everyone is lying around with all his or her erotic generators hanging out. Conversely, cold requires more clothing, which exposes fewer of the body's erotic generators, but increases desire for one of the byproducts of sexual activity—the creation of warmth.

14. Swimsuit competition in beauty contests is the most obvious exploitation of these overlap points. Note that underwear is never substituted for swimsuits in these contests, even though both show approximately the same amount of flesh (actually underwear usually shows a little less). Bathing suits are designed to encapsulate the body from the outside, underwear to encapsulate the outside from the body, particularly its soiling exudations. Like bathing suits, the colors and designs on underwear today indicate that it is meant to be seen; unlike bathing suits its stains indicate that it is not meant to be studied.

15. Moralists use the distinctly different erotic experiences evoked by uncovering more and more parts of the body to justify preventing the pubic from appearing in public; for instance, by permitting topless but not bottomless dancing. The movie rating categories are perhaps our society's most precise attempt to draw the line at different points along the sensual slide. Originally, a G-rated movie presented an uninterrupted continuum of everyday reality; a GP-rated movie presented only a verbal intrusion of erotic reality through sexually suggestive words; an R-rated movie presented a visual intrusion through such secondary sex characteristics as naked breasts; and an X-rated movie presented a complete reality replacement through the appearance and use of genitals in intercourse. In "soft-core" pornography the camera focuses mostly on the transition between clothed and partial nudity, shyly shifting away when the genitals were about to appear; in "hard-core" pornography it stares straight ahead unblinking, even when erotic experience rapidly intensifies as the genitals come into focus and go into action. Recently, however, the hemline of movie censorship has once again crept upward. Brief flashes of secondary sex characteristics in GP-rated movies and of primary ones in R-rated movies are now allowed—apparently based on the theory that these glimpses of another realm are too transient to actually generate it in consciousness, for the erotic perception needs some time to develop.

Since the beginning of the code in 1968, an automatic language rule has required an R-rating for movies that contain the "four-letter" obscene words. But as sensory inflation has pushed visual depictions of erotic generators into GP movies, requiring an R for movies that contain merely verbal allusions to sex has led to increasing questions about the rating system's consistency.

16. Problems for philosophers usually present no problem for laymen because

these problems seem to lie in the categories philosophers use to cut up the cosmos, not in the cosmos itself. The Cartesian mind-body problem is no exception. While philosophers have long wondered how something so nebulous as a mind can become coextensive with a body, copulators have always used specific practical techniques to make mental life coextensive with physical existence, at least temporarily.

17. The "laying-on-of-hands" technique used to maneuver someone into erotic reality is very similar to that used to manipulate someone in everyday reality. For this reason "massage" is a tactile overlap point between everyday and erotic reality, encouraging prostitutes to disguise themselves as masseuses or masseurs (instead of, say, palm readers). Masseuses and masseurs have already finessed the resistance points usually found along the path from clothed to nude and from hands-off to hands-on, for their fingers have prior permission to wander in the vicinity of secondary and primary erotic generators.

18. The main event of the center ring—genital insertion—should be distinguished from the diversions of the side rings—kissing and caressing body parts still within reach after each copulator has become tethered to the other's genitals. These secondary sexual activities prevent the identity from coagulating around the genitals too completely, allowing the seething psychological interchange processes occasionally to eject selfhood back onto the rest of the body, just as the sun sporadically releases a buildup of boiling gases into its corona.

19. Since the muscular tension/release rhythms of erotic reality are similar to the aural tension/release rhythms of music, the latter can reinforce the former. Today stereos have replaced blindfolded musicians as a seducer's prime erotic accoutrement. Conversely, musical rhythms can interfere with erotic rhythms. Adult book stores often play excessively loud and irritating music to interrupt their customers' natural drift into erotic reality, encouraging them to buy pornography for future use instead of consuming it on the spot.

20. The ethologist Hediger distinguishes two groups of mammals on the basis of their copulatory behavior: (1) most herbivores and aquatic mammals (such as whales and dolphins) whose orgasm occurs almost immediately after insertion; (2) most carnivores whose orgasm occurs a long while after insertion (De Ropp 1969, pp. 84–85). Although this distinction between mammals presents no problem for intraspecies sex, it might do so for human beings who attempt to practice bestiality.

21. The English critic John Atkins observes that intellectuals in particular often overshoot (more precisely, undershoot) their mark. They are so caught up in other realms that they find their focus on erotic reality difficult to sustain:

> It is said that men who are preoccupied with spiritual and mental problems tend to suffer from sexual incapacity because scientific ideas pass through their minds at the moment when coition requires complete attention. Apparently lust is a demanding beast and will brook no dilution of effort. There was once a mathematician who never succeeded in completing his embrace because his whole being was so taken up by problems of geometry and calculus that he would be shunted from the labour of Venus to the solution of SSSRpdpdOdz. [1972, p. 282]

22. Prostitutes have more vested interest in becoming proficient in techniques that accelerate their partners' orgasm than in those that decelerate it. A London prostitute describes this as one of the secrets of her profession:

There's some of them lies still as stones, they think it's more ladylike or
something; but I say they don't know which side their bread's buttered.
Listen; if you lie still the bloke may spend half the night sweating away. But
if you bash it about a bit he'll come all the quicker and get out and away and
leave you in peace. Stupid to spin it out longer than you need, isn't it? . . .
And then, you know, there are all sorts of little gentle things you can do to a
client so that with a bit of luck they come before they even get into me.
When they do I look ever so loving and say: "Traitor." [Young, 1959,
pp. 20, 21]

23. In *The Art of Love*, the poet Kenneth Koch provides a technical manual for
overcoming the difficulties encountered by someone trying to actualize more
fanciful fantasies:

Nailing a woman to the wall causes too much damage
(Not to the wall but to the woman—you after all want too
enjoy her and love her again and again). You can, however, wrap
    tape around her arms, waist, ankles, and knees
And nail this to the wall. You'll enjoy the pleasure of nailing
And the very thought of it should make her scream. You can fit
    this tape
On her like tabs, so your girl will be like a paper doll. . . .
If she is able to talk she will probably ask you to take her down,
Which you then can do. However, if she wants to stay up there . . .
    leave her there and run up against her
As hard as you can, until the very force of your bumping
Breaks tape from nail or girl from tape or breaks great chunks of wall
So you and she lie tumbled there together
Bruises on her body, plaster on your shoulder, she
    bloody, she hysterical, but joy in both your hearts. [1975, pp. 78, 79]

24. Perhaps the most effective nonverbal reassurance ritual is kissing. John Gagnon
and William Simon note that kissing is especially important after sexual activities that seem much less savory in everyday reality than they do in erotic reality:

Whether the act continues to orgasm or does not, there is the problem of
how to manage the oral kissing behavior that often follows mouth-genital
contact of any sort. Vaginal fluids or semen have meanings that are partially rooted in feelings about excretion, and for both partners such kissing
frequently becomes an act of reassurance and denial. The act of oral kissing
also returns the behavior to a more conventional sequence, coincidentally
returning the bodies to immediately pre-coital positions. [1973, p. 90]

25.
It is when two actors return to the world of speech that they must now
begin to integrate the sexual performance into their other expectations of
each other. The first words that they exchange must be assuring of continued pleasure and linked to further desire. What does one say when
returning to the conventional world? There are phrases that are routinely
used: "That was good," "Hello," or some other reestablishment of conventional realities. [Gagnon and Simon 1973, p. 79]

26. Erotic reality differs from everyday reality not only in the static ways described
in chapter 1 but also in its dynamic pushes and pulls. Those in erotic reality feel

different tugs and pressures than those in everyday reality. Therefore coitus interruptus will suddenly reorganize experience even more severely than orgasm because the latter usually occurs after most of these erotic tensions have been worked out.

The difference between these static and dynamic aspects of erotic reality also account for two types of impotence. In one, an individual has no erotic organization of experience at all. In the other, an individual experiences the static aspects of erotic reality but has no ability to organize its dynamic aspects enough to bring it to a conclusion. Merleau-Ponty contrasts the "pathological" absence of erotic experience in an impotent man with the "normal" experience of a sexually active man:

> It is the very structure of perception or erotic experience which has undergone change in Schneider. In the case of a normal subject, a body is not perceived merely as any object . . . : the visible body is subtended by a sexual schema, which is strictly individual, emphasizing the erogenous areas, outlining a sexual physiognomy. . . . But for Schneider a woman's body has no particular essence: it is, he says, pre-eminently character which makes a woman attractive, for physically they are all the same. . . . Perception has lost its erotic structure, both spatially and temporally. What has disappeared from the patient is his power of projecting before himself a sexual world, of putting himself in an erotic situation or, once such a situation is stumbled upon, of maintaining it or following it through to complete satisfaction. [1962, p. 156]

27. Van de Velde warns copulators to avoid imitating these low-status behaviors even accidently:

> In coitus, the rush of air into the vagina has an unfortunate effect. . . . The piston-like backwards and forwards motion of the phallus may occasionally force some of the air out of the vaginal cavity again, to the accompaniment of unpleasantly suggestive and quite audible whistling sounds. . . . The process is only too audible and extraordinarily repulsive in its effect. [1965, p. 215]

28. If one is going to immigrate to "death reality" permanently, one might as well have a more enjoyable embarkation point than everyday reality. Ovid suggests that the sensual slide into erotic reality is the best way to leave ordinary life behind:

> But as for me, let me go in the act of coming to Venus;
>   In more senses than one, let my last dying be done.
> And at my funeral rites, let one of the mourners bear witness:
>   "That was the way, we know, he would have wanted to go." [1966, p. 55]

29. Those who are raped usually remain in everyday reality because rapists refuse to remove any impediments to the victims' journey into erotic reality, while threatening them unless they facilitate the rapists' own journey there ("Do as I say and you won't get hurt"). (Although people may be drawn out of everyday reality by the powerful appeal of eros, most people are pushed back into it by the even more powerful fear of death or harm, for one can respond to this threat effectively only in everyday reality.) On the other hand, those who are seduced

are more likely to accompany seducers on a trip to erotic reality because seducers try to remove as many impediments to the journey of the seduced as possible, while promising to continue to do so ("If you'll grant me this one wish, I'll love you forever").

30. Since the largest number of technical problems must be overcome to operationalize complex or violent sexual activities, they are the ones most often relegated to fantasy, as in this letter to the *Village Voice* (3 May 1976, p. 4):

> Dear Editor:
> Women have rape fantasies . . . for the same reasons that men patronize prostitutes: Because they believe in the possibility of sex without complications. The fantasy rapist (unlike a real rapist, or a real lover) knows exactly what to do to arouse and satisfy the fantasist. It is embarrassing to ask a sexual partner for a particular attention; humiliating if he refuses; frustrating if he never quite gets is right. . . . The fantasy rapist does not expect a hot breakfast in the morning. Nor does he expect his victim to display the sexual virtuosity recommended by Xaviera Hollander (or Marabel Morgan). No fantasy rapist ever called his victim frigid. . . .

Sex and Dirt

1. Although experience and interpretation are too tightly intertwined in actual human existence to be easily unraveled, I have found it useful to distinguish them for the purpose of this analysis. Future researchers, however, may wish to show how even our erotic experiences themselves are colored by our interpretation of them.

2. In fact, the sexual organs and the organs of excretion have been both closer and farther apart during the course of evolution. Robert S. de Ropp summarizes the uneven development of this bifurcation:

> One may regret that the pattern we see in the snail, the spider or the squid, in which the sexual function is separated from that of excretion, failed to become established among vertebrates. . . . The words "dirty" and "filthy," so commonly used in connection with sexual behavior, clearly show that the distaste man feels for his excrements has rubbed off on the sexual function. . . . This problem would not have arisen if men, like squids, had sex organs on the end of their arms and could offer their sperm to the female with no more danger of fecal contamination than is involved in shaking hands. . . .
>
> With the development of the vertebrate pattern [however,] a link was established between defecation, urination and reproduction. . . . Sperm and urine were voided through a common duct (the urethra), often by a special organ (the penis). Entrance to the female tract became localized *inter feces et urinam* and birth took place through the same lowly chamber, a fact that impressed St. Augustine as offering irrefutable evidence of the fallen state of man. . . .
>
> The cloaca, the common sewer, . . . for amphibians, birds and reptiles forms the sole exit both for excrements and for the products of the sex

glands. . . . As the mammals evolved, the cloaca became divided into two openings. The anus, now sole exit of the intestine, retained from the old cloacal days certain sexual associations which make it one of the erogenous zones of the mammalian body. But the focal point of sexual awareness was shifted forward, becoming concentrated on the clitoris of the female and the glans penis of the male. [1969, pp. 58–59, 82–83; see also Carr 1971, pp. 59–61]

3. These inquiries originated in the Gestalt psychology of Wertheimer, Koffka, and Kohler, who believed that people view the phenomena of their world not as isolated elements, but as wholes. These early Gestaltists, however, were more interested in how one brings elements together into a coherent whole than in how one reacts to some element that cannot be fitted into this system.

4. I will use "disgusting" and "dirty" (or "unclean" or "obscene") as synonyms, following Herold Stern in "The Ethics of the Clean and the Unclean" (1957). In "The Sublime and the Obscene" (1968, pp. 162–64), R. Meager tries to distinguish these terms. Building on Kant's conception of disgusting art, which represents an object as "intruding itself for our enjoyment while we strive against it with all our might," Meager restricts "disgust" to successful strivings while reserving "obscene" for unsuccessful ones. But since such success is always a matter of degree, it is difficult to see how to apply this distinction empirically in particular cases. Both Stern and Meager agree, however, that both the disgusting and the obscene attack human dignity. In this part, I will be attempting to specify the conception of human dignity they attack.

5. The sociologist Alan Segal describes the spread of cognitive contamination from another source in his parallel investigation of Phillip Roth's novel *Portnoy's Complaint*:

> The breaking of one rule involves an attack on the whole system of rules, rituals, personal identity and community. This can be seen clearly in the episode in which Portnoy . . . refuses to go to synagogue with his family. His refusal provokes from his father . . . a series of abusive claims: that Portnoy is wearing *unclean* if not indecent clothes, that he start looking like a *human being*, . . . that he has no respect nor love for his father, nor any respect for the Jewish people, their learning, their suffering and their history. . . . By one specific attempt at independence, Portnoy . . . invokes upon himself a devasting and total attack. [1971, p. 264; emphasis added]

6. These dimensions constitute an entire "cosmos" because they concern the nature, internal structure, and external relations of both the individual and the society. By constructing our cognitive map of the obscene, then, we are in effect delineating a cosmos in which sex can be found dirty; delineating the only possible cosmos, in fact, in which the specific forms of sex that our society condemns could logically be condemned. (In part three, I will adumbrate the requirements for another cosmos in which sex cannot be found dirty.)

I also want to stress that we are not seeking the structure of "reality" here, but only the structure of a *conception* of reality. Reality may be all flux and process, but conceptions of reality endure long enough to develop more static structures. Moreover, I have minimized the constructionist aspects of sexual interpretations in order to emphasize their structuralist aspects. Like interpretations of other phenomena, interpretations of sex are constructed anew in every situation (even if out of old pieces). But because the basic processes of constructing interpretations of all phenomena are so similar ("universal," according to ethnomethodology), the particular process of constructing an interpretation of sex is far less interesting than the particular interpretation actually constructed, which may differ greatly from other possible interpretations.

7. The same approach could be used to determine the fundamental categories held by other groups as well. The *relation* between a group's normative category system and the aspects of sex it finds dirty is everywhere a constant—even though the particular category violated, and consequently the particular aspect of sex regarded as revolting, varies from group to group. The legal theorist David Richards notes that the "form" of the obscene is transcultural, even if its "content" is culturally specific:

> To the extent people in different cultures take different attitudes to certain bodily functions, those cultures will take different views of those things that are obscene, though the cultures both share the concept of the obscene as abuse of bodily function. . . . Thus for Tahitians, displays of coitus are not obscene, but displays of eating are obscene. [1974, pp. 52–53]

For the beginnings of research into cross-cultural generalizations about sexual taboos, see Marshall and Suggs's (1971) review of anthropological studies on this topic.

8. Note that sexual ideology is not necessarily related to political ideology. Radicals may be as sexually restrictive as conservatives; communists as prudish as Catholics:

> Sex is about to enter the classroom for the first time at selected Moscow schools in the latest sign of a changing official attitude to the once taboo subject. . . .
>
> The magazine "Health" which led the break from the orthodox view that sex and communism do not mix, advised a couple of years ago that intercourse should ideally last two minutes. . . .
>
> "The word is just never mentioned, ever, at school," one Muscovite woman commented. "Biology teachers have the greatest difficulty getting around subjects like cats and kittens without mentioning sex."
>
> [*Los Angeles Times* 26 February 1978, part 1, p. 16]

9. Admittedly, "Jehovanism" is an ugly name, but then it represents an ugly view of sex or, rather, a view of sex as ugly. This term designates those whose reaction to sex is violent, either outwardly or inwardly. I felt a neologism like Jehovanism would be better than the more common puritanism or Victorianism because, being less historically specific, it can stand for a more fundamental and more inclusive tradition.

10. From its inception, the Jehovanist world view has been concerned with classifying all aspects of the world—including sex—as either "pure" or "polluting." According to Herold Stern (1966, p. 89): "Biblical ethics concerns itself primarily with the classification of material things and acts into the Disgusting and the non-Disgusting . . . the 'Clean' and the 'Unclean.'"

Chapter Three

1. Sartre criticizes Freud mainly for differentiating part of the person from the rest. Lionel Trilling's excellent summary states:

   "By the distinction between the 'id' and the 'ego'," Sartre says, "Freud has cut the psychic whole into two." The bad faith of psychoanalysis follows from this dicotomy. It consists of one part of the psychic whole regarding the other part as an object and thereby disclaiming responsibility for it. . . . The psychic facts which are made manifest to him, although they are represented as being of decisive importance in their effect upon him, he apprehends as external phenomena, having their existence apart from the consciousness which constitutes his being. "I am not these psychic facts," Sartre says, "insofar as I receive them passively . . . ," that is, insofar as he receives them as objects. [1972, pp. 144–45]

   Trilling (1972, pp. 147–49) points out, however, that Sartre's attack applies only to Freud's early work, for in his later work Freud tried to overcome his previously absolute distinction between ego and id.

2. In *The Ritual Process* (1969, pp. 94–107, 172–78), Victor Turner was the first to specify the actual operation of Durkheim's thesis that social ceremonies renew community energy. The Ndembu (and implicitly other primitive communities and, to a lesser extent, modern societies), he discovered, periodically set aside their usual social structure on certain ceremonial occasions. They go into these "liminal" (i.e., extreme or boundary) states to relieve the tensions generated by their usually rigid social structure, allowing it to function more efficiently after it returns to normal.

3. A more extensive study provides additional support for what may seem merely one madam's opinion:

   A study of high-priced prostitutes showed that 60 percent of their clients are political leaders or powerful corporate chieftains who usually prefer "kinky" sex, according to a report delivered yesterday to the American Psychiatric Association.

   Public figures frequently seek flagellation while they are held in bondage, and indulge in fetishism, exhibitionism, and voyeurism, the study said. . . .

   Drs. Samuel S. Janus and Barbara Bess said they interviewed 42 call girls and 10 madams in New York City, California, and Las Vegas. [*Boston Globe*, 14 May 1976, p. 2]

4. Members of the women's movement find one version of the compensation model of sex disturbing: that in which the more equality and freedom women achieve in society, the more disparity and domination they wish to experience in bed. This model would explain why women who become the most liberated socially sometimes become the least liberated sexually, either in fact, as in Elizabeth McNeill's confession *Nine and a half Weeks* (1978) or in fantasy, as in Nancy Friday's survey *My Secret Garden*:

   It seems that the more liberated I become (I'm really digging Women's Lib now) the more I fantasize about the spanking and the bondage. Since I'm fully liberated in my work situation, social life, etc., it's almost as if I'm trying to achieve some sort of counterbalance to this liberation in my sexual life. I've always had the first two fantasies (spanking and bondage), but never so intensely as since I've been involved in Women's Lib, or rather, since I've embraced the principles behind the movement. I am sure there are other women like me who having emerged from being under male domination crave to return to it in bed. [Friday 1974, p. 130]

5. The increase in sexual attraction to strangers in modern society may result simply from increased contact with them, especially on public transportation:

"Before the appearance of omnibuses, railroads, and street cars in the nineteenth century, [people] were not in a situation where for periods of minutes or hours they could or must look at each other without talking to one another." [Simmel 1921, p. 360]

The narrowly visual nature of our interaction with these strangers allows us to complete their unknown social statuses and personality characteristics with our ideal ingredients, transforming them into gourmet food for fantasy.

6. The only comparable activity that temporarily opens identity is the drug experience, particularly with psychedelic drugs. This similarity prompts public opinion to associate illicit drugs with sex ("drug taking leads to orgies") and—for reasons put forth in the introductory section to part two—with dirt as well ("drug taking occurs in filthy surroundings").

7. Sex seems to transfer identity material at the social level in almost the same way that it transfers genetic material at the biological level. In an essay entitled "The Origin of the Kiss," C. M. Beadnel points out a biological function of this exchange of essential material:

Among some of the earliest and simplest of the animals, such as the protozoa, he wrote, certain individuals come into contact for a brief while, part company and then go their own way. During such surface apposition—for that is all it has been—a slight exchange of material has taken place, so that after separation each organism contains within itself particles of living matter that have been subjected to the impacts of two different sets of environments. Such dual experience enables the organism to adapt itself better to the varying circumstances of its ever-changing surrounding. [Summarized in Atkins 1972, p. 285]

It may be that identity exchange during sex performs a similar social function. By allowing one human being to experience vicariously the foreign social environments of other human beings, sex expands his or her own awareness and adaptability.

8. Whoever conducts his sex life "discreetly" will, of course, prevent his social group from becoming aware of any alteration in his identity. As soon as the social group discovers its oversight, however, it will redefine the individual's identity, stabilizing its transformation. Occasionally an observation of the mere associaton between potential sex partners will cause their social group to regard them as having mutated sexually, even though they have not. But as long as their group believes they are sleeping together, it matters little whether or not they actually are insofar as their social identity is concerned. Such misinterpretations are especially likely to occur if the couple is seen together in certain settings (e.g., bohemian neighborhoods) or at certain times (e.g., early Sunday

morning) or if they exhibit certain status combinations (e.g., a middleaged man
and an unrelated young woman). Both those reputed to swing sexually and
those reputed to be sexually shy may discover that their social groups' definition of their identities has gotten out of line with their own.

9. This is not to assert that the quest for physical pleasure plays no part in sex.
Lower organisms, which presumably have no social psychological motivation
for copulation, will literally die for sex (deRopp 1969, pp. 37–43). But perhaps
one reason these motives are stronger in human beings is that *Homo sapiens* is
one of the few species to fuck face to face, facilitating the exchange of identities
since identity is centered chiefly on the face.

Moveover, the importance of physical pleasure relative to social psychological satisfaction may be greater for some human groups than for others. Kinsey
found that the lower classes use their imaginative-identificative faculty in
copulation and masturbation less than do the middle classes (1948, pp. 363ff)
and that women use it less than do men (1953, pp. 649ff), though the latter
finding remains in dispute (see Robinson 1977, pp. 110–15).

Finally, social-psychological satisfaction varies with the individual's approach to each sex partner. In his felicitously titled article "The Phenomenology
of Fucking," Michael Kosok (1971) distinguishes *fucking*, in which the individual tries to "merge to oneness" by aggressively "possessing" the sex partner
as a "centered object," from *intercourse*, in which the individual tries to "retain
the twoness" by reluctantly merging merely a "projected image" with the sex
partner. Neither fucking nor intercourse produces maximal mental fulfillment,
according to Kosok. Only in the approach that he calls "love" is the individual's
separation from a sex partner overcome enough for a fully satisfying identity
merger to take place and maintained enough for a fully satisfying identity
transformation to occur.

10. In addition, the more components of her sex partner's identity a woman knows,
the more intercourse with him will affect her:

> Women raped by men they know suffer greater psychological damage
> than those raped by strangers, a University of Illinois Medical School
> sociologist says.
> Dr. Pauline B. Bart . . . analyzed 1070 questionaires returned by rape
> victims in a survey by Viva magazine. . . .
> "The more intimately the victim has known the attacker, the more likely
> she is to suffer sexual problems after the attack," Dr. Bart said in her
> analysis.
>
> [*Los Angeles Times*, 2 June 1975, section III, p. 3]

11. Some prostitutes, however, claim that copulating with their lovers still affects
their self, even though copulating with their customers affects only their
bodies:

> At least my real lovers *do* understand one thing about me: when I make
> love to a regular customer, nothing happens to *me*, just to my body. . . .
> Thus, if you have someone you truly feel close to, I believe that this love
> is a complete giving and taking of the mind, the soul, and the body. I have
> to give and receive all three or there is no relationship. It's just ships
> passing in the night. [Hollander 1972, pp. 294–95]

This gradual decline in the power of sex to affect the prostitute essentially is the main reason prostitution is one of the few professions with a negative seniority system, a career in which attractiveness—and consequently earning power— decreases with experience. (Of course, the prostitute may compensate for the depreciation of her physical resources by developing greater skill at bargaining or by eventually becoming a madam.)

12. Yet, except for gender, youth remains the component most sought by American men for identity reversal during sexual intercourse. (American women, conversely, tend to prefer experience, which is commonly associated with age.) The paradoxical tendency of members of our society both to shelter and to seduce the innocent stems from its child-rearing practices. Loss of innocence has long been a powerful theme in modern American society because it has segregated its young from the adult world. This quarantine seems to produce two opposite tendencies in those reared under it: to preserve the next generation of youth from the "evils" of adult life and to pollute youth with them. The result is hypocritical laws such as those that forbid adolescents to see the large proportion of X-rated movies in which they themselves star as sex objects, such as *Teenage Hitchhiker*, *Teenage Runaway*, *Teenage Tramp*, and (my favorite title) *Wet Teenagers*.

13. The degree of psychological disintegration caused by physical violation, however, has always been problematic. Augustine argued that the self can remain pure even though the body becomes polluted; but not vice versa:

> The body is not holy just because its parts are intact. . . . During a manual examination of a virgin a midwife destroyed her maidenhead, whether by malice, or clumsiness, or accident. I do not suppose that anyone would be stupid enough to imagine that the virgin lost anything of bodily chastity, even though the integrity of that part had been destroyed. . . .
>
> Now suppose some woman, with her mind corrupted . . . , in the act of going to her seducer to be defiled. Do we say that she is chaste in body while she is on her way . . . ? Of course not! We must rather draw the inference that just as bodily chastity is lost when mental chastity has been violated, so bodily chastity is not lost, even when the body has been ravished, while the mind's chastity endures. [1972, p. 28; see also Petras 1973, p. 40]

The transition from Judaism to Christianity reflected a shift in the primary locus of the self from external behavior to internal beliefs, as the source of threats to personal continuity shifted from the physical environment to the social environment.

14. Artists idealize the naked human body by portraying it without the exterior blemishes—particularly its gentials and body hair—that interrupt its otherwise smooth and integrated surface. Jehovanists are not quite so repulsed by a naked human body that lacks these surface flaws because its boundary between inside and outside appears more intact:

> When John de Andrea's statue "Standing Man 1970" was exhibited at the Art Institute in Chicago, its realistic portrayal of the naked human body elicited a reaction from onlookers that differed considerably from their reaction to the museum's other, idealized, nude statues.

A latter-day David by some struggling Michaelangelo, you say? Hardly—more like David on The Morning After. This body with all its imperfections is standing there, daring you to deny it. Certainly, it is not an example of the body glorified, which is somehow easier for people to take. No, the wrinkles, the scars, the slightly bulging waistline, the body, the members—they're all there, intact. One wonders, is this why one hears snarls of 'disgusting!' floating down the halls in this section but hears only footsteps padding through other arrays of creative nudity.

[Maria Traska, *Chicago Reader*, 23 March 1974, p. 3]

15.

A new city ordinance against nudity has gone into effect in Dallas and one of its first effects was to force bookstore owners to paste a white label across the cover of Newsweek magazine.

The magazine's cover showed a picture of a Vietnamese mother carrying a nude child with the genital area showing. . . .

An assistant city attorney, asked to interpret the ordinance, said, "Covering the genitals of the child on the cover of the magazine, under the literal terms of the ordinance, would be correct."

According to the law, pictures of human genitals and buttocks cannot be displayed where a person under 17 might see them unless they are "completely or opaquely" covered.

[*Los Angeles Times*, 31 March 1975, p. 12]

16. The German poet and social scientist Christian Enzensberger points out the ability of smell to penetrate the defenses of the body:

The skin is all very well . . . but there are holes. If something tries to break in and a person cannot close himself up, seal himself off, batten himself down, then he is in a bad way. . . . In ascending order of importance [are] hearing, sight and smell: because, of all dirt, anything that smells bad probably gets closest to a person, gets furthest inside him. [1972, p. 20]

17. This penetration need not be physical. R. J. Levin notes that people can experience a merely visual penetration of certain areas of their personal space as a sexual assault:

When a female wears a skirt she creates a distinct space between the medial aspects of her thighs. In many respects females treat this space, in relation to their public behaviour patterns, as if it were an artificial extension of their vaginal cavity. This extension becomes a defensible private space. The embarrassment of inadvertant exposure of the crotch area under the skirt at the apex of the space may . . . be . . . generated by the male visual penetration of the surrogate vagina. In essence the female feels that a 'visual rape' takes place and she becomes sexually demeaned by its occurrance as she would in a carnal rape situation. [1975; p. 351]

18. Unconsidered by Weber, Husserl, and Schutz—to my knowledge—is the question whether intersubjectivity is not merely possible but in fact inescapable, whether the individual not merely *can* but actually *must* get into the mind of others. (The difficulty in disengaging from empathy with others is also indicated by the widespread horror at patients undergoing surgery, at mangled victims of major accidents, and at newly deceased corpses.) At least as much as

the "problem of other minds," the "problem of avoiding other minds" is the "scandal of philosophy."

To even begin to deal with this latter problem we must supplement the relatively solipsistic theories of Weber, Husserl, and even Schutz—which assume that the individual ego is the fundamental unit of society while making problematic its connection with other minds—with the relatively social theories of Simmel, Mead, and Buber—which assume that the empathetic connection between minds is the fundamental unit of society while making problematic its reduction to the individual ego.

19. Intersubjectivity establishes one kind of experiential border for a society be-cause it occurs only between its citizens. Even for anthropologists, establishing intersubjectivity with those in other societies is a difficult task. (The recent development of world society, however, has decreased the importance of this phenomenological boundary.) Consequently, members of each society experi-ence the subjective correlates of the sexual behavior of members of other societies much less than that of members of their own society. Being less affected psychologically by even the (to them) bizarre aspects of foreign sexual behavior, they can treat it more as an object of curiosity than of condemnation. (Except for missionaries, of course, who are charged with the task of imposing the Jehovanist scheme on everyone, especially on members of other societies.) This is perhaps the reason *National Geographic* was the sole mass-circulation magazine permitted to show unclothed human bodies in the United States during the greater part of the twentieth century. (Its pictures of "naked sav-ages," in fact, were the only photographic depictions of human sexual parts ever seen by many Amercian adolescents during this sexually repressive period—giving their image of sex a foreign, primitive flavor.) Even in the 1970s, according to *The New York Times* (19 October 1975, p. 9), South African censors demonstrated their conviction that blacks and whites constituted two distinct societies by prohibiting magazines from featuring photographs of white breasts while permitting them to publish pictures of black breasts.

20. This reduction in frequency of coitus between long-term couples and their consequent pursuit of new partners (in fantasy or actuality) has been observed in both heterosexuals and homosexuals in Western society (Gagnon and Simon 1973, pp. 83, 173) as well as in anthropological and even animal studies (deRopp 1969, pp. 109–10). This search for sexual variety is also indicated by such small details of erotic culture as most "pinup" calendars, which renew their models on a monthly cycle instead of retaining the same picture for the entire year—a much less expensive procedure.

The cause of this reduction in coital frequency is unclear. But it is at least plausible that the more (real or imagined) intercourse with the same partner, the less effectively one can reintegrate all the parts of one's identity by looking at it from this partner's perspective. Some parts remain disparate, causing the individual to feel "unfulfilled." Since such self-revitalization is one of the main motivations for sex, desire to continue to copulate with this partner will decline.

21. The power of marriage to contain the chaos of sex is limited, however, for the effects of any sexual activity that is too passionate may break through the marriage buffer, menacing both self and society:

The belief that even within marriage the sexual act should not be per-formed for pleasure, still persists to the present day. . . . This led to the

incontravertible proposition that no man should love his wife. In fact, Peter
Lombard maintained, in his apologetic *De excusatione coitus*, that for a man
to love his wife too ardently is a sin worse than adultery. . . . [Taylor 1973;
p. 51–52]

22.

The desire a man has for a woman is not directed toward her because she is
a human being, but because she is a woman; that she is a human being is of
no concern to the man; only her sex is the object of his desires. . . . The sole
condition on which we are free to use our sexual desire depends on the
right to dispose over the person as a whole—over the welfare and happi-
ness and generally over all the circumstances of that person. . . . But how
am I to obtain these rights over the whole person? Only by giving that
person the same rights over the whole of myself. This happens only in
marriage. [Kant 1930, pp. 164, 166–67].

23.

In fact, love is often in contradiction . . . with the lover's own individuality,
since it casts itself on persons who, apart from the sexual relation, would be
hateful, contemptible, an even abhorrent to the lover. But the will of the
species is so much more powerful than that of the individual that the lover
shuts his eyes to all the qualities repugnant to him . . . and binds himself
forever to the object of his passion. He is . . . completely infatuated by that
delusion, which vanishes as soon as the will of the species is satisfied, and
leaves behind a detested partner for life. [Schopenhauer 1958, p. 555]

24.

To ensure a fully normal attitude in love, two currents of feeling have to
unite—we may describe them as the tender, affectionate feelings and the
sensual feelings. . . . [Since] the whole current of sensual feeling . . . may
remain attached in the unconsciousness to incestuous objects, . . . sexual
activity. . . [may] avoid all association with feelings of tenderness. . . . The
impression made by someone who seems deserving of high estimation
leads, not to a sensual excitation, but to feelings of tenderness which
remain erotically ineffectual. The erotic life of such people remains dissociated, divided between two channels, the same two that are personified in
art as heavenly and earthly (or animal) love. Where such [people] love they
have no desire and where they desire the cannot love. [Freud 1963, pp.
59–62].

25. The cosmos that lies behind Judeo-Christian marriage, of course, is not the only
one in which sexual intercourse can be situated. In fact, Paul Ricoeur points out
that it was much easier to integrate copulation into the primitive cosmos, which
was based on an earthly, biological, and imminent conception of the sacred,
than into the Judeo-Christian cosmos, which is based on a celestial, geomet-
rical, and transcendent conception of the sacred:

By the standards of the starry archetype of order, sexuality appears as an
aberrant phenomenon, deprived of its own sacredness by the demytholo-
gizing of infernal and vegetative gods. . . . [Such a transcendent understanding of the sacred] can only sustain the institutional discipline of
marriage, itself considered as merely a fragment of the total order. It is as

order, as institution, the sexuality is justified within this order as best it can. [1964, p. 134]

And the French critic Denis de Rougemont points out that the cosmos in which "love" locates sexual intercourse is actually antagonistic to the one in which marriage locates it, rather than complementary, as most people today believe:

> Passionate love . . . actually became in the twelfth century . . . a religion in the full sense of the word, and in particular a Christian heresy. . . . Underlying the modern breakdown of marriage is . . . a struggle between two religious traditions. . . . Passion and marriage are essentially irreconcilable. . . . Romance feeds on obstacles, short excitations, and partings; marriage, on the contrary, is made up of wont, daily propinquity, growing accustomed to one another. . . . In countless nauseating novels there is now depicted the kind of husband who fears the flatness . . . of married life in which his wife loses her "allure" because no obstructions come between them. [1966, pp. 145, 291, 298, 301, 307]

26. Jehovanists condemn adulterers more than fornicators because the former present more of a threat to others. By separating the two main sources of their identity components—the sexual and the intimate—adulterers disintegrate their own identity while contaminating ("adulterating") the identity of their spouses as well:

> [As] a result of living together the woman becomes part of the body of her husband by receiving his physical substance into it. . . . Thus by uniting their bodies the male and female "become one flesh. . . ." Therefore, if a man feels a natural disgust in coming into contact with another man's semen, he feels the same disgust when his wife does. From the viewpoint of Biblical man, a woman who receives another male pollutes the husband's flesh. . . . Since he once felt that his wife formed part of himself, her infidelity is now felt as a kind of amputation or castration of his own being. Adultery is, therefore, considered by Biblical society a far more horrible crime against the husband than the lack of virginity in a newly married wife. . . . Therefore, in the Bible the prohibition of adultery achieves the status of one of the Ten Commandments. [Stern 1966, p. 197]

27. In his poetic exegesis of the nature of "smut," Christian Enzensberger reaches a similar conclusion about the kind of person who would be bothered by it:

> [The] individual sees himself . . . [as] islolated, untouchable, homogeneous, structured, [and] unique. . . . Dirt is anything that threatens the proper separateness of the individual. . . . Apart from the dirt produced by contact and excretions, he also . . . has a horror of intermingling. . . . [Hence] the ineradicable association with dirt in . . . the prime example of intermingling, which is sex. . . . The threat involved . . . is the disintegration . . . of identity and structure. . . . [1972, pp. 22, 32, 52]

28. The idea of a sharply bounded body also explains the obsessive desire for cleanliness exhibited by many Jehovanists. Dirt disfigures the body's surface, combines inner secretions with external additions, spreads and smells, and in general blurs the body's boundary. Any group that believes the human form to

be almost as distinct and important a stuctural element in the cosmos as its transcendental divinity will rank "cleanliness" next to "godliness."

29. The implications of losing physical integrity frighten Jehovanists so much that Augustine posited a utopian paradise where even procreation could occur without breaking into the body:

> [In the garden of Eden] the sexual organs would have been brought into activity by the same bidding of the will as controlled other organs. Then, without feeling the allurement of passion goading him on, the husband would have relaxed on his wife's bosom in tranquility of mind and with no impairment of his body's integrity. Moreover, . . . the male seed could have been dispatched into the womb with no loss of the wife's integrity, just as the menstrual flux can now be produced from the womb of a virgin without loss of maidenhead. [1972, p. 591]

Chapter Four

1. Ever since de Sade's *120 Days of Sodom* (1967), both the great pornographers and the great sexologists—Ashbee, Ellis, Freud, Kant, Krafft-Ebing, and others— have been preoccupied with classifying the varieties of condemned sexual practices. Anything that cannot be located in some conceptual scheme will threaten to undermine the conceptual organizations in which everything else is located. Thus the attempt to catalog the forms of illicit sex—like the attempts to catalog the forms of sin or madness—is an attempt to defend the frontier of rationality from the insidious intellectual wilderness beyond its border. Those who can find a rational order behind even the seemingly irrational aspects of human existence have at least spared the integrity and dignity of the human mind, even if their abstract schemes have little practical consequence for human life.

   Sex catalogers, then, are the "custodians" of intellectual life, carrying out the duties of both guardianship and sanitation. By constructing new systems in which to sort the sordid, they help to tidy up the universe (even if they sometimes sweep some difficult-to-classify particle of disorder under the rug of a "residual category"). It is no wonder that sex catalogers have had the same social status as janitors—untouchable, but necessary to have around.

2. Kant (1930, pp. 169–71) considered prostitution, concubinage, polygamy, adultery, and incest "crimes against second (or social) nature" because their aim is procreation but not marriage. He considered masturbation, bestiality, and homosexuality "crimes against (first or) animal nature" because their aim is not even procreation. The former are contrary to reason, but the latter are also contrary to biology because (Kant asserts) even animals do not engage in them:

> All *crimina carnis contra naturam* degrade nature to a level below that of animal nature and make man unworthy of his humanity. He no longer deserves to be a person. . . . These vices make us ashamed that we are human beings and, therefore, capable of them, for [even] an animal is incapable of all such *crimina carnis contra naturam*. [1930, pp. 170, 171]

As we saw in the last chapter, Jehovanists believe that this "nature" against which these sexual activities are "crimes" requires people to prolong the transitory identity mergers of their sexual activities with the abstract social bonds of marriage and the concrete temporal bonds of children.

3. Freud saw perverted sex as intimately related to normal sex—a view that would horrify Kant and did horrify many of Freud's contemporaries: "Perhaps the sexual instinct itself may be no simple thing, but put together from components which have come apart again in the perversions" (1972, p. 53). Like Kant, however, he divides all sexual perversions into two groups: (1) "deviations in respect to sexual object," which he defines as the "person from whom sexual attraction proceeds"; and (2) "deviations in respect to sexual aim," which he defines as the "act toward which the instinct tends" (1972, p. 22). In order to focus on the various blockages of the sexual instinct, however, he minimizes the importance of the sexual object:

> Under a great number of conditions and in surprisingly numerous individuals, the nature and importance of the sexual object recedes into the background. What is essential and constant in the sexual instinct is something else. [1972, pp. 37–38]

Thus his classification of sexual perversions is confined to deviant sexual aims, which are divided according to spatial and temporal criteria:

> Perversions are sexual activities which either (a) extend, in an anatomical sense, beyond the regions of the body that are designed for sexual union, or (b) linger over the intermediate relation to the sexual object which should normally be transversed rapidly on the path towards the final sexual aim. [1972, pp. 38–39]

4. Some people, however, do not come to experience the genitals of their sex partners as embodying their essential identity. According to the TV movie *Hustling*, prostitutes and masseusses dislike kissing their customers on the mouth, although they don't seem to mind kissing them on their genitals. And in *The Happy Hooker*, Xaviera Hollander reports that johns don't like to kiss hookers on the lips even though they often want to "eat pussy" [1972, p. 182]

5. Ellis's explanation of masochism as merely an ordinary intensifier of erotic energy was more simple and elegant than Freud's, who tried to explain its peculiar character by postulating a second, nonsexual instinct—the aggressive (1972, pp. 47–50; 1962, pp. 7–8, 58ff).

6. Clothing fetishes are usually designed to exaggerate the differences between the hard and soft parts of the embodied identity. Boots, gloves, and heavy stockings intensify the "heaviness" of the extremities while lace, gauze, or mesh underwear intensify the "lightness" of the genital region. Consequently, wearing one or both kinds of these clothing fetishes functions on the phenomenological level to accelerate the sensual slide of attention from the body's periphery to its center.

Although passé in everyday reality, a dark garter belt and nylon stockings are still the most common female attire in visual pornography. Many men regard them as sexier than more modern female underclothes because they appear to cut the genital region off from the torso and legs, transforming it into a stage set that draws the attention to where the action will take place.

7. "Do not profane your daughter by making her a harlot, lest the land fall into harlotry and the land become full of wickedness" (Leviticus 19:29). See also Deuteronomy 23:17–18 and 1 Corinthians 6:15–16.

8. Cynics, however, have pointed out that dating and even marriage involve the indirect exchange of money for sex:

> Municipal Court Judge George Crawford in effect urged prostitutes yesterday to lobby for liberalization of laws against the oldest profession.
> Crawford, in commenting on a new law passed by the state legislature and signed by Gov. Brown, noted that it legalizes "all homosexual conduct" but continues to outlaw solicitation of sex acts for money. . . . In his ruling, Crawford commented that while some persons spend money "wining and dining" to engage in sex acts, an "honest exchange" of money for sex is prohibited. [*San Diego Evening Tribune*, 9 July 1975]

9. Sex for money also muddles the distinction between our society's sexual system and its economic system. Every transaction between prostitute and customer is an overlap point at which each social system exchanges characteristics: sex becomes commercialized while commerce becomes sexualized. Our society's attempt to avoid this cross-system contamination helps explain why it forbids us to sell our bodies but not our time, energy, thought, and behavior—even though most people identify with the latter at least as much as with the former.

10. "If a man lies with a beast, he shall be put to death; and you shall kill the beast. If a woman approaches any beast and lies with it, you shall kill the woman and the beast; they shall be put to death, their blood is upon them" (Leviticus 20:15–16; see also Leviticus 18:23).

11. The growing non-Jehovanist segment of Western society, of course, has begun to treat bestiality as a joke. Lynda Schor, for instance, now feels free to portray a suburban couple's *menage à trois* with a stallion in soap-opera style:

> Isobel realized that the horse was the best lover she'd ever had. Yet her life and his were so different, he could never become part of hers. She couldn't think how to integrate this affair with the rest of her life. She wondered whether the horse liked her. She'd been so passive, but she really'd felt free to enjoy herself for the first time. [1975, p. 198]

12. The sociologist Alan Segal (1970, pp. 66–67) notes that partially human, partially animal creatures are either very unsexy, like circus freaks and monsters, or very sexy, like centaurs and Pan-figures. Both sexual attraction and repulsion, then, are alternative responses to the possibility that one's identity may be altered by cross-category creatures.

   Although the issue has not yet arisen, Jehovanists would no doubt regard it as perverted to copulate with extraterrestrials, especially those somewhat "humanoid" in form. And, like all sexual activities, what repulses some will attract others:

> Dressed in pure Martian style, British Rock Singer David Bowie and the Spiders from Mars packed in 6,000 in two nights at a marijuana-smoke-filled Radio City Music Hall in Manhattan. . . . One of Bowie's fans, an 18-year-old girl, looking a little like a Martian herself with green, orange and purple feather boas, red glitter around her eyes and black lipstick, spoke for the sqealers: "I wish David Bowie were from Mars. It would be so sexy." [*Time Magazine*, 26 February 1973]

13. Another way to transform people into animals is to force them to imitate other bestial characteristics such as paralinguistics, kinesics, or apparel. In Boorman's movie *Deliverance*, one character is made to grunt and posture like a pig. In Mawra's classic pornographic movie *Olga's House of Shame*, a character is saddled and bridled like a horse.

14. Although the gods and devils of the Bronze and Middle Ages are no longer with us, our Electric Age seems to have spawned its own eligible deities. The present stars of stage, screen, and stereo have replaced the gods of the past as focal points of meaning-generating activity, and consequently of sexual interest. Recent journalistic (Gross 1975) and psychiatric (Willis 1972) reports on "groupies," who choose their sex objects exclusively from this category of suprahuman "idols," attest to the permanence of theogamy's perverse appeal.

15. Havelock Ellis invented the term but used it in a somewhat different sense to mean "spontaneous sexual emotion generated in the absence of an external stimulus . . . from another person" (1942, "Auto-Eroticism," p. 11). Freud gave it its current meaning of self as the sexual object rather than self as merely the generator of excitation in the absence of any sexual object (1972, p. 76 n.1). On this controversy between Ellis and Freud, see Robinson (1977, p. 39).

16.
> Then Judah said to Onan, "Go in to your brother's wife, and perform the duty of a brother-in-law to her, and raise up offspring for your brother." But Onan knew that the offspring would not be his; so when he went in to his brother's wife he spilled his semen on the ground, lest he should give offspring to his brother. And what he did was displeasing in the sight of the Lord and he slew him also. [Genesis 38:8–11]

17. Promiscuity seems an appropriate sexual activity in a society with our socioeconomic organization, since it is the sexual parallel to the individual's relations with the many partners in his role set, who continually "turn over." One expression of the close connection between sexual activity and socioeconomic organization may be found in the root of the term "orgy" —from the Greek *ergon*, work.

18. Immanuel Kant, for instance, knew it would be difficult to explain why his contemporaries abhorred "wanton self-abuse" even more than suicide. Nevertheless, he gave it a try:

> It is not so easy to produce a rational demonstration of the inadmissability of that unnatural use . . . of one's sexual attributes as being a violation of one's duty to himself. . . . The ground of proof surely lies in the fact that a man gives up his personality (throws it away) when he uses himself merely as a means for the gratification of an animal drive. But this does not make evident the high degree of violation of the humanity in one's own person by the unnaturalness of such a vice, which seems . . . to transcend even the vice of self-murder. The obstinate throwing away of one's life as a burden is a least not a weak surrender to animal pleasure, but requires courage; and where there is courage, there is always respect for the humanity in one's own person. On the other hand, when one abandons himself entirely to an animal inclination, he makes himself an object of unnatural gratification, i.e., a loathsome thing, and thus deprives himself of all self-respect. [1964, pp. 86–87]

19. Even today, many of those raised in the Jehovanist tradition, like the protagonist of Phillip Roth's novel *Portnoy's Complaint*, fear that "self-abuse" will lead to
bodily affliction:

> It was at the end of my freshman year of high school . . . that I discovered
> on the underside of my penis, just where the shaft meets the head, a little
> discolored dot that has since been diagnosed as a freckle. Cancer. I had
> given myself *cancer*. All that pulling and tugging at my own flesh, all that
> friction, had given me an incurable disease. And not yet fourteen! . . . If
> only I could cut down to one hand-job a day, or hold the line at two, or even
> three! But with the prospect of oblivion before me, I actually began to set
> new records for myself. [1969, p. 19]

20. "None of you shall approach anyone near of kin to uncover their nakedness"
(Leviticus 18:6). The kin prohibited by the incest taboo are extensively specified
in Leviticus 18:7–18, and 20:11, 12, 14, 17, 19–21. "If a man lies with a male as
with a woman, both of them have committed an abomination; they shall be put
to death, their blood is upon them" (Leviticus 20:13). Other biblical injuctions
against homosexuality occur in Leviticus 18:22; Romans 1:26–27; 1 Corinthians
6:9–10.

21. For instance, see Duberman 1972, and Gould 1974 for thorough reviews of the
literature on the alleged association between homosexuality and mental illness.
What this literature discovers directly about the origin of homosexuality—with
regard to biology (hormones), psychology (psychogenetics), or sociology
(group dynamics)—is less interesting than what it discloses obliquely about the
origin of the Jehovanist taboo against homosexuality.

22. In regard to the connection between copulation and contamination that I have
been trying to establish here, it is not insignificant that Jehovanists refer to
someone who desires sex with a partner far beneath his (or her) own age as a
"dirty old man (or woman)."

23. Alan Segal (1971) attempts to analyze the sex in *Portnoy's Complaint* structurally.
His conclusion, unfortunately, faults an otherwise perceptive discussion:

> Portnoy's sexuality is, in fact, an expression of his search for power, a
> power that he feels he can acquire personally through erotic contact with
> the WASPS. . . . Portnoy is impotent with [Israeli women] because he sees
> them as members of the socially powerless Jewish community. [1971, pp.
> 226–67]

Yet this interpretation fails to account for Portnoy's choice of shikses (like
Monkey) from socially powerless groups in America or his choice of physically
powerful Jewesses who are either lieutenants in the Israeli army or six-foot-tall
kibbutzniks. Although it is true that Portnoy could easily copulate with outgroup shikses in America but "couldn't get it up in the State of Israel" (Roth
1979, p. 257) with ingroup Jewesses, it is not so much differences in power that
attracts Jews and Christians as simply their differences in general.

24. A women shall not wear anything that pertains to a man, nor shall a man put on
a woman's garment; for whoever does these things is an abomination to the
Lord your God" (Deuteronomy 22:5). On the components and rigidity of

gender categories, see Harold Garfinkle's brilliant study of a transvestite who became a transexual, "Passing and the Managed Achievement of Sex Status in an Intersexed Person" (Garfinkle 1967, pp. 116–85, 285–88).

25. There is a sharp, fundamental difference between "B&D"—bondage and discipline—and what the public knows as "S&M"—sadism and masochism. Although both interests involve the domination of one individual by another through physical restraint, they express it in quite different ways. In S&M it is expressed through control of how much *pain* the partner feels; in B&D it is based on control of the partner's *pleasure*. [Editorial in *Country Bound*, vol. 1, Los Angeles: House of Milan, 1975]

26. Employing these other social hierarchies to stratify sexual partners has resulted in the reciprocal sexualization of these hierarchies. Hierarchical roles originally erotically neutral—such as boss-secretary, doctor-nurse, or teacher-student— have consequently developed sexual overtones. If pornographers can exploit authority figures to heighten eroticism, social critics can exploit eroticism to humiliate authority figures:

> [In] pornography current in socialist countries . . . bureaucrats get buggered. . . . [In] the older type [of pornography] in church oppressed countries . . . nuns are sexually defiled or priests pictured as satyrs. [Slade 1971, p. 42; see also Segal 1970, pp. 67–68]

27. Thus the foregoing Periodic Table of Sexual Perversions can be seen as the outline for a basic text in sociology ("Sociology through Smut"), for it lays out many of the main topics covered in introductory courses, from microsocial interaction to macrosocial differentiation, stratification, and deviance.

28. Of course, normal sex may also threaten social relations and social structure: sexual arousal may occasionally interfere with the role performances that maintain the former, and sexual intercourse may occasionally produce illegitimate children who have no place in the latter. But the threats to social organization from normal sex are trivial compared with those from perverted sex—more a cause for annoyance than alarm. For instance, if normal sex were feared only for its potential to disrupt social inheritance patterns by producing illegitimate children, perverted sexual linkages would be urged instead, for they are all contraceptive. But since these prophylactic perversions are obviously tolerated even less than ordinary intercourse, the "illegitimacy potential" of sex must not be the principal factor behind its prohibitions.

29. Such a threat to their sociocosmic order, however, may motivate Jehovanists to work even harder to maintain it. Neo Durkheimians would point out that, like other forms of deviance such as delinquency or witchcraft, perverted sex functions indirectly to support this order. Those committed to a specific social and cosmic arrangement react to any sexual violation of its normative organization by recalling its constitution and reasserting its boundaries. But whereas some contact with its antithesis encourages Jehovanists to reaffirm their sociocosmos, too much contact undermines its legitimacy for them. A weak, unappealing opponent may enhance a group's *Geist*, but a strong, enticing antagonist can destroy it.

30. Fellatio, for instance, reinforces gender stratification:

A series of symbolic meanings . . . heighten the significance of fellatio as a form of sexual contact [:] the images of filling up, choking, dominating, controlling, degrading. . . . The couple may act out conventional gender role models, he dominating, she submitting, while the transgression of the taboo gives both persons a heightened sense of erotic power. . . . [Gagnon and Simon 1973, p. 87]

Sexuality and Ideology

1. Modern Jehovanists, such as Harry Clor (1969, pp. 225ff) and Walter Berns (in Rist 1975, pp. 48–50), criticize pornography for the Augustinian reason that people should not be observed during their least controllable, and therefore most vulnerable, moments. As we will see in our discussion of Gnosticism, however, this is precisely the appeal of pornography—for people's least controllable responses are presumably their most authentic ones.

2. Aquinas's teleological conception of sex has remained influential. Modern Catholic theologians, like Harold Gardner, S.J., still condemn any form of sex such as masturbation, homosexuality, prostitution, or premarital sex—that does not continue all the way through to what they take to be its "completion":

   Moral teaching on the whole process of sex holds, as a basic and cardinal fact, that complete sexual activity and pleasure is licit and moral only in a naturally completed act in valid marriage. All acts which, of their psychological and physical nature, are designed to be preparatory to the complete act, take their licitness and their morality from the complete act. If, therefore, they are entirely divorced from the complete act, they are distorted, warped, meaningless and hence immoral. [Rist 1975, p. 164]

3. If Catholic Jehovanists today take their reasons for criticizing particular forms of sexuality from Augustine and Aquinas, Protestant Jehovanists like Ernst van den Haag draw on Kant:

   The characteristic focus of pornography is precisely that it leaves out all human context and reduces the action to interaction between organs and orifices—and that I find obscene, degrading to sex and dehumanizing to its audiences. . . .

   Human solidarity is based on our ability to think of each other not purely as means, but as ends in ourselves. Now the point of all pornography. . . is that it invites us to regard the other person purely as a subject of exploitation for sexual pleasure. (*The New York Times* 21 November 1976, section II, pp. 1, 26]

4. These other factors include:
   1. The growth of Wesleyan Methodism as an evangelical religious revival (Perrin 1969, pp. 17–18; Taylor 1973, pp. 204ff).
   2. The rise of the middle class, which emphasized sexual restraint to distinguish itself from the less inhibited lower class (Marcus 1967, p. 147). Even the very terms for obscene sexual behavior, such as "lewd," "vulgar," or "common," were synonymous with "lower-class."
   3. The artistic revival of neoclassicism, with its aesthetic ideal of the human body as a perfect form without vitality (Clark 1956, pp. 50–52, 221). Those, like

Dr. Bowdler (Perrin 1969), who believed that the human body should have no apertures, expurgated all bodily effusions or intrusions—excretions, farts, belches, smells, and spit, as well as sexual organs and activities.

4. The influence of Lockean psychology, with its conception of personality as a "blank slate." Even the slightest contact with anything sexual, therefore, might leave an indelible "stain" on it (Perrin 1969, p. 237).

5. The Romantic movement, which stressed feeling over thinking. Together with Lockean psychology it created a "cult of delicacy," especially to sexual inputs that overpower emotional stability, producing blush or faint (Perrin 1969, pp. 10ff).

5. Foucault (1980) would agree that hierarchy and power pervade all aspects of sex, though even more extensively and inherently than these radical feminists would care to acknowledge.

6. Obviously, a typology comprising only three sexual ideologies is too simple. More refined research will of course be necessary to articulate the multiplicity of sexual ideologies that actually occur in our society and to delineate the subtle ways they shade into one another. But only from such crude distinctions as this tripartite typology can we at least begin to understand the interplay of different interpretations of sex.

Chapter Five

1. Huysmans points out that only the deeply religious can perform a sexual perversion properly:

> The truth of the matter is that if it did not involve sacrilege, sadism would have no *raison d'etre*; on the other hand, since sacrilege depends on the existence of a religion, it cannot be deliberately and effectively committed except by a believer, for a man would derive no satisfaction whatever from profaning a faith that was unimportant or unknown to him.
> The strength of sadism then, the attraction it offers, lies entirely in the forbidden pleasure of transferring to Satan the homage and prayers that should go to God; it lies in the flouting of the precepts of Catholicism, which the sadist actually observes in topsy-turvy fashion when, in order to offend Christ the more grievously, he commits the sins Christ most expressly proscribed—profanation of holy things and carnal debauch. [1971, p. 162]

2. The hero of the other major branch of Gnosticism is the ascetic. Both the libertine and the ascetic are hostile toward the world. But the ascetic fears the world so much that he tries to reduce contact with its contamination whereas the libertine fears the world so little that he feels free to break its laws (Jonas 1963, pp. 46, 295). Bullough and Bullough (1977, pp. 18ff) showed the effect of both schools of Gnosticism on the development of Christian sexual doctrines. Eric Voegelin (1952) pointed out that many radical political movements are based on the ascetic branch of Gnosticism, and traced their development from Puritanism to Marxism. Wilhelm Reich tried to combine political radicalism with the sexual branch of Gnosticism by attacking the asceticism of most modern political revolutionaries—without much success.

3. Earlier, de Sade treated Nature better. He had used Nature to replace God as the creator of the world (1966, *Philosophy in the Bedroom*, pp. 209–10) and to defend

perverted sexual activities against the restrictions of society (1966, *Philosophy in the Bedroom*, p. 237). Like Rousseau, he began by playing off the more basic natural part of human beings against their less basic social part. Eventually, however, like the ancient Gnostics, he came to conceive of human beings as fundamentally alien to Nature as well—though he regretted that they cannot outrage Nature as easily as God or society (See Blanchot, de Beauvoir, and Klossowski in de Sade 1966, pp. 62–65; 1967, p. 45 and pp. 72–77.)

4. Perhaps the figure most sacred to Christian Jehovanists whom Gnostics would like to contaminate through copulation is Christ himself. It can't be said they haven't tried:

> London—Britain's traditional tolerance for eccentrics has been strained to the breaking point by Jens Jorgen Thorsen. He is the bearded Danish director who wants to make a film here of the sex life of Jesus Christ.
>
> He announced he would film a life of Christ to include episodes showing him embracing John the Baptist, Mary Magdalene and a modern Palestinian girl. Thorsen was about to get a subsidy from the Danish Film Institute when the Pope denounced the scheme as "an ignoble and blasphemous outrage." [*Los Angeles Times* 25 August 1976, part II, p. 9]

5. But by shifting the emphasis from deviant sexual objects to deviant sexual linkages, George Steiner can counter that the limited number of sexual modalities possible will inevitably make pornography boring:

> Given the physiological and nervous complexion of the human body, the number of ways in which orgasm can be achieved or arrested, the total modes of intercourse, are fundamentally finite. The mathematics of sex stop somewhere in the region of *soixante-neuf*; there are no transcendental series. . . . This is the obvious, necessary reason for the inescapable monotony of pornographic writing, for the fact well known to all hunters of . . . bookstalls that dirty books are maddeningly the same. [1965, p. 14]

Pornography seems to be the only social phenomenon that critics find simultaneously dangerous, disgusting, and dull.

6. Jehovanists occasionally use "nature" to justify distinguishing normal sex from perverted sex (e.g., Romans 1:26–27), and Gnostics occasionally use it to justify equating them (e.g., de Sade, 1966, *Philosophy of the Bedroom*, p. 237). But both groups are too theologically oriented to regard nature as their sole criterion for interpreting and evaluating sexual activity, as do true Naturalists.

Note that Naturalists conveniently forget that the "nature" they use to justify their conception of sex has already been conceptualized in human terms. This is another instance of the way many kinds of social phenomena—such as territoriality or survival of the fittest—have been legitimized by being first projected onto nature and then read back again into society as an underpinning a particular kind of social arrangement.

7. But even Roman sexual commentators such as Lucretius (96?–55 B.C.), Ovid (43 B.C.–A.D. 17?), and Petronius (first century A.D.), still believed that the gods must have some connection with sex, however slight, for something out of the ordinary must motivate a person to become attracted to those to whom he has no rational reason to be attracted.

8. Although he viewed sex as a positive force in human affairs, D. H. Lawrence differed from other modern Naturalists by still regarding it with primitive awe. By connecting copulation to larger cosmic rhythms and organic principles, he implicitly criticized the secular aspect of Naturalism:

> But . . . marriage is no marriage . . . that is not linked up with the sun and the moon and the fixed stars and the planets, in the rhythm of days, in the rhythm of months, in the rhythm of quarters, of years, of decades and of centuries. Marriage is no marriage that is not a correspondence of blood. For the blood is the substance of the soul, and of the deepest consciousness. . . . The great river of male blood touches to its depths the great river of female blood—yet neither breaks its bounds. . . . And the phallus is the connecting link between the two rivers, that establishes the two streams in a oneness, and gives out of their duality a single circuit, forever. And this, this oneness gradually accomplished throughout a life-time in twoness, is the highest achievement of time or eternity. [Lawrence 1968, p. 349]

9. Leslie Farber describes how sex became materialized even more during the next century:

> In the second half of the 19th century. . . . it was entirely appropriate to regard the human body as still another natural object with many of the vicissitudes of the machine. . . . For the first time the scientists, in their intoxication, could forget the duality previous centuries knew: namely, that the body is both a natural object and not a natural object. . . . With the suppression of the second half of the dialectic, sexology and psychoanalysis could—with the assistance of the Romantics—claim the erotic life as their exclusive province, removing it from all the traditional disciplines, such as religion, philosophy, literature, which had always concerned themselves with sex as human experience. Qualities such as modesty, privacy, reticence, abstinence, chastity, fidelity, shame—could now be questioned as rather arbitrary matters which interfered with the health of the sexual parts. And in their place came an increasing assortment of objective terms like *ejaculatio praecox*, foreplay, forepleasure, frigidity—all intended to describe, not human experience, but the behavior of the sexual parts. [1964, p. 53]

10. Scientists, we have recently learned from Thomas Kuhn, not only study their subject matter but can actually create it in the process. If prestigious social scientists continue both to assert and to imply that behavior is the only real characteristic of copulation, ordinary people may begin to perceive their copulation only as behavior. Today, for instance, we find many people becoming so preoccupied with the "adequacy" of their sexual behavior that they forget the purpose that originally motivated them to engage in it—the experience of erotic reality.

11. This is not to say that these sexual surveys are intellectually worthless, for they often reveal unexpected contradictions between attitudes and actions. For instance, some studies have reported how sexual ideology has changed over the past few generations while actual sexual behavior has remained the same, although other studies have reported the opposite finding.

12. Jehovanists, however, remain unconvinced by this Naturalist attack, for they can "feel" components of their sex partners' identity taking root in their own. Consequently, they would respond to the Naturalist charge that anxiety about identity exchange is "all in the head" by observing that identity itself is "all in the head," and therefore more easily affected than Naturalists might think.

13. Like Jehovanists, some Naturalists still cannot accept sexual modes that transport sensory stimulation and identity components too intensely for their tastes. Thus they "draw the line" at sadism, which spices sex with violence.

14. Like Jehovanists, some Naturalists still cannot accept sexual objects that are too impressionable or hierarchical. Thus they "draw the line" at pedophilia, which can sexually pollute children, or bondage, which conflicts with their democratic ideal of equality.

15. In a scathing attack on sex researchers who advocate incest, *Time* magazine (14 April, 1980, p. 72), accused these Naturalists of finally going "too far:"

> But most of the pro-incest thought rises logically enough from the premises of the sex-research establishment: all forms of consensual sexuality are good, or at least neutral; problems arise not from sex, but from guilt, fear, and repression. That kind of faith is bound to lead its believers in crusades against all sexual prohibitions, including incest.
>
> Traditional academics have tended to look down on sex researchers as pushy, ham-handed amateurs, and the arguments for incest will do little to change that view. . . .

16. Donald Levine pointed out to me that, although these theorists do regard social differentiation as increasing, they also regard it as cross-cutting, and therefore undermining, traditional moral (including sexual) differentiations. Thus they may not be so far off the mark as my interpretation suggests.

17.
> Certainly the most interesting implication of [Havelock] Ellis's emphasis on courtship was the suggestion that sexual arousal constituted a problem. In traditional theory it was not the stimulation but the control of sexual activity that posed difficulties: satyriasis and nymphomania rather than impotence or frigidity seemed to represent the greatest threats to sexual equilibrium. All modern theory, by way of contrast, makes exactly the opposite assumption, and, in characteristic fashion, Ellis's work stood at the beginning of this revolution in sexual perspectives. [Robinson 1977, p. 16]

18. Naturalists have usually argued against censoring sex by opposing all forms of censorship. But recently they have begun to argue for censoring violence. The criminologist James Q. Wilson (1971) pointed out this inconsistency by comparing the procensorship recommendations of the National Commission on the Causes and Prevention of Violence with the anticensorship recommendations of the Commission on Obscenity and Pornography.

19. Even the hyper-Naturalist editors of the pornographic newspaper *Screw* discovered that their usually broad tolerance of sexual diversity has limits. It is uncertain, however, whether they joined the snuff-out "snuff" crusade as a matter of principle or—as the last sentence implies—of expediency:

> The latest development in 8mm porno sends a chill down our spines. Newspaper and television accounts of "snuff films"—porno films thought

to have been made in Latin America in which the participants are literally murdered at the climax of the film—are horrifying. . . . Although we're aware of the intimate connection between sex and death, we're outraged by snuff films. As yet, none has been sent to us. Should they be, we won't review them, contrary to our open policy of reviewing every product we receive. In general, we believe that paying anything to see a snuff film makes a person an accomplice to murder, and the morality of viewing them at all is open to question. There is also the possibility that public revulsion will associate snuff films with 8mm porno in general—the public is seldom good at making distinctions—resulting in increased prosecution of porno dealers. [John Milton's mail-order review column in *Screw*, issue no. unknown]

20. Naturalists who believe that sex is good but violence is bad are extremely ambivalent about activities that combine them, like rape. The only way they can condemn rape wholeheartedly is if it is redefined as having nothing to do with sex, shifting it totally into the violence category. Currently, feminists are engaged in a massive campaign to relabel rape for Naturalists in just this way. A fine example of their technique can be found in a letter to the editor of *The New York Times Magazine* (10 February 1980, p. 86):

> Fox Butterfield remarks on the widespread problem of rape in China. Unfortunately, he . . . perpetuated the myth of rape as an act of sex, which it is not. . . . Rape is an expression of power. . . .
>
> In an article which explores sexual values, it is distressing to find a continuation of distorted notions about rape. Rape is an act of anger, aggression and assertion of dominance, and has nothing to do with the expression of sexuality.

Chapter Six

1. Linnaeus based his classification of plants particularly on their differential modes of sexual reproduction, corroborating the close connection between copulation and classification, sex and order, that I have been trying to establish. It is interesting to note that, although confined mostly to plants, Linnaeus's research was regarded during his lifetime and later as somewhat risqué.
2. See Paul Ricoeur (1970, pp. 345–75) for a summary of the ways Freud's system fails to satisfy the criteria of a science. Ricoeur concludes that Freud's approach to psychology resembles the historian's more than the natural scientist's.
3. Freudians also use these low-status perverted inclinations to "unmask" high-status social activities (though Freud himself did this more insightfully than his followers). For instance, Ernest Jones (1951) claims to have found homosexual and incestuous desires lurking behind the competitive success of the first American chess champion, Paul Murphy.
4. Kinsey's students at the Indiana Institute for Sex Research, John Gagnon and William Simon, have elaborated this elementary behaviorism by inserting a stage of cognitive definition (derived from sociocultural sources) between the internal sexual drive and its behavioral externalization (1973, p. 262). (Hence the title shift from Kinsey's *Sexual Behavior. . .* to Gagnon and Simon's *Sexual*

Conduct.) They regard sexual inclination as amorphous until channeled by socially produced "sexual scripts," which prescribe objects of sexual satisfaction and patterns of sexual activity. They contend that sexual desire is influenced more by these sociocultural factors than by biological factors in order to deny Freud's assumption that the individual's sexual desire is necessarily antagonistic to society (1973, pp. 19–26, 262ff). But neo-Freudians like Denis Wrong (1961) would reply that this theory "oversocializes" the sexual instincts, which are essentially recalcitrant to social shaping. Gagnon and Simon also fail to explain why society would come up with antisocial sexual scripts and why someone chooses to follow one sexual script rather than another. Nevertheless, their theory is an admirable attempt to enlarge behaviorism to include mental phenomena, particularly sexual experience; although I believe it is better to begin with sexual experience and work toward sexual behavior than the other way around.

5. Dr. Thomas Cottle, quoted in *Time* (9 July 1973, p. 64); Carol Kleiman, "Caught in a Web of Conflicting Sexual Values," *Chicago Tribune* (23 March 1973, section II, p. 2).

6. Dr. Max Levine, quoted in *The New York Times* (27 December 1972, p. 36); reported by Gagnon and Simon (1973, p. 278).

7. Dr. Joyce Brothers, "Prostitution Quiz," *Chicago Tribune* (3 March 1973, pp. 13–14)); Dr. David Gorton, quoted in the *Los Angeles Times* (30 May 1977, part I, p. 3).

8. Dr. Robert Kolodny, quoted in the *Los Angeles Times* (29 January 1975, part II, p. 8).

9. Dr. James Ford, letter to the editor, *Los Angeles Times* (9 May 1975, part II, p. 4).

10.
   HOLLYWOOD: COMMUNITY AT CROSSROADS
   As the sex shops proliferated, both male and female prostitutes descended in unprecedented numbers to prey on the patrons of the porn parlors.
   With the hookers came their pimps, a rough breed that took over some Hollywood barrooms and all-night restaurants.
   Given such an influx, what followed was inevitable: street bandits, thieves, drug dealers and other violence-prone elements invaded Hollywood in unprecedented numbers.
   [*Los Angeles Times*, 30 May 1977, p. 17]

11.
   U.S. PROBES MOB LINK TO SEX FILMS
   A move by the crime syndicate to take over theaters showing pornographic films by arson and bombings is under investigation by federal authorities.
   Investigators say they have found cases of bombings and arson fires during the last two years while checking the mob's reported move into the multimillion-dollar smut film business.
   [*Chicago Tribune*, 3 March 1973, p. 11]

12. Of course, most social scientists emphatically deny the association between sexual phenomena and criminal activities (see, for instance, *The Report of the Commission on Obscenity and Pornography*, 1970, pp. 142–43, 256–69). They argue that pornography and prostitution in particular are connected with crime only because Jehovanists have forced them to be. By making these activities largely illegal, Jehovanists have made it difficult for noncriminals to engage in them,

but easy for criminals to do so. Prostitution and pornography are associated with crime much less in most European countries where they are regulated or at least tolerated by government.

13. Gnostics also augment their arguments—though less so than Jehovanists and Naturalists—by minimizing their cosmological assumptions in order to appeal to common concerns. "Civilized" Gnosticism merges with Marxism by contending that our society is so corrupt and our self-consciousness so false that both should be overthrown by any means, including sexual excess.

14. Censorship is most effective in controlling the experience of middle-class viewers and readers. Even under the most stringent censorship conditions some pornography will continue to circulate outside the usual economic exchange system of society. The lower and upper classes acquire most of this illegal but tolerated pornography "under the counter" because it cannot be merchandised "over the counter" to ordinary bourgeois buyers.

15. With the most recent Jehovanist revival of the late 1970s, many American newspapers such as the *Los Angeles Times* and even the *New York Times* have returned to suppressing pornographic movie advertising entirely, restoring the uninterrupted continuity of their media's presentation of everyday reality.

16. Jehovanists and Naturalists use their respective techniques of containment and dilution to neutralize not only sexual "evil" but other kinds of "evil" as well. Many Jehovanists, for instance, have attempted to segregate blacks into separate schools and housing in order to prevent them from "contaminating" the rest of society. Many Naturalists, on the other hand, have passionately advocated integrated schools and scattered public (i.e., black) housing. Whatever inherent or acquired "taint" blacks carry, these Naturalists seem to believe, its dangers can be swamped out by diluting tinctures of blacks with larger concentrations of "pure" whites.

17. Cf. Goffman's "frames" (1974). For Goffman's use of "frames" to analyze pornography, see 1974, pp. 55–56. The term "frame" directs the researcher's attention to the different organizations of experience within and without a boundary. I prefer the term "filter," which directs attention to the modifications experience undergoes as it passes through a contextual scheme.

18. If pornography purveyors were as imaginative as their lawyers are in devising ploys for dodging antiobscenity laws, dirty pictures would be a lot less boring. In Indianapolis, . . . the attorneys for one bookstore claim that their client should be protected from prosecution under the same Indiana statute that exempts hospitals, physicians, psychiatrists, and museums from the state's obscenity regulations. If 'Belmont's Adult Museum' wins its case, you'll probably see smut shops tacking up museum shingles over their doors from coast to coast. . . . [*Village Voice*, 26 January 1976, p. 20]

19. This is not to imply that pornography is a transparent medium that simply re-presents sex unaltered; it too is a distorting lens. But rather than being a "filter" like art or science that screens out the dangerous erotic aspects of sex, pornography is a "magnifier" that enlarges them—making them appear even more alluring than they do during sexual activity itself.

20. *The Lancet*, a well-known English medical journal, justified its failure to review Havelock Ellis's *Sexual Inversion* in the following way:

We believe that the book would fall into the hands of readers totally unable to derive benefit from it as a work of science and very ready to draw evil lessons from its necessarily disgusting passages. It must be pointed out, too, that a more than ordinary danger is attached to Mr. Havelock Ellis's work as a book for laymen in that the author's views happen to be that sexual inversion is far more prevalent than we believe it to be and that the legislature does injustice to many by regarding as crimes the practices with which it is bound up. . . . Be that as it may, it is especially important that such matters should not be discussed by the men of the street. [Quoted in Ruitenbeek 1974, p. 37]

21. If gynecological and other comparable medical examinations can remind the erotically experienced of sex, sex can remind the erotically inexperienced of these examinations. In *The Group*, Mary McCarthy uses a medical scenario to describe how Dottie loses her virginity to Dick:

> When her dress was gone, she felt rather faint for a minute, but he left her in her slip, just as they did in the doctor's office. . . . Perhaps it was going to the doctor so much or perhaps it was Dick himself, so detached and impersonal, the way they were supposed to be in art class with the model, that made Dottie brave. He had not touched her once, all the time he was undressing her, except by accident, grazing her skin. Then he pinched each of her full breasts lightly and told her to relax, in just the tone Dr. Perry used when he was going to give her a treatment for her sciatica. [1964, pp. 36–37]

22. Gnostic humor, however, intensifies rather than reduces eroticism, greatly increasing its anarchic potential. Thus the satanic laughter of the rapist.

23. The following description of the relation between sexual ideology and social-psychological change in the Western world is very crude, of course, because Western society is complex and its subgroups participate in its overall development at different rates. In effect, I will be characterizing all of Western society at a particular time by the ideology of one of its subgroups, which I take to be representative of the whole. Future researchers might wish to specify the variety of sexual ideologies held by other social groups at a particular historical period as well as the fluctuations in sexual ideology over shorter temporal intervals. Nevertheless, I believe that some hypothesis about an overall phenomenon, however uncertain, is better than none, for at least such a general hypothesis orients other researchers toward what to look for in the phenomenon's components—a necessary preliminary for refining or refuting it.

24. Not unrelated to the fear that unbridled sexual license was "polluting" our society, which developed after Vietnam and Watergate, was the fear that unbridled economic development was "polluting" our natural environment, which also increased dramatically after this latest social crisis.

Conclusion

1. For instance, compare Freud's output model of sadism and masochism, in which "masochism is nothing more than an extension of sadism turned round upon the subject's own self" (1972, p. 48) with the input analysis presented in chapter 4, in which masochism is primary and sadism is secondary.

2. Kinsey, too, discussed sex mainly in terms of "outlet" (1948, p. 1953).

3. Sex is a member of a large class of activities—including games and theater—in which participants depart from everyday consciousness and eventually return to it. Many of these activities pay deference to some more encompassing collectivity through social rituals. Major sports events, for instance, often begin with a religious or patriotic gesture—like a moment of silent prayer or the singing of "The Star Spangled Banner"—to refresh the participants' and spectators' memory of the larger orders from which their attention will soon be distracted.

   In *Escape Attempts: The Theory and Practice of Resistance to Everyday Life* (1978), Stanley Cohen and Laurie Taylor have developed a general theory of the relation between everyday and other realities. Though marred by an inadequate treatment of sex (pp. 106–13)—which my examination of erotic reality is intended to rectify—their work is one of the most interesting discussions of this relation since Alfred Schutz's essay "On Multiple Realities" (1962, pp. 207–59), originally published in 1945.

4. I have been examining in this book the point of contact between experience and ideology, process and structure, life and form. To do so I have had to draw on two entirely different techniques of investigation. We will not betray human experience only if we describe it as a dynamic whole, which is best accomplished through a phenomological-interpretive-interactional perspective. But to understand a static ideology we must take it apart, which is best accomplished through a structural perspective. Both approaches are necessary for the study of sex, for its human experiential side can help us to articulate its unhuman ideological side, and vice versa.

5. Since Victorian times, Jehovanists have referred to sexual characteristics and activities only indirectly, as something *not* everyday: "*un*chaste," "*in*continent," "*dis*reputable." Their mania for euphemism becomes self-defeating, however, when they find they cannot even describe what they want to condemn:

   SMUT HANDBOOK TOO SPECIFIC FOR PASTORS
   A religious handbook mailed to all Southern Baptist pastors in Texas to aid them in urging their congregations to oppose pornography is being criticized as too graphic and may be banned by the church as pornography. . . .
   (*Los Angeles Times*, 21 October 1974, section I, p. 5]

6. Without mentioning them by name, Susan Sontag seems to have grasped the utility of pornography for Gnostics:

   What pornographic literature does is precisely to drive a wedge between one's existence as a full human being and one's existence as a sexual being—while in ordinary life a healthy person is one who prevents such a gap from opening up. Normally we don't experience, at least don't want to experience, our sexual fulfillment as distinct from or opposed to our personal fulfillment. But perhaps in part they are distinct, whether we like it or not. Insofar as strong sexual feeling does involve an obsessive degree of attention, it encompasses experiences in which a person can feel he is losing his 'self.' [1970, p. 58]

7. Although they are not given to arguing from social calculus, Gnostics could contend that changing the final arbiter in sexual decision-making would shift

power from the attractive to the less attractive, from the minority who are desired to the majority who desire them. Conversely, it would shift displeasure from the larger group, who now often have to abstain from the sex they desire, to the smaller group, who will often have to submit to the sex they dislike. Of course, the repercussions on the fashion, cosmetic, and celebrity industries would be enormous, for as many would then try to avoid looking like one of the "beautiful people" as now aspire to do so.

8. The legal theorist David Richards, for instance, has attacked the Supreme Court's refusal to grant pornographers the right of free speech:

> Within the perspective of the evolving national debate over sexual morality and the Supreme Court's repeated support of an "uninhibited marketplace of ideas," it is difficult to see why the pornographic vision should not have a place in the marketplace of ideas besides other visions that celebrate the life of the mind, the sanctity of ascetic piety, or the usefulness of prudent self-discipline. In excluding the pornographic vision from the market-place, the Court fundamentally fails to make a morally neutral judgment of obscene material, for . . . it affirms one moral and political view and denies another. [1974, pp. 81–82]

9. Freud could have completed his search for continuities between erotic and everyday activities by looking for the opposite influences, for the ways one's ordinary activities can affect one's sexual practices:

> Part of the legacy of Freud is that we have all become adept at seeking out the sexual ingredient in many forms of nonsexual behavior and symbol-ism. We are suggesting what is in essence the insight of Kenneth Burke: it is just as plausible to examine sexual behavior for its capacity to express and serve nonsexual motives as the reverse. [Gagnon and Simon 1973, p. 17]

For instance, those who hold submissive positions in work may consequently want to assume dominant positions in bed, or those who are treated too personally during the day may consequently want to be treated solely as sex objects during the night. To complement his theory of sexual repression, then, Freud might have developed a theory of "quotidian repression": what is repressed in daily life will reappear (in distorted form) in sexual life.

10. Pornography can be used for general education as well as for sex education. Marian Borouch suggested to me that if our schools really wanted to teach adolescents—especially lower-class ones—to read, they would put lots of por-nography in their curriculums. An obviously practical suggestion, considering that students who find, say, *Silas Marner* more appealing than, say, *Candy*, have always been very much in the minority. It will never be put into practice, of course, because the Jehovanists who control most school systems would rather retard their pupils' ability to read than impair the integrity of their own cosmos.

11. Rather than from merely their economic class anchorage, the characterization of the less broadly compassed "free floating intellectuals" stressed by Karl Mann-heim (1936, pp. 153ff).

References

Atkins, J. 1972. *Sex in literature.* New York: Grove Press.

Augustine. 1972. *City of God.* Baltimore: Penguin.

Albee, E. 1958. The zoo story. In *The American dream and the zoo story.* New York: Signet.

Bartell, G. 1971. *Group sex: A scientist's eyewitness report on the American way of swinging.* New York: Peter H. Wyden.

Barthes, R. 1972. *Mythologies.* New York: Hill and Wang.

————. 1976. *Sade/Fourier/Loyola.* New York: Hill and Wang.

Bateson, G. et. al. 1972. Toward a theory of schizophrenia. In *Steps to an ecology of mind,* pp. 201–28. New York: Ballantine.

Beauvoir, S. de. 1961. *The second sex.* New York: Bantam Books.

Berger, P. and T. Luckmann. 1967. *The social construction of reality.* Garden City, N.Y.: Doubleday Anchor.

Bergson, H. 1956. Laughter. In *Comedy,* ed. W. Sypher, pp. 61–190. Garden City, N.Y.: Doubleday Anchor.

Birdwhistle, R. 1972. *Kinesics and context.* New York: Ballantine.

Blum, S. 1976. The re-mating game. *The New York Times Magazine*, August 29:10ff.

Boswell, J. 1980. *Christianity, social tolerance, and homosexuality*. Chicago: University of Chicago Press.

Brown, N. 1959. *Life against death*. New York: Random House.

Bullough, V. and B. Bullough. 1977. *Sin, sickness, and sanity: A history of sexual attitudes*. New York: New American Library.

Burtt, E. 1954. *The metaphysical foundations of modern science*. Garden City, N.Y.: Doubleday Anchor.

Byrne, D. 1970. Continuity between the experimental study of attraction and real-life computer dating. *Journal of Personality and Social Psychology* 16:157–65.

Cameron, J. 1976. Sex in the head. *New York Review*, May 13:19–28.

Carr, D. 1971. *The sexes*. London: Heinemann.

Clark, K. 1956. *The nude: A study in ideal form*. Garden City, N.Y.: Doubleday Anchor.

Clor, H. 1969. *Obscenity and public morality*. Chicago: University of Chicago Press.

Cohen, J. ed. 1967. *The essential Lenny Bruce*. New York: Ballantine.

Cohen, S. and L. Taylor. 1978. *Escape attempts: The theory and practice of resistance to everyday life*. New York: Penguin.

Commission on Obscenity and Pornography. 1970. *The report of the commission on obscenity and pornography*. New York: Bantam Books.

Cummings, E. 1968. *Complete poems*. Volume I. Bristol, England: Macgibbon and Kee. Ltd.

Davis, K. 1961. Prostitution. In *Contemporary social problems*, eds. R. Merton and R. Nisbet, pp. 262–88. New York: Harcourt, Brace and World.

Davis, M. 1971. That's Interesting! Towards a phenomenology of sociology and a sociology of phenomenology. *Philosophy of the Social Sciences* 1:309–44.

———. 1973. *Intimate relations*. New York: The Free Press.

———. 1979. Sociology thru humor. *Symbolic interaction* 2:105–10.

Doctorow, E. 1975. *Ragtime*. New York: Bantam Books.

Donleavy, J. 1976. *The unexpergated code*. New York: Delta.

Douglas, J. and P. Rasmussen. 1977. *The nude beach*. Beverly Hills: Sage.

Douglas, M. 1970. *Purity and danger: An analysis of concepts of pollution and taboo*. Baltimore: Penguin.

Duberman, M. 1972. Homosexual literature. *The New York Times Book Review*, December 10:6ff.

Durkheim, E. 1951. *Suicide: A study in sociology*. Glencoe, Ill.: The Free Press

Durrell, L. 1962. *The black book*. New York: Pocket Books.

Dworkin, A. 1981. *Pornography: Men possessing women*. New York: Putnam.

Ellis, H. 1936. *Studies in the psychology of sex*. Volumes 1 and 2. New York: Random House.

Emerson, J. 1970. Behavior in private places: Sustaining definitions of reality in gynecological examinations. In *Recent sociology no. 2: Patterns of communicative behavior*, ed. H. Dreitzel, pp. 73–97. New York: Macmillan.

Enzensberger, C. 1972. *Smut: An anatomy of dirt*. New York: Seabury.

Erickson, E. 1968. *Identity: Youth and crisis*. New York: Norton.

Farber, L. 1978. *Lying, despair, jealousy, envy, sex, suicide, drugs, and the good life*. New York: Harper.

Fielding, H. 1963. *Tom Jones*. New York: Signet.

Flaubert, G. 1959. *Madame Bovary*. New York: Bantam.

———. 1968. *The dictionary of accepted ideas*. New York: New Directions.

Fleming, K. and A. Fleming, eds. 1975. *The first time*. New York: Berkley Medallion.

Foucault, M. 1980. *The history of sexuality. Volume 1: An introduction*. New York: Vintage.

Freud, A. 1946. *The ego and the mechanisms of defense*. New York: International Universities Press.

Freud, S. 1960. *Jokes and their relation to the unconscious*. New York: Norton.

———. 1960a. *The ego and the id*. New York: Norton.

———. 1961. *Beyond the pleasure principle*. New York: Norton.

———. 1962. *Civilization and its discontents*. New York: Norton.

———. 1963. *Sexuality and the psychology of love*, ed. P. Rieff. New York: Macmillan.

———. 1972. *Three essays on the theory of sexuality*. New York: Avon.

Friday, N. 1974. *My secret garden*. New York: Pocket Books.

Gagnon, J. and W. Simon. 1967. Pornography—raging menace or paper tiger? *Transaction*, July/August:41–47.

———. 1973. *Sexual conduct*. Chicago: Aldine Publishing.

Garfinkle, H. 1967. Passing and the managed achievement of sex status in an intersexed person. In *Studies in ethnomethodology*, pp. 116–85, 285–88. Englewood Cliffs, N.J.: Prentice-Hall.

Genet, J. 1958. *The balcony*. New York: Grove Press.

———. 1964. *Our lady of the flowers*. New York: Bantam.

———. 1965. *The thief's journal*. New York: Bantam.

Gerson, W. and S. Lund. 1971. Playboy magazine: Sophisticated smut or social revolution? *Journal of Popular Culture* 1:218–27.

Goffman, E. 1959. *The presentation of self in everyday life*. Garden City, N.Y.: Doubleday Anchor.

———. 1961. *Encounters: Two studies in the sociology of interaction*. Indianapolis: Bobbs-Merrill.

———. 1974. *Frame analysis*. New York: Harper and Row.

Gould, R. 1974. What we don't know about homosexuality. *The New York Times Magazine*, February 24:13ff.

Greene, G. and C. Greene. 1974. *S-M: The last taboo*. New York: Grove Press.

Greer, F. 1976. My scene: Balling on a bus. *Screw*, # 373:19.

Gross, M. 1975. *I, a groupie*. New York: Pinnacle.

Harmetz, A. 1978. The year TV turned to sex (sort of). *TV Guide*, May 6.

Harton, B. 1973. The sexual fantasies of women. *Psychology Today*, March:39–44.

Hechinger, F. and G. Hechinger. 1978. Homosexuality on campus. *The New York Times Magazine*, March 12:15ff.

Henslin, J. and M. Biggs. 1971. Dramaturgical desexualizations: The sociology of the vaginal examination. In *Studies in the sociology of sex*, ed. J. Henslin, pp. 243–72. New York: Appleton-Century-Crofts.

Hite, S. 1976. *The Hite report*. New York: Macmillan.

Hollander, X. 1972. *The happy hooker*. New York: Dell.

Husserl, E. 1970. *Cartesian meditations*. The Hague: Martinus Nijhoff.

Huysmans, J. 1971. *Against nature*. Baltimore: Penguin.

———. 1972. *Là-bas (Down there)*. New York: Dover.

Jesser, C. and L. Donovan. 1969. Nudity in the art training process: An essay with reference to a pilot study. *Sociological Quarterly* 10:355–71.

Jonas, H. 1963. *The gnostic religion*. Boston: Beacon.

Jones, E. 1951. The problem of Paul Murphy: A contribution to the psychology of chess. In *Essays of applied psychoanalysis*. Volume 1. London: Publisher unknown.

Jong, E. 1974. *Fear of flying*. New York: New American Library.

Kant, I. 1964. *The metaphysical principles of virtue*. Indianapolis: Bobbs-Merrill.

————. 1930. *Lectures on ethics*. London: Methuen.

Kendall, E. 1976. *Peculiar institutions: An informal history of the seven sister colleges*. New York: Putnam.

Kenton, M. (pseud. for Southern, T.). 1965. *Candy*. New York: Lancer.

Kilpatrick, W. 1975. *Identity and intimacy*. New York: Delta.

Kinsey, A. et. al. 1948. *Sexual behavior in the human male*. Philadelphia: W. B. Saunders.

————. 1953. *Sexual behavior in the human female*. Philadelphia: W. B. Saunders.

Knight, B. 1976. Don't the girls all get prettier at closin' time. Recorded by Mickey Gilley for Playboy Records, Singletree Music Co. Nashville, Tennessee.

Koch, K. 1975. *The art of love*. New York: Vintage.

Kosinski, J. 1976. *Cockpit*. New York: Bantam.

Kosok, M. 1971. The phenomenology of fucking. *Telos* 8:64–76.

Krafft-Ebing, R. von. 1965. *Psychopathia sexualis*. New York: Bell.

Kronhausen, P. and E. Kronhausen. 1970. *Erotic Fantasies: A study of the sexual imagination*. New York: Grove Press.

Lane, J. 1978. A pinch of porn. *San Diego Reader*, June 22:1ff.

Lawrence, D. 1968. *Lady Chatterley's lover* (including A propos of Lady Chatterley's lover). New York: Bantam.

Leach, E. 1966. Anthropological aspects of language: Animal categories and verbal abuse. In *New directions in the study of language*, ed. E. Lenneberg, pp. 23–63. Cambridge, Mass.: MIT Press.

Lély, G. 1970. *The Marquis de Sade*. New York: Grove Press.

Levin, R. 1975. Facets of female behaviour supporting the social script model of human sexuality. *The Journal of Sex Research* 11:348–52.

Luker, K. 1976. *Taking chances: Abortion and the decision not to contracept*. Berkeley and Los Angeles: University of California Press.

MacDonald, R. 1967. The frightful consequences of onanism: Notes on the history of a delusion. *Journal of the History of Ideas* 28:423–31.

Mailer, N. 1960. The time of her time. In *Advertisements for myself,* pp. 427–51. New York: Signet.

Malamud, B. 1975. *Pictures of Fidelman.* New York: Pocket Book.

Mann, T. 1936. The blood of the Walsungs. In *Stories of three decades,* pp. 292–319. New York: Knopf.

Mannheim, K. 1936. *Ideology and utopia.* New York: Harvest.

Marcus, S. 1967. *The other Victorians.* New York: Bantam Books.

Marcuse, H. 1964. *One dimensional man.* Boston: Beacon.

Margolis, J. 1974. Perversions. *Los Angeles Free Press,* February 22:6, 31.

Marx, K. 1967. *Writings of the young Marx on philosophy and society,* eds. L. Easton and K. Guddat. Garden City, N.Y.: Doubleday Anchor.

Masters, W. and V. Johnson. 1966. *Human sexual response.* Boston: Little, Brown.

May, R. 1969. *Love and will.* New York: Dell.

McCarthy, M. 1964. *The group.* New York: New American Library.

McNeill, E. 1978. *Nine and a half weeks.* New York: Dutton.

Mead, G. 1934. *Mind, self and society.* Chicago: University of Chicago Press.

Meager, R. 1968. The sublime and the obscene. In *Aesthetics in the modern world,* ed. H. Osborne, pp. 148–65. New York: Weybright and Talley.

Merleau-Ponty, M. 1962. *The phenomenology of perception.* New York: Humanities Press.

Michaels, L. 1969. City boy. In *Going places,* pp. 13–30. New York: New American Library.

Miller, H. 1965. *The world of sex.* New York: Grove Press.

Montaigne, M. 1958a. *Essays,* ed. and trans. J. M. Cohen. Baltimore: Penguin.

————. 1958b. *The complete essays of Montaigne,* ed. and trans. D. Frame. Palo Alto: Stanford University Press.

Musil, R. 1965. *The man without qualities.* New York: Capricorn.

Nabokov, V. 1958. *Lolita.* New York: Fawcett.

Nagel, T. 1969. Sexual perversion. *The Journal of Philosophy* 66:5–17.

Ovid. 1966. *The art of love.* Bloomington: University of Indiana Press.

Partridge, E. 1969. *Shakespeare's bawdy.* New York: Dutton.

Perrin, N. 1969. *Dr. Bowdler's legacy: A history of expurgated books in England and America.* New York: Atheneum.

Petras, J. 1973. *Sexuality in society*. Boston: Allyn and Bacon.

Polsky, N. On the sociology of pornography. In *Hustlers, beats, and others*, pp. 183–200. Garden City, NY: Doubleday Anchor.

Réage, P. 1967. *Story of O*. New York: Grove Press.

———. 1973. *Return to the chateau*. New York: Grove Press.

Ricoeur, P. 1964. Wonder, eroticism and enigma. *Cross Currents*, Spring:133–41.

———. 1970. *Freud and philosophy: An essay on interpretation*. New Haven: Yale University Press.

Richards, D. 1974. Free speech and obscenity law: Toward a moral theory of the first amendment. *University of Pennsylvania Law Review* 123:45–91.

Rist, R. ed. 1975. *The pornography controversy*. New Brunswick, N.J.: Transaction.

Robinson, P. 1977. *The modernization of sex*. New York: Harper.

Ropp, R. de. 1969. *Sex energy*. New York: Delta.

Rosebury, T. 1973. *Microbes and morals: The strange story of venereal disease*. New York: Ballantine Books.

Roth, P. 1969. *Portnoy's complaint*. New York: Random House.

———. 1975. *My life as a man*. New York: Bantam Books.

———. 1977. Interview. *The New York Times Book Review*, September 18:1ff.

Rougemont, D. de. 1966. *Love in the western world*. Greenwich, Conn.: Fawcett.

Ruitenbeek, H., ed. 1971. *Sexuality and identity*. New York: Dell.

Ruitenbeek, H. 1974. *The new sexuality*. New York: New Viewpoints.

Sade, M. de. 1966. *Justine, philosophy in the bedroom, Eugenie de Franval, and other writings* (including introductions by J. Paulhan and M. Blanchot), eds. and trans. R. Seaver and A. Wainhouse. New York: Grove Press.

———. 1967. *The 120 days of Sodom and other writings* (including introductions by S. de Beauvoir and P. Klossowski), eds. and trans. R. Seaver and A. Wainhouse. New York: Grove Press.

———. 1968. *Juliette*, eds. and trans. R. Seaver and A. Wainhouse. New York: Grove Press.

Sartre, J.-P. 1956. *Being and nothingness*. New York: Philosophical Library.

———. 1960. Erostratus. In *Intimacy and other stories*, pp. 41–58. New York: Berkley.

————. 1964. *Nausea*. New York: New Directions.

Scholem, G. 1961. *Major trends in Jewish mysticism*. New York: Schocken.

Schopenhauer, A. 1958. The metaphysics of sexual love. In *The world as will and representation* 2:531–67. New York: Dover.

Schor, L. 1975. *Appetites*. New York: Warner.

Schutz, A. 1962. *Collected papers 1: The problem of social reality*. The Hague: Martinus Nijhoff.

————. 1964. *Collected papers 2: Studies in social theory*. The Hague: Martinus Nijhoff.

————. 1966. *Collected papers 3: Studies in phenomenological philosophy*. The Hague: Martinus Nijhoff.

Schutz, A. and T. Luckmann. 1973. *The structures of the life-world*. Evanston, Ill.: Northwestern University Press.

Segal, A. 1970. Censorship, social control, and socialization. *British Journal of Sociology* 21:63–74.

————. 1971. Portnoy's complaint and the sociology of literature. *British Journal of Sociology* 22:257–268.

Sigerist, H. 1962. *Civilization and disease*. Chicago: University of Chicago Press.

Simmel, G. 1921. Sociology of the senses: Visual interaction. In *Introduction to the science of sociology*, eds. R. Park and E. Burgess, pp. 356–61. Chicago: University of Chicago Press.

————. 1971. *Georg Simmel: On individuality and social forms*, ed. D. Levine. Chicago: University of Chicago Press.

Slade, J. 1971. Pornographic theaters off Times Square. *Transaction*, November/December:35–43, 79.

Slater, P. 1963. On social regression. *American Sociological Review* 28:339–64.

Sontag, S. 1970. The pornographic imagination. In *Styles of radical will*, pp. 35–73. New York: Dell.

Steiner, G. 1965. Night words: High pornography and human privacy. *Encounter*, October:14–19.

Stendhal. 1970. *The red and the black*. New York: Signet.

Stern, H. 1957. The ethics of the clean and the unclean. *Judaism* 6:319–27.

————. 1966. The concept of chastity in biblical society. *Journal of Sex Research* 2:89–97.

Sterne, L. 1967. *The life and opinions of Tristram Shandy*. Baltimore: Penguin.

Sullivan, H. 1953. *Conceptions of modern psychiatry*. New York: Norton.

Taylor, G. 1973. *Sex in history*. New York: Harper and Row.

Trilling, L. 1953. The Kinsey report. In *The liberal imagination*, pp. 216–34. Garden City, N.Y.: Doubleday Anchor.

———. 1972. *Sincerity and authenticity*. Cambridge, Mass.: Harvard University Press.

Turner, V. 1969. *The ritual process*. Chicago: Aldine.

Tynan, K. 1969. *Oh! Calcutta!* New York: Grove Press.

Ullerstam, L. 1966. *The erotic minorities*. New York: Grove Press.

Van Kaam, A. 1970. Sex and existence. In *Sexuality and identity*, ed. H. Ruitenbeek, pp. 123–45. New York: Delta.

Van de Velde. 1965. *Ideal marriage: Its physiology and technique*. New York: Random House.

Vassi, M. 1976a. *The saline solution*. New York: Manor.

———. 1976b. *The metasex manifesto*. New York: Bantam.

The Vatican Congregation for the Doctrine of the Faith. 1976. Declaration on certain questions concerning sexual ethics. *The New York Times*, January 16:11.

Verene, D. ed. 1972. *Sexual love and western morality*. New York: Harper and Row.

Voegelin, E. 1952. *The new science of politics*. Chicago: University of Chicago Press.

Weber, M. 1968. *Economy and society*. New York: Bedminster Press.

Weinberg, M. 1965. Sexual modesty, social meanings, and the nudist camp. *Social Problems* 12:311–18.

Willis, S. 1972. Falling in love with celebrities. *Sexual behavior*, August:3–8.

Wilson, C. 1966. *The origins of the sexual impulse*. London: Granada.

Wilson, J. 1971. Violence, pornography, and social science. *The Public Interest* 22:45–61.

Winch, R. 1974. Complementary needs and related notions about voluntary mate selection. In *Selected studies in marriage and the family*, pp. 399–410. New York: Holt, Rinehart and Winston.

Wrong, D. 1961. The oversocialized conception of man in modern sociology. *American Sociological Review* 26:183–93.

Young, W. 1959. Sitting on a fortune: The prostitute in London. *Encounter*, May:19–31.

Zetterberg, H. 1966. The secret ranking. *Journal of Marriage and the Family* 28:134–42.

Index

condemns transvestism, 148–49; condemns voyeurism, 128–30; cosmos of, 157; distinguishes normal from perverted sex using nature, 280n6; doubts art sufficient filter for sex, 218–19; doubts medicine sufficient filter for sex, 222–25; doubts science sufficient filter for sex, 222; draws upon social science to support position, 210; equates sex with procreation, 245; evolution of attitudes toward sex, 165–71; fears political freedom, 199; fears sex as destructive of cosmos, 124, 206–7; fears sex as disintegrating the self, 104, 123, 196, 282n12; influence of, increases after social crises, 231–32; major contributions of, 244; mania of, for euphemism, 287n5; neo-, 171–72; obsessive desire for cleanliness in, 271–72n28; opposes Naturalists' sex education, 243; prohibits bestiality, 137–39; prohibits distribution of contraceptive drugs and devices, 208; refuses to accept sex as part of the human experience, 242; rejected *Report of Commission on Obscenity and Pornography*, 187; restricts access to legal abortions, 208; retreats to deterrent of distraction, 213–14; sexual beliefs of less influential, 231; sexual judgments of produce guilt, 225–26; sexual restrictions by, 120, 124, 134, 193; stresses marriage as diminishing damage of sex, 118–19, 122; theory of concomitant evil in, 207; transition from to Naturalism, 202, 225–26; using technique of containment, 214–15; world view of, 123–24, 127, 165–72, 239–40, 263n9, n10
Jerome, Saint, 88
Jesser, C. and L. Donovan, 56, 217
Johnson. *See* Masters and Johnson
Jonas, Hans, *The Gnostic Religion*, 174–75
Jones, Ernest, 283n3
Jong, Erica, 11; *Fear of Flying*, 84, 102
Joyce, James, *Ulysses*, 216–17

Judaism, 167, 171, 174, 176, 231, 232, 233, 267n13, 270–71n25
Jung, Carl, 100, 187

Kant, Immanuel, xx, 120, 136, 171, 262n4, 270n22, 272n1, n2, 273n3, 275n18, 278n3; on sexual perversions, 126; sees sex as undermining distinction between humans and beasts, 170, 171
Kendall, E. 24
Kenton, Maxwell, *Candy*, 109–10, 224–25, 288n10
Kilpatrick, J., 89, 189
Kinsey, Alfred, xix, xxvi, 70, 184–85, 186, 188, 198, 219, 236, 287n2; behavioristic Naturalism of, 202–3; equates sex with pleasure, 245; favorably disposed toward all forms of sex, 205; *Sexual Behavior*, 283n4
Kissing, 61, 259n24, 265n7
Kissinger, Henry, 29, 55
Knight, B., 17, 31
Koch, Edward, 82
Koch, Kenneth, 36–37; *The Art of Love*, 259n23
Koffka, 262n3
Kohler, Wolfgang, 262n3
Kosinski, Jerzy, *Cockpit*, 76, 82
Kosok, Michael, "The Phenomenology of Fucking," 266n9
Krafft-Ebing, Richard von, 210, 272n1; *Psychopathia Sexualis*, 202, 221
Kronhausen, Phyllis and Eberhard Kronhausen, xxiii, 131–32, 138, 153
Kuhn, Thomas, 281n10

Laclos, Choderlos de, *Dangerous Liaisons*, 176
Lancereaux, E., 214
Lane, J., 8
Lautréamont, 194
Lawrence, D. H., 184, 281n8; "A Propos Lady Chatterley's Lover," 251n5; *Lady Chatterley's Lover*, 8, 63, 73, 74–75, 98, 99, 147–48, 151
Leach, Edmund, 92–93
Lély, G., 162
Leo XII, Pope, 207

ments, 53, 63–64; corrupted by ordinary life, 240; disintegration of during sex, 96–107, 119, 120, 122–23, 267n13, 287n6; embodied in sexual act, 49, 56, 60–61; embodiment of, as threatening, 49–53; endangered by isolation created by Protestantism, 169; as evil or unreal, 182; false, peeled away to reveal inner self, 179; as highly structured and unique, 123; ideal, 123; integration of, 124; locus of, in erotic reality, 79; made mutable through sexual arousal, 239; maintenance of, 98; new, created by new social conditions, 231; not threatened by perverted sex, 205; polluted by sex, 167; of prostitute as affected by sex, 266–67n1; renewal of, through sex, 97, 99, 100; saved from disintegration through laughter, 226; social, essential to sexual arousal, 106; softened in erotic reality, 65, 72–74; splintered or strengthened by promiscuity, 140; struggle to maintain, against sexual temptations, 169; threatened through body by sex and violence, 195–96, 197; true, as conceived by Gnostics, 174–75, 179. *See also* Identity

Semen, 114–15, 123, 168, 259n24
Sex education, 89, 243
Sexual act: as biological activity detached from sacred, 183–84; 186–88; business metaphors for, 227; as connected with crime and degeneracy, 202; contaminates God within, 123; draws consciousness into world antithetical to ordinary world, 238; as evil, 168, 179; extramarital, 120, 122, 166–67, 190, 205, 270n26, 272n2; extreme forms of, decorticate false self, 179–80, 182; for the first time, 46–47, 61, 65; genital, preferred over perverted sex, 128; has greater potential for eliciting condemnation, 237–38; interpersonal interpenetration during, 64, 116, 117; as lead-

ing to mental problems, 209; legislation against, 170; loss of control during, 116; marriage as remedy for, 119; modern conception of, 183, 186; as part of cosmic cycle of birth and rebirth, 184; premarital, 122, 205, 209, 210; reiterative nature of, 119; social perils from, 119; technization of, 242; threatens to disintegrate self, 118, 120, 121, 124, 131; transforms self, 119, 129; warned against in the Bible, 124

Sexual act, terms for: coitus, xxiv, xxv, 65, 75, 78, 162, 226, 260n27, 269n19; copulation, 2, 3, 45, 46, 59, 80, 103, 107, 116, 119, 120, 122, 134, 141, 146, 162, 168, 180, 185, 186, 187, 188, 189, 190, 191, 193, 202, 205, 207, 214, 215, 224, 225, 226, 230, 241, 242, 244, 245, 246, 253n18, 266n9n11, 270n25; fornication, xxiii, xv, 119, 122, 124, 167, 168, 219, 271n26; fuck, xix, xxiii, xxv, xxvi, 14, 20, 26, 31, 46, 61, 74, 76, 80, 105, 182, 195–96, 226, 227, 266n9; intercourse, xxiii, 37, 47, 61, 65, 67, 69, 84, 98, 103, 112, 115, 116, 117, 118, 119, 123, 124, 128, 131, 134, 141, 160, 162, 169, 172, 186, 187, 188, 190, 191, 217, 223, 236, 239, 244, 253n17, 266n9, n10, 267n12, 269n20, 270–71n25; "zipless" fuck, 84, 102

Shakespeare, William, xxii, xxiv; *Hamlet*, 228; *Henry IV, Part I*, 22; *King John*, xxii; *Macbeth*, 64; *Romeo and Juliet*, 51
Shaw, George Bernard, *Pygmalion*, 135
Sigerist, Henry, *Civilization and Disease*, 207
Silas Marner, 288n10
Simmel, Georg, 136, 141, 249n9, 265n5, 268–69n18
Simon, William. *See* Gagnon, John and William Simon
Slade, Joseph, 137, 229
Slater, Phillip, 237
Smut, sex transformed into, 87–95